LAND TENURE
IN OCEANIA

ASSOCIATION FOR SOCIAL
ANTHROPOLOGY IN OCEANIA
Monograph Series

Vern Carroll, Editor
Everett A. Wingert, Associate Editor
    for Cartography

Previously published in this series:
No. 1 *Adoption in Eastern Oceania,*
    edited by Vern Carroll

ASAO Monograph No. 2

LAND TENURE IN OCEANIA

Edited by Henry P. Lundsgaarde

THE UNIVERSITY PRESS OF HAWAII

HONOLULU

ERINDALE
COLLEGE
LIBRARY

Library of Congress Cataloging in Publication Data

Lundsgaarde, Henry P
  Land tenure in Oceania.

  (ASAO monograph ; no. 2)
  Bibliography: p.
  1. Land tenure—Oceanica—Addresses, essays, lectures. I. Title. II. Series: Association for Social Anthropology in Oceania. ASAO monograph, no. 2.
  HD1126.L85   333.3'2'099   73-90854
  ISBN 0-8248-0321-3

Copyright © 1974 by The University Press of Hawaii
All rights reserved
Manufactured in the United States of America

CONTENTS

	Editor's Preface	vii
1.	An Approach to the Analysis of Land Tenure Systems *Ron Crocombe*	1
2.	Melpa Land Tenure: Rules and Processes *Andrew Strathern*	18
3.	Land Tenure in the Woleai *William H. Alkire*	39
4.	Land Tenure on Kapingamarangi *Michael D. Lieber*	70
5.	Landholding on Namu Atoll, Marshall Islands *Nancy J. Pollock*	100
6.	Land Tenure in the Ellice Islands: A Changing Profile *Ivan Brady*	130
7.	The Evolution of Tenure Principles on Tamana Island, Gilbert Islands *Henry P. Lundsgaarde*	179
8.	Land Tenure in a Test Tube: The Case of Palmerston Atoll *Ron Crocombe*	215
9.	Pacific Land Tenure in a Nutshell *Henry P. Lundsgaarde*	265
	References	277
	Contributors	287

EDITOR'S PREFACE

Discussions of land tenure in social anthropology have usually been deeply embedded in broader empirical and theoretical explanations of social, economic, legal, and political institutions. In this volume we have sought to correct the emphasis of previous studies by focusing our attention directly on land tenure, without, it must be added, losing sight of the connections between land tenure principles and general social structure.

We have deliberately looked for similarities by analyzing each tenure system from the same analytical and conceptual perspective. Chapters 1 and 9 specifically discuss the methodological and theoretical framework that evolved in the course of analyzing the seven tenure systems described in chapters 2 through 8. The difficulties and problems encountered by the contributors in presenting their data in comparable form is reflected by the more than three years of analysis, writing, editing, and rewriting necessary to complete this volume.

The seven substantive ethnographic chapters illustrate the range and diversity in the land tenure practices which are found within the vast culture area of Oceania. The similarities in basic tenure principles between all seven systems seem all the more remarkable in light of the varied geographical and cultural settings of the seven societies. In all of these societies we find a complete absence of fee simple ownership and a corresponding presence of entailed family estates.

The ethnography reveals tenure principles that detail an impressive number and variety of separate categories of property. Each category, in turn, includes an even greater number of rights and duties that symbolize different forms of proprietorship. The differential allocation of these rights and duties among persons and groups represents the exact point of connection between land tenure and social structure. For example, kinship principles that specify the distribution of authority within age, sex, descent, and status categories converge on such tenure principles as land use, land distribution, succession, and inheritance. Principles of political organization concerning the relative scaling of authority and power within the society have clear parallels in the land tenure system, where corporate and individual tenure privileges are differentiated. Economic principles subtly merge with land tenure principles in social domains, where land as a resource and land as a value intersect.

It is a pleasure to acknowledge the cooperation received from all the contributors to this volume. Professor Vern Carroll has excelled in the performance of his duties as A.S.A.O. Monograph Series editor. I also wish to thank a number of anonymous scholars who helped to evaluate early drafts of individual chapters.

My very special gratitude is reserved for Kenneth G. Norman, who, in his dual capacity as law student and research assistant, undertook the most demanding bibliographical and editorial assignments without complaint.

I also wish to acknowledge my indebtedness to Professors William W. Elmendorf and Homer G. Barnett, who jointly supervised my early fieldwork in the Gilbert Islands, and to Professors Harry E. Maude and Martin G. Silverman for their continuous encouragement of my studies of Gilbertese culture. Finally, generous fellowship stipends from the American Council of Learned Societies and Harvard Law School allowed me the freedom to plan and organize this volume during 1969 and 1970 in a stimulating atmosphere of productive scholarship.

LAND TENURE
IN OCEANIA

NOTE

Single quotes are used consistently throughout this book for glosses of native words, concepts, and conventional phrases.

AN APPROACH TO THE ANALYSIS OF LAND TENURE SYSTEMS

Ron Crocombe

INTRODUCTION

The term land is used here to refer to space on, above, and below the surface of the earth. Although land area is usually thought of in two dimensions, human societies invariably recognize rights and relationships that deal with land as though it continued both above and below the earth's surface, though the distance and circumstances of this extension vary greatly. In addition, land rights apply in greater or lesser degree to things growing in, living on, attached to, or contained in the land or water.[1]

Land tenure may be broadly defined as the system of relationships between men in respect of land. In describing land tenure as a system it is not intended to suggest that it is a discrete entity. On the contrary, it is a product of diverse forces and is merely one of the means through which man's total relationship to his environment is mediated. Land rights are a subcategory of property rights, and the relationships established by property rights are merely a subcategory of social relations generally. Regarding land tenure as a system is an abstraction—a convenient way to draw boundaries around particular phenomena on which we wish to focus attention. Any land tenure system is, nevertheless, defined by a quantifiable human population and a quantifiable area of land.

Each society classifies its land according to various criteria, some of which are explicit and some of which are not.[2] An external observer will also, quite appropriately, additionally classify the land, and relations to it, by his own criteria and for his own analytical purposes. For example, land rights and relationships in a particular society frequently differ in relation to the land's natural qualities and also in relation to the use to which the land is put. Differing natural qualities permit classification according to such factors as terrain, soil or water type, altitude, or microclimate. Classification by use leads to distinctions among rights to land for hunting, fishing, foraging, gardening, grazing, sacred purposes, burial, residence, access, and so on. These various rights are not necessarily discrete, and they frequently overlap.

Land tenure then is a system of patterns of behavior that specifically serve to control a society's use of environmental resources. But land tenure is distinct from land use, which is the physical exploitation of land by man. Land use is conditioned by tenure, but tenure does not necessarily result in particular uses, though it often makes them more likely.

DETERMINANTS OF A LAND TENURE SYSTEM

The form and function of any system of land tenure is determined by the interaction of a number of variables. There is a biological factor in that the territorial drive, which is almost universal in vertebrates, appears to be manifest in man. Geographical variables include the nature of the land and the physical environment. Biotic variables include the fauna and flora sharing this environment and the extent to which they are used by man. Technological factors include the skills, facilities, and equipment available to a particular people. Socio-cultural influences include the nature and distribution of various forms of power both now and in the past, the beliefs, values, and aspirations of the people. Economic influences include the productive potential of the land in relation to the level of technology, patterns and types of production, and distribution. The demographic structure, the system of land use, and a number of other factors influence not only the nature but also the operation of any tenure system.

Ethological factors. It is accepted that almost all vertebrates manifest, in varying forms and with varying degrees of intensity, territorial behavior.[3] That is, when placed into an environment with others of the same species, vertebrates engage in various forms of behavior which result in different individuals or groups having different relationships with different portions of that environment. Since this territorial behavior is so widespread it presumably relates to the adaptation and survival of vertebrate populations.

The main implication of ethological findings is that in most creatures, and probably in man, tendencies to dominate, to space, and to demarcate are at least partly genetic in origin. But the tendency to dominate and expand one's area of influence can be conditioned and channeled through a wide range of behavioral alternatives. It is difficult to distinguish precisely between the biological and cultural components of territoriality because both processes are operating simultaneously on the same individuals. Moreover, people are only partly conscious of either.

Incidentally, I have long been fascinated by territoriality among social scientists who undertake fieldwork, and in the territorial reactions of people, including myself, when traveling on the decks of inter-island schooners. In both instances individuals demarcate general territories for themselves, recognize hierarchies of access, or privilege, and systems of transfer (and sometimes inheritance), and accept that different individuals and groups may exercise rights to exploit different resources in the same area at the same or at different times.[4] Research teams in the field, like teams of islanders on a schooner, draw interior boundaries of area, subject matter, or use within the outer boundaries of the group.

Environmental factors. The nature of the environment facilitates or inhibits the degree to which the people of a given culture can physically demarcate boundaries, the extent to which, given their cultural values, they will want to claim and exercise rights over the land, and the kinds of uses to which they can put the land. The physical environment poses limits within which any tenure system must function, and it makes certain choices more likely than others.

Technological factors. These include the nature of the recording devices available to a particular people both for marking the ground and for documentary and cartographic recording of arrangements between people in respect of the land. They also include the landworking technology and economic infrastructure such as roads and bridges, ships and trucks, banks or other financial institutions, markets, and extension services.

Socio-cultural factors. These are the most complex and can be examined from a number of points of view. The most readily ascertainable are the overt principles and practices including the laws, rules, and conventions relating to land. But we must know also the social, economic, political, and religious context within which they operate. A people's perception of what constitutes land, what relationships in respect to it are right and proper, what values and aspirations they have with respect to it, the history of the land and people's perception of that history, all influence the nature of the tenure system.

These conceptual notions about nature, man, and land are of great significance. It is necessary to seek not only what is meant by particular words as demonstrated by actual behavior but also the mental patterns with which people are accustomed to think about such things as the validity or inevitability of various systems of social and power relations, the feasibility or rightness of physical mobility, the degree of attachment to locality, and the propriety of particular ways of transferring land rights.

The interaction of these and other variables in any society at any given time leads to a particular set of relationships between men in respect of land as one aspect of the total relationships between man and his environment. These factors do not necessarily result in any predetermined pattern, for any physical or cultural environment can be exploited in a variety of ways. But the more limited the environment, the technology, and the number of people, the greater the influence environment is likely to be in determining land tenure patterns. Cultural patterns further modify or restrict the tenure choices theoretically available.

Where industrial technology with its concomitants of literacy, bureaucracy, and mobility is widespread, the principles and practices governing relationships in respect of land tend to be spelled out in considerable detail and to relate specifically to land. Behavior with respect to land is determined largely by reference to these principles, and land tenure may be differentiated relatively easily from other aspects of culture. Moreover, land rights tend to be clearly distinguishable from other rights and relationships existing in industrial societies.

In preliterate societies, however, the relationships between men as regards land are much more direct but much less directly specified. That is, they are not mediated through as complex a series of persons, institutions, or processes. In most Oceanic societies before contact with industrial technology, the bulk of food and other resources were extracted from land and water directly by the consumer and his family. Relations with others in respect to land were complex, but diffuse and imprecise, even though they involved only a relatively small number of people over a limited area. Most important, land relationships were so closely integrated with relations of social, economic, and political kinds as to be almost fused with them in many cases. The influence of environment was so great that man-land relations were mediated through ecological cycles which were often interpreted in ritualistic terms (e.g., see Rappaport 1968). In such situations land tenure is an abstraction of the pattern of expectations of human behavior in a much wider context.

CLASSIFICATION OF TERRITORIAL RELATIONSHIPS

Territorial behavior is of two types: that aimed at keeping others out and that aimed at admitting others or seeking admittance into a hierarchy of subordination or a network of interaction. In some animals it manifests itself in the well-known pecking order; in man it is reflected in hierarchies of power, the payment of rent and tribute, the differential distribution of prestige, or in networks of mutual commitment. These relationships may be precise and enforceable, in which case they are properly termed rights, or they may be vague and unenforceable but nevertheless recognized and accepted, in which case they are more properly expectations in the light of past behavior. But even these vague expectations are rights in the sense that their fulfillment can be fairly safely predicted, and some direct or indirect sanctions can usually be exercised if they are not. For want of a better term to describe these diverse relationships that result in actual or potential advantage to the holder the word *rights* will be used.[5]

Land rights may be classified into the following six categories:

1. Rights of or claims to direct use, which include the rights to plant, to harvest, to gather, or to build. It should be noted that various rights of direct use may be held by various persons in respect of the same parcel of land. For instance one person may have rights to collect wild

fruits, another to plant short-term cash crops, and another to harvest tree crops. Apart from the above rights which govern production from the land, we may recognize subsidiary rights of users, which include rights of access and rights to the use of water.

2. Rights of indirect economic gain such as those to tribute or to rental income.

3. Rights of control. Rights of use are almost invariably limited by rights of control, which are held by persons other than the user. For instance, a man with the exclusive right to plant land may nevertheless be required to plant a specific crop or to conform to certain technical requirements of husbandry or to erect a specific type of house. On the other hand, the control may be negative, restraining the user from allowing the land to be used for such purposes as the growth of noxious plants. Other rights of control include those held by land courts, chiefs, or others with authority over land.

4. Rights of transfer, which are the effective power to transmit rights, either those in the land itself or those in other property attached to the land, by will, sale, mortgage, gift, or other conveyance.

5. Residual rights include the reversionary interest acquired in the event of death of the former right holders without descendants or collateral heirs; of noncompliance with specified conditions, as when persons are evicted for breaches of social norms; and of extreme need by the holder of the residual rights, such as the power of eminent domain which is held by governments.

6. Symbolic rights or rights of identification. In many societies there are clearly recognized relationships between men and land which have no apparent economic or material function, though they may serve important psychological or social purposes. Maori chiefs, for example, often named particular places after parts of their bodies, thus forming a symbolic and sacred relationship between themselves, or themselves and their people jointly, and the areas concerned. In many cases this had a spacing function, as outsiders were inviting trouble if they trespassed on the symbolic "backbone" or "head" of the chief concerned. But on many occasions it did not—prominent rocks jutting from unused seas were also thus named.

Likewise, in many islands, churches are built on land which was informally given to them over a century ago. In most instances the churches are still there and show every prospect of remaining there, but I have seen numerous examples in both Polynesia and Melanesia where the great-grandchildren of the donors of the land proudly point out that the church land is theirs. They have never used it, do not want to use it, and have no wish to ever take it back. Nor do they derive rent or compensation of any material kind. But they do derive prestige and some personal satisfaction from this symbolic right. The word *right* is considered appropriate, for both they and others consider it proper for the donor's descendants to make such claims and would vigorously condemn any unentitled person who made such a claim. The possession of colonial or dependent territories appears in some respects to have involved symbolic rights of a similar order, associated with similar psychological satisfactions.

Each right is associated either with reciprocal duties or with a total network of relationships. Rights to inherit are paralleled by social obligations of the heir during the testator's lifetime or ritual obligations after his death. Rights to derive rent are paralleled by the obligation to grant usufruct to the lessee. Rights to build on a particular plot are paralleled by the duty of other members of the society to refrain from doing so. The right and its opposite or correlative duty is not necessarily of the same magnitude. In fact, rank systems include institutionalized differences between rights and their related obligations, though in a static situation the relative magnitudes of the total rights and obligations must be in constant proportions.

It is necessary to specify the source of all rights and the machinery for their enforcement. Where land tenure rules are codified as laws, a distinction needs to be made between relationships that are subject to constraints of statute, those that are quasi-legal, and those that are outside statute law but still subject to customary constraints. The sanctions applicable to each category should be noted.

DIMENSIONS OF LAND RIGHTS

Each specific land right and each duty may be measured in four dimensions:

An area dimension, which defines the limits of area to which any right, duty, privilege, or disability applies. These are defined in different societies, with varying degrees of accuracy, by means of natural or artificial marks on the ground, in written records and unwritten traditions, and known cultural patterns, such as *marae* and named seating stones in much of central Polynesia. Boundaries among men as among other animals are determined by actual or potential competition between neighboring individuals and groups. The situation at any moment is the balance between the desire and ability to expand, on the one hand, and the wish and ability to defend on the other. This applies to both the areas and the kinds of influence of the interacting parties. The competition may be expressed in overt aggression but is usually mediated through complex spacing mechanisms. In the case of man, these mechanisms include such elaborate institutions as markets, law-courts, registries, and treaties as well as physical barriers. Once established, boundaries are learned and recognized by those concerned until a change in the balance of power results in their alteration.

A time dimension denotes the period during which the right or other relationship has force. This may be a specified number of years, a lifetime, a period dependent on occupation, or on the fulfillment of obligations on which the right is dependent.

A population dimension enumerates the persons and groups involved and classifies them in relevant categories, statuses, and social classes, each different category having specific rights. Rights only exist in situations of interaction; that is, one invariably holds rights as against other persons, and it is sometimes necessary to specify who is excluded as well as who is included in a particular right or obligation.

A complex of legal and customary dimensions specify the legal and customary criteria by reference to which the distribution, transfer, and exercise of rights are conditioned. A full understanding of these dimensions is impossible without an understanding of the social and political structure within which the rights are organized.

DISTRIBUTION OF RIGHTS

The use of the term ownership in connection with land tends to be misleading—in common usage in capitalistic societies, though not in practice in any society, it connotes the absolute possession of all rights or almost all rights by a single party. The ownership of any material object refers to the possession of a right or rights in respect of that object and ultimately the legal or customary power to exclude other persons from exercising such rights. But there is no land tenure system in existence wherein all rights to any parcel of land are held by a single party, and it seems preferable to avoid the term ownership altogether and examine the tenure system by reference to the various types of rights and duties that are recognized and the parties by which they are held.

Although it is not property, but rights in relation to property, that are owned, popular usage speaks of the property itself as being owned. Alternately, some people speak of rights as being *held* and use the word *ownership* to refer to the holding by someone of a cluster of the most important rights. But as rights in land are held at so many levels and are so widely distributed, particularly in tribal societies, use of the word *ownership* tends to oversimplify a complex reality and to prevent understanding the true nature of the relationships involved.

Likewise, the terms *individual tenure* and *communal tenure* are misleading, for they are based on the false assumption that all rights to the land are held in the one case by individuals and in the other by the community. They obscure the fact that in all tenure systems there are multiple rights to all land. Some types of rights to most parcels of land are held by individuals; some by persons by virtue of their particular status in the community, such as chiefs, judges, mortgagees, and so on; some by groups such as local bodies, communes, committees, lineages, and village councils; and others by the community or nation as a whole, usually through its formally or informally constituted governing body.

The terms *individual tenure* and *communal tenure* are at times used in a relative sense to indicate that in the particular system the rights of individuals or of the state, respectively, are the more pronounced. In this sense the term has a measure of validity but the terms are used with such diverse and imprecise connotations that they are confusing. For example, we find the term *communal tenure* being used to describe classic communistic, cooperative, and a wide variety of tribal tenure systems. Such catchwords oversimplify a complex situation. For the sake of clarity they are better avoided altogether, in favor of deciding, for each specific society, the actual rights that are held by individuals, groups, and communities.

The distribution of land rights in any society may be examined in terms of relations between right holders. Some such relationships are hierarchical with certain categories of right holder having superior rights to others. A description of this hierarchical distribution should show the nature and extent of rights held at various levels in social, governmental, or economic hierarchies. This would include, for example, those rights held by commoners and various categories of chiefs; those held by citizens and local, state, and federal governments and statutory authorities set up by each; and those held by tenants and landlords. Other relationships carry no necessary hierarchical connotation and may be spoken of as horizontal relationships. These comprise the relationships existing between co-owners, members of a landholding descent group, or tenants in common. The importance of non-hierarchical rights is often overlooked or skimmed over because they are difficult to measure and classify.

Patterns of expectation and ideological values determine land relationships in addition to formal rights; for example, I may have a legal right to evict my mother-in-law but be quite unable or unwilling to carry it out in practice for social and psychological reasons. The classification of relationships as hierarchical or horizontal is conceptually useful but is far from absolute. The relationships between the hierarchies, moreover, are very diverse and do not lend themselves to simple classification. The above relationships may be measured and compared in terms of frequency of occurrence, or percentage of persons and resources in each category.

In addition to the legal relations in respect to land, we must also consider other relations which influence the distribution and exercise of legal rights. Moreover, we must take cognizance of the political and psychological goals, values, and pressures which influence the nature of the system as well as the manipulation of rights within it. This necessitates determining the distribution of rights and privileges among various members in the community and those outside having influence in it. That these groups may not necessarily be within the community itself may be seen, for example, in that international opinion has altered the pattern of land alienation and the land rights of foreigners in New Guinea and Nauru very greatly in the last decade and has led to changes in the functioning of the legal framework as well as in the framework itself. In other words, not only contractual relations, but also status and values, can influence the distribution of rights.

ACQUISITION AND TRANSFER OF LAND RIGHTS

Each land tenure system provides some series of recognized processes whereby land rights may be acquired from or transferred to other parties. These processes may be classified in terms of the circumstances which initiate or cause their occurrence, for the transfer that takes place as a result of particular circumstances is secondary. Warfare may lead to the transfer of rights by conquest, and death to the transfer of rights by inheritance. As expressions of social obligations there are transfers of land rights at marriage, at adoption, or by will. Where an act requires reciprocity (e.g., a reward for service, an attempt to gain a privilege, or a gratuitous act to a person in need—which usually carries an obligation to reciprocate), gifts and loans of land rights may be made. The following chapters are full of examples.

Where the circumstance is economic incentive, land rights may be transferred by purchase, lease, or mortgage. In the absence of other claimants, reversion takes place to the State; to the recognized "source," "root," or "origin" of the title; or to some other *ultimus haeres*. Similarly, where existing resources are inadequate, there may be exploration, voluntary departure, or banishment; land rights may be acquired by discovery and settlement of undeveloped or unoccupied land.

The proportion of rights obtained by each method in any particular society may be stated in terms of percentages of the total number of transfers of each type and of the area or value of land involved.

In analyzing the processes of acquisition of rights, the conditions of transfer must be carefully specified. In capitalistic societies the conditions associated with the sale of land are endlessly variable. The relationship between the contracting parties is highly specific, particularly in terms of price or value at the time of sale. The fact that the transfer must be negotiated in great detail, as specified in the wealth of documents needed to effect the transfer, and through a variety of technical experts (realtors, lawyers, financiers, registrars) indicates the enormous body of relationships which are affected by the fact of sale.

In industrialized societies, a written legal framework, extensive documentation, registries, and technical specialists help perpetuate the system and stabilize decisions. In societies without these facilities, transfers of land rights are often less secure. There may be greater difficulty in upholding the transfer, though this will depend to a considerable extent on the institutions (e.g., chiefs and courts) and traditional precedents available to give security to the parties involved. The difference is not only that in simpler societies relations are primarily based on status and in complex societies more by contract—it is also that contractual relations in societies without an effective bureaucracy often need more reinforcement more frequently.

For example, the parties cannot say precisely what rights are transferred when a customary sale takes place. Only by detailed study of past sales can this be determined. This is partly because the rights are conditional on the relations between the two persons or groups remaining the same, on the dominance or subordination of the one group or the other, on population change, and so on. Under these circumstances the best degree of permanence is obtained by continued use of the land and by periodic exchanges of gifts, or reenactment of agreements, to refresh memories and by the spreading of rights, and thus the obligation to support the other right holders, over as wide a group as possible.

The retention of rights is always to some extent conditional, and occupation is often a necessary condition. There are normally obligations to be observed whether to a taxing authority, or to a local council, or to a family group, or whatever. In customary tenure systems, in which the precise circumstances of retention of rights is not specified, there is usually a degree of group conformity required if rights are to be retained. This often continues to apply in practice for a considerable time after formal legal systems have been introduced.

Land rights in customary tenure systems are never acquired by reference to a single principle, although each society has one or more dominant themes or patterns. For example, a patrilineal ideology or bias (as among the Melpa, see chapter 2) or a matrilineal ideology (as among the Woleai, see chapter 3) does not mean that all land is inherited through the father or through the mother, it means that there is a dominant or ideal pattern which the people feel to be right and proper.[6] But even in societies characterized by unilineal descent, it is normally possible, and sometimes common, to acquire some rights to land through the other parent, or through other processes.

If a system of patrilineal land inheritance functioned strictly patrilineally, it would only survive intact if every individual had one male child and only one male child, and of course this does not happen.[7] In ambilineal inheritance systems, most rights are transferred either through the father (or alternatively, through one or more members of his family or group), or through the mother but normally not through both, at least not to the same extent. The southern Gilbert Islands (chapter 7) are unusual in the frequency of inheritance from both parents. The important thing to remember is that these are relative terms. Patrilineal simply means that *most* people acquire *most* rights from their fathers, and ambilineal means that there is considerable flexibility concerning which side one acquires one's major rights from.

Systems in which the land is inherited from both parents are sometimes called bilateral. But the term must be used cautiously for, although one can acquire some rights from both the mother and father, one cannot acquire all the mother's rights and all the father's rights.

In most systems some land rights are acquired from each parent. The Orokaiva of New Guinea are usually spoken of as exclusively patrilineal in descent and inheritance, but almost every Orokaiva whom I have worked with has acquired some rights from his mother's line. These are usually quite subordinate rights, such as the right to get sago, to take refuge in the event of eviction, or to take produce, but sometimes rights to plant on the mother's land are also given, particularly if it is near at hand.

Subsidiary principles which modify those of descent in the acquisition of land rights include residence, use, conformity to social codes, adoption, family size, land resources, and so on. The following chapters demonstrate the relative significance of such factors in particular societies. In inheritance there is usually a degree of both obligation and choice. Although a man cannot usually give land to a person outside the community, and is usually obliged to provide for particular relatives, generally he has also an element of choice within these limitations. Questioning informants directly is likely to reveal the ideal pattern, but an analysis of a number of actual cases invariably shows that it is modified by a number of subsidiary principles. Their existence makes it possible for individuals to manipulate the system to their individual advantage.

In traditional tenure systems in the Pacific islands, which rights are acquired depends first upon one's affiliation to a landholding descent group or local group. Primary rights are acquired through the group with which the person concerned affiliates and in which he resides as a married man and are subject to such questions as occupation and number of children among whom the rights have to be divided; they are usually divided and not held by the group.[8] In each generation, the land is allocated in some detail. Persons do not acquire all the rights or shares in all the land of their parents, their grandparents, their great-grandparents, and so forth. There is a constant process of allocation according to such criteria as line of descent, residence, occupation, affiliation, need, and use.

Why do human groups so often speak of inheritance of land rights—and often group membership as well—in terms of descent alone, when research may show other factors to be more important?

Perhaps it is because the kinship idiom confirms one's self-identity. Our first interest is in ourselves; next, we feel closest identification with those whose interests contribute most to our own (spouses, children, kin, colleagues, etc.). Many ideologies focus on a common origin, common seed, common blood, or common spirit as the unifying theme. Claims to land in many Oceanic societies are legitimized by reference to the ancestor from whom they were ultimately derived. This has social validity irrespective of its historical accuracy.

Moreover, Robin Hide (personal communication) has suggested to me that in the absence of writing, kinship reckoning is an easy idiom of legitimation. It can be manipulated or adjusted by such processes as emphasizing one of the four grandparental descent lines, various types and degrees of adoption, the use of classificatory kinship terminology, and so on, in response to changes in residence, land resources, social compatibility, or other factors. This negotiable characteristic of kinship systems increases their value as symbols of the changing reality.

In traditional societies, what matters most in determining where one gets one's rights, and which rights one gets is one's status in respect to the particular right-holding group or right-holding individuals. Status is differentiated in most societies by sex and age: females are eligible to acquire certain rights and males to acquire certain others and adults can obtain some rights for which children are not eligible. Status which derives from membership in a lineage, clan, or other right-holding group may be classified into one of four categories on the basis of two major criteria: descent and residence.[9]

A person who belongs to a right-holding group by both descent and residence may be termed a primary member of it. He was born in it, lives in it, and identifies with it. This is normally where he acquires his primary rights. A person who was a primary member but has moved out (e.g., at marriage) or has not yet moved in (for example, an unmarried person in a matrilineal society in which premarital residence is patrilocal and postmarital residence avunculocal, such as in the Trobriand Islands) may be termed a contingent member. Such a person has certain rights while absent, but their nature changes according to whether or not he is resident in the landholding group concerned.

A person whose parent is or was a contingent right holder may be classified as a secondary member of the group. For example, in a society with patrilineal rules of descent and virilocal postmarital residence, a woman resides in her husband's village, and her children are primary members of their father's descent group (i.e., they are members by both descent and residence) but they are secondary members of their mother's descent group (i.e., they are members by descent but not by residence). Their rights in the land of the mother are normally quite different from those of the father—they may have rights to get sago or to take refuge or to be able to adopt a child.

Finally, we get marital and permissive status in a right-holding group. These are acquired by residence, usually as a by-product of marriage, assistance, or other acts, and not by descent. These rights include those of a wife or other affine, a refugee, or a person who is otherwise accepted into a group.

To sum up, primary right holders belong to a group by virtue of both descent and residence; contingent right holders, by descent and by past or future residence; secondary right holders, by descent but not residence; and marital and permissive right holders, by residence but not descent. Many land authorities have erred by working from the false assumption that a person either is or is not a member of a descent group, whereas in fact there are several distinct statuses and the rights of persons in each status are quite different. Although a person has only one status with respect to any one descent group, he usually belongs to, that is, has recognized links with and status in, two or three different descent groups. One is usually a primary member of the father's descent group in a patrilineal society and a secondary member of the mother's. A woman who is married out will be a permissive member of her husband's group, a contingent member of her father's, and a secondary member of her mother's.

CONCLUSION

Land tenure is seen as a system of interpersonal and intergroup relationships through which man's relationship with part of his environment is mediated. Any comparison, evaluation, or modification of tenure systems can be effected most adequately if the system(s) concerned are accurately described and analyzed and if the context within which they operate is understood. Categories of land rights are suggested. Their main dimensions and systems of distribution and transfer are outlined as a basis for approaching the study of tenure patterns.

NOTES

1. I have benefited from comments on the draft of this chapter from Dr. Vern Carroll, Mr. Robin Hide, Dr. Henry Lundsgaarde, Dr. Gerard Nash, Dr. Anton Ploeg, and Dr. Peter Sack.
2. Pospisil (1965) gives a valuable example of land classification by the Kapauku of Irian Barat (west New Guinea).
3. Perhaps the best summary of the data is by Carpenter (1958) and the fullest exposition of the facts is by Wynne-Edwards (1962). More popular, and much less satisfactory, summaries and descriptions are given in Ardrey (1966), Lorenz (1966), and Morris (1967). A critique of these views is contained in Montagu (1968).
4. A large body of tacit understandings, threats, signalling devices, appeals, and ethical judgements govern the operation of these principles. Many people manifest such behavior without being conscious of it, and I had done so in schooner travel for many years before becoming aware of the unwritten and largely unspoken language with which all passengers exercised and recognized rights to space.
5. In Hohfeld's system of classification of property rights those in category 1 would also be "rights" or "claims." Those in category 2 would be closer to Hohfeld's concept of "privileges" for the recipient and "liabilities" for the payer. Those in category 3 would correspond reasonably closely to "powers" for those exercising control and "liabilities" for those subject to it. Rights of transfer (4) would fall into various Hohfeldian categories according to circumstance (e.g., in some cases parties have a right to receive which is at least as strong as the transferrer's right to give). Residual rights (5) and symbolic rights (6) would both fall into the category of "privileges" in the Hohfeldian sense.

   For discussion of both the merits and pitfalls of the analyses of Hohfeld and those who have modified his scheme see Dias (1964, chap. 9). Such an omnibus term as rights does indeed need to be refined and divided into components, but I find as many inadequacies in Hohfeld's system of classification when applied to land rights as in the simpler classification used here.
6. When referring to inheritance, it may be more accurate to use the terms patrilateral (i.e., from the father's side), matrilateral (from the mother's side), ambilateral (from either side), etc., rather than patrilineal. The latter term is more commonly used, but it, strictly speaking, refers more specifically to descent and to a particular descent line, than to a group associated with such a line.
7. A very common problem following European contact is that the colonizing group grasps the ideal pattern, but does not fully understand (or consciously ignores) all the subsidiary processes which are concurrently

ANALYSIS OF LAND TENURE SYSTEMS

at work in the system. Then the ideal becomes ossified by law or administrative practice and becomes dysfunctional and unrelated to needs. A knowledge of the normative system (or the statistical frequency of various rules being applied) helps to reveal the principles, but in a time of change, rigid adherence to such frequency patterns would be equally hazardous.

8. In many matrilineal systems, he resides in his father's descent group until marriage and his mother's group thereafter.
9. Various subcategories can be introduced by the introduction of other criteria such as occupation, use, etc.

MELPA LAND TENURE: RULES AND PROCESSES

Andrew Strathern

INTRODUCTION

This chapter discusses land tenure among the Melpa speakers of the Mount Hagen area, Papua New Guinea.[1] Basic land rights of individuals in this area depend on their consanguineal and affinal ties with clan groups. The core of each clan consists of a group of men who usually hold a single territory and who combine for certain ceremonial exchanges and cult festivals. In the past, clansmen also supported each other in warfare. The clan is exogamous, and its members regularly use kinship terms in addressing each other. Membership of a clan is ordinarily obtained through patrifiliation, but sons of female group members and others can also be admitted in a variety of circumstances. Clansmen speak of themselves, in the idiom of descent, as 'sons of an original clan founder,' although in practice they are not much concerned about maintaining genealogies tracing their links with the founder.

Most of the Hagen Sub-District has been under the control of the Australian administration in Papua New Guinea since 1945 or earlier. However, before control was established warfare was frequent and resulted in migration, resettlement, and the reaffiliation of individuals to groups, the results of which can still be seen in group alignments today. Hence it is not possible to discuss the contemporary situation of any clan in relation to landholding without some reference to its recent

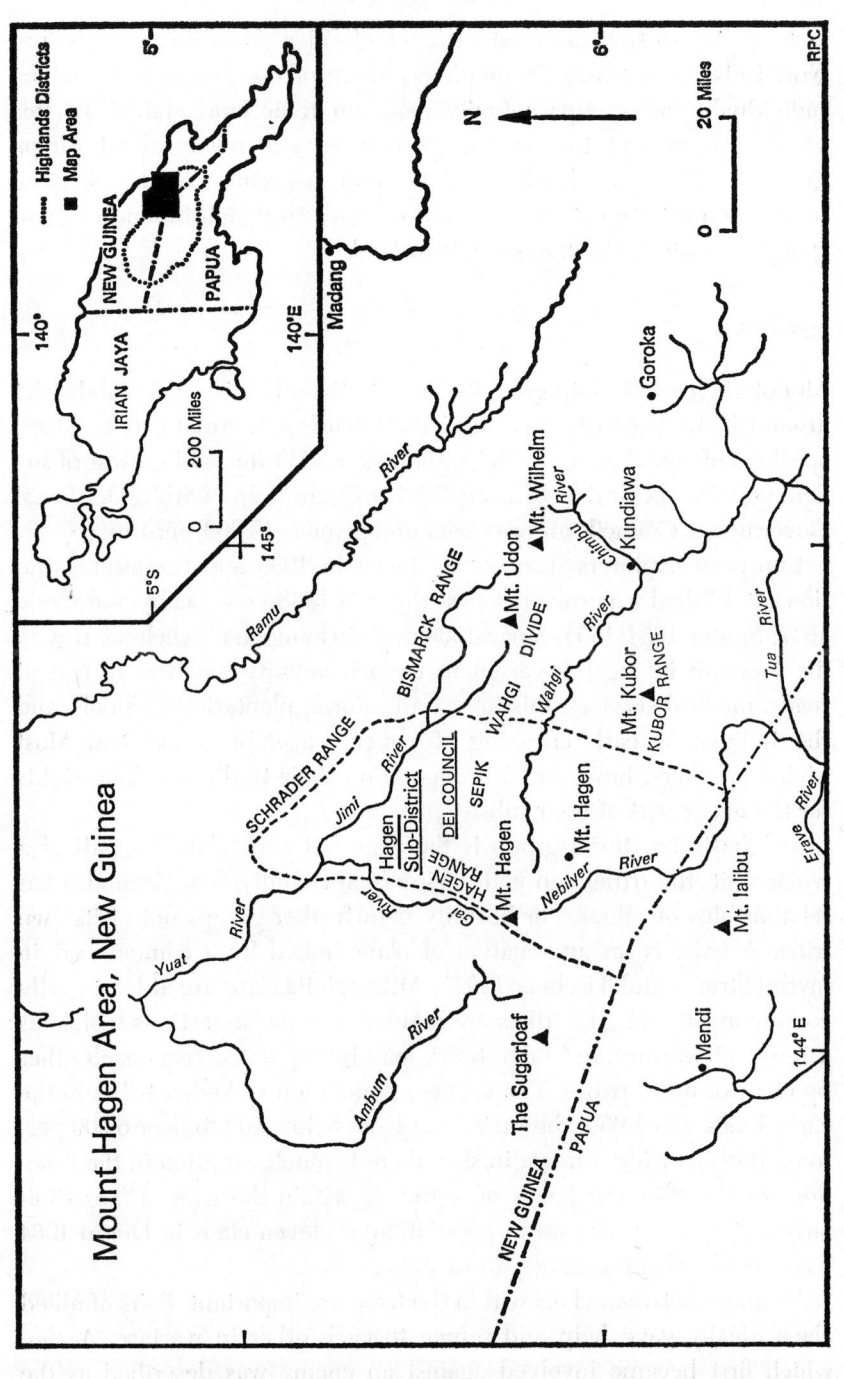

history. An abstract account of a set of rules governing land tenure would also give a very incomplete picture of the processes by which individuals and groups actually maintain their land claims. In this chapter, I attempt to combine generalized statements about Melpa group structure and land tenure with some account of the effect of warfare on settlement patterns and of cases in which individuals and groups dispute each other's rights to land.

GROUPS

Mount Hagen township gives its name to the administrative subdistrict around it. Living mainly north of the township, there are some 60,000 speakers of the Hagen, or Melpa, language (Wurm 1964). Most of my fieldwork has been done among the Northern Melpa within Dei Local Government Council, an area containing some 18,000 persons.

European explorers discovered Hagen in 1933 and the administration established a permanent post there in 1938 (see Leahy and Crain 1937; Souter 1964:185). Since 1960, social change has accelerated with the increase in local government council activity and the spread of roads, medical services, missions, trade stores, plantations, schools, and the indigenous cash cropping of coffee, vegetables, and tea. Most Melpa speakers, however, still depend on their traditional land rights for the major part of their subsistence.

The basic territorial group is the clan, but each clan is a part of a wider unit, the tribe, and is itself internally subdivided. Each also has relationships of alliance or hostility with further groups not of its own tribe. A tribe is an aggregation of clans linked by a common origin myth (Strauss and Tischner 1962). Although its clans are at least partly contiguous, the largest tribes are divided into major sections which, as a result of warfare and migrations, may be separated from each other by clans of other tribes. The average population of Melpa tribes in the early 1960s was 1,059; the range was from below 100 to over 6,000 persons. With so wide a range in size, there is much variation in the functions of the different levels of segments within the tribe. Clans similarly vary in size. The mean population of eleven clans in Dei in 1964 was 258 persons; the range, 45 to 463.

Alliances between clans within the tribe are important. Pairs of allied clans ideally gave help and refuge to each other in warfare. A clan which first became involved against an enemy was described as the *el pukl wu*ᵉ 'root man of war,' while its ally was called *kui wu*ᵉ 'the dead man,' from the fact that it was likely to lose men in fighting for the 'root man.' 'Root men' had to pay 'dead men' for their losses, and these payments are still made the basis for elaborate exchanges nowadays. Also, some new battles have occurred since 1970. Pairs of allies speak of themselves as exchanging wives, and friendship between them is also indicated by interdigitation of their garden land at certain points along their borders. A basic distinction is made between a clan's allies and minor enemies and its major traditional enemies. With the latter, intermarriage and sharing of land are less frequent.

Within a clan's territory there are areas, more or less discrete according to the stage of segmentation which the clan has reached, associated through repeated use with its sections and subclans. Where a clan has divided into separate sections, they are likely to have more clearly distinct territories than the subclans within them, but this pattern is also modified by shifts of residence within the wider territory of the clan as a whole.

Subclans are most often spoken of in two ways: first, as descendants of different wives of the clan founder or simply of his different sons and second, as separate *manga rapa* 'men's house groups,' whose adult male members gather together for joint discussions on ceremonial exchange activities. Subclans in turn may include *manga rapa kel* 'small men's house groups,' themselves divided into congeries of men conceptualized as *tepam-kangemal* 'father-son units' or lineages. These smaller units are important in arranging bridewealth payments and also in land inheritance. The lineages are the only groups within which most men can state a genealogical connection with each other, and it is within the lineage that land claims are usually passed on by inheritance. The transmission of land in this way is usually confined to those who are close relatives. Despite the agnatic idiom in which the lineage is conceptualized, such relatives are not always patrilineal kin. In one Northern Melpa tribe, the Kawelka, nonagnates comprised 37 percent of the adult male members in 1964, the percentages in separate clans ranging from 18 percent to 51 percent.

In each clan there are also a number of prominent *wu*ᵉ *nyim* 'big-men,' that is polygynists and self-made leaders who are important in ceremonial exchanges. These are the men who actually negotiate and organize payments between allied groups and who in the past offered protection and the use of land to refugee groups. They also welcome from other groups incoming kinsmen who will stay and support them in their exchange activities in return for the use of land. Newcomers are also often brought in by divorced or widowed sisters who return home to their brothers, bringing young children with them.

SETTLEMENT AND GARDENING

The Melpa area divides into hills and plains. Altitudes range from about 3,000 feet above sea level to 13,000 feet at the summit of Mount Hagen, but most settlement is concentrated within the 5,000 to 7,600 foot range. On the hilltops stands of primary forest occur; elsewhere grassland and planted or self-sown secondary fallow trees predominate.

Settlement follows the pattern found in other societies of the Western Highlands—homesteads dotted over group territories. A typical homestead may comprise a man with his married sons, and possibly other associates, along with wives and children. Each homestead is surrounded by some of its staple gardens; others, owing to land availability or previous changes of residence, may be elsewhere. Within the homestead men and women sleep in separate houses. Partitioned-off areas in the women's houses accommodate pigs at nighttime. The reason for the maintenance of separate houses for the sexes is that men consider they may be endangered by too regular and close contact with their women. Menstruating women spend four or five days in seclusion huts, during which time they may not feed their menfolk or weaned sons.

Two main garden types are distinguished: the sweet potato garden and the mixed vegetable garden where one finds a variety of greens, hibiscus, cucumbers, cane inflorescences, maize, bananas, and New Guinea asparagus growing together. Sugar cane, taro, and cassava are also planted, sometimes in separate plots. After a full set of crops has been harvested from a mixed vegetable garden, it is left to a long fallow of five to fifteen years or else may be reworked and converted into a sweet potato garden. Mixed vegetable plots are said to require better soil than those planted in sweet potato. To ensure the recovery of soil fertility they may be planted with casuarina seedlings and left until these have grown tall before recultivation. Sweet potato gardens, by contrast, may be planted three times before they are allowed to revert to fallow through the invasion of sword grass. Ground covered by sword grass or cane grass fallow is considered unsuitable for replanting with mixed vegetables, but may be taken into cultivation for sweet potatoes again after only a few years. Men retain individual claims to fallow land, and disputes arise if a man's rights to fallow are infringed.

Gardens cut from primary forest are only roughly prepared. Men fell the trees and either allow their trunks to lie across the garden and rot or use them to form part of a fence. Women clear the soil of some of its roots. Vegetation is burned in heaps. Men plant crops classified as tall, especially sugar cane and bananas; women plant those which are short, especially greens. Gardens cut from fallow are more carefully tilled. They are likely to be trenched, and the soil is thoroughly cleared. Earth from the trenches, which are laid out in a distinctive crisscross pattern, is placed on top of the garden beds themselves. Before Europeans came, various kinds of wooden spades and stone axes were employed; now all major tools are of steel.

Women do most of the harvesting, cooking, and pigherding. Each household within a homestead raises its own pigs, which are required for a large number of ceremonial occasions. The production of sweet potatoes for pigs to eat and the provision of land for their pasturing are integral requirements of the economic system. Some pigs are pastured on land to which men have individual fallow claims; they may also run in areas of forest or cane grass over which only communal claims are exercised.

LAND RIGHTS

A principal category which the Melpa employ in talking about land rights is that of *møi pukl wuᵉ* 'ground root man.' *Pukl* may be glossed as 'root, link, cause, reason.' The 'root man' of a piece of land is a man who has a true reason for his association with it. Clansmen as a whole are spoken of as 'root men' of their territory. They are also 'root men' of each other, that is, each other's true associates. Their links with each other and with a common territory are thus conceptually blended.

In analyzing the system of land rights which flows from this concept of the 'root man,' it is important to make two distinctions: first, between individual and communal rights and second, between the rights of 'root men' proper whether individual or communal and the claims which others can exercise to the use of a piece of land by virtue of a kinship tie with the 'root man.'

Clansmen as a whole have "guardianship" rights (see Lawrence 1967). That is, an individual may not entirely alienate his rights to a piece of land over which his clansmen have a communal right without their agreement. He may, however, grant the use of strips of his garden land to others for one or more cropping seasons without consulting his clanmates. Further, if his clansmen agree, he can encourage a sister's son to live with him and eventually join his group. Sisters' sons have strong claims on their mother's clansmen and are sometimes spoken of as 'ground root men' when they come to live at their mother's natal place. They are thus in a good position to convert their claims on their mother's brothers into full membership of the latter's clan, which brings with it access to the communal rights enjoyed by clansmen in relation to their territory.

Clan rights. Clansmen have guardianship rights over the whole of their territory. They jointly hold the right to cut down trees in forest stretches for building purposes. Men of paired clans may, however, grant access to each other's forests for hunting birds and marsupials and for gathering mushrooms, lianas, and plants used for personal decoration at festivals. In most areas an individual clansman should ask his group mates before he converts an area of communal forest or pig pasture land into a garden. Where land is becoming short, areas may be specifically set aside for communal pasture, and numbers of clansmen cooperate in digging large ditches or building fences in these areas. Clansmen also maintain joint rights over cemeteries and ceremonial grounds. The sanction against cutting into the cemeteries in order to make gardens lies in the fear not only of rebuke from one's living clansmen but also of attack by the ghosts of ancestors buried there. Clans often maintain more than one cemetery, but there is usually no strict association of cemeteries with particular subclans as there is in the case of ceremonial grounds. One ceremonial ground within a clan's territory is likely to be spoken of as being used for large ceremonies by all clansmen, while smaller ones are specific to subclans. The smaller ones are often created and used especially by individual 'big-men,' who may convert them back to garden land after a particular prestation has been completed. Thus, these smaller grounds do not fall so clearly into the communal domain as do cemeteries and larger ceremonial grounds. After a 'big-man's' death, his personal ceremonial ground may fall into disuse and become overgrown unless he has a son or other lineage mate who can adequately succeed to his position.

Individual personal rights. A clansman has an unambiguous power over the exclusive exercise of personal rights over pieces of currently used garden land and fallow within the clan territory to which he has claims by inheritance or by undisputed tillage. Provided there are no complicating disputes and there has been no disruption in a clan's occupation of its territory, most of a man's land rights are likely to be obtained by patrifiliation. Transmission occurs both postmortem and inter vivos. A father cannot deny rights to a son unless the son neglects him and runs away to join another group. As his sons grow up, they are expected to help with the work of preparing gardens and are allocated strips which their mothers plant and harvest. After they marry, their father provides new areas for them. Brothers and lineage mates cooperate in garden work, but each also progressively establishes rights to separate strips or to whole gardens as he grows older. Each allocates strips or plots to his mother until she dies. Brothers may continue to share rights over certain gardens even after their father's death, for the father need not divide his land exhaustively—he may simply say before he dies, "Share the gardens out and live together." This situation can lead to disputes.

When a polygynist with a number of sons dies, ideally, as well as usually in actual practice, the older sons should reallocate their father's gardens and pigs between themselves and should also recognize any of his debts which they or their mother knew about before the father's death.

There are three points to note about this process. First, there is no true system of succession whereby a single person steps into a large number of statuses and roles occupied by a previous possessor. That is, no son automatically assumes precedence over the others, although all of them may in fact be guided by the advice and decisions of a brother of their dead father. Rather, sons are expected to make the reallocation together by discussion.

Second, if the sons are already grown and married, they are likely to have made a number of gardens on their father's land before he dies and thus to have established rights to continued cultivation of these gardens after his death. If there are sons who are not yet grown, the elder brothers should keep gardens for them. In one case, an aging polygynist father has retained certain gardens for himself and his wives and told his grown sons to make gardens on other plots within their subclan's area if they need more than they have obtained from him. The older sons agree that the gardens the father has retained should go to his two youngest sons when he dies. These two can expect to obtain plots used by their mothers while the father was alive.

This brings us to the third point—the youngest son's situation is likely to depend on what his mother does when she is widowed. If she elects to stay in her dead husband's place, she looks after pigs for her young son and sees that he obtains pieces of land from his elder brothers. If she remarries within her dead husband's subclan, as is common, her son can later claim land both from his father's and from his stepfather's estate. A further possibility is for her to return to her own natal kin. If she does so, her son can expect to obtain land rights from his mother's people.

Group claims which can be made on 'root men.' Whole groups or sections of groups can be accommodated as enclaves of immigrants or refugees within the territory of another clan. Before 1945 such moves were often made as a result of warfare; nowadays, groups still migrate in search of good land or pig pasture. In doing so, their men may make use of generalized alliance or friendship between their group and their hosts, but one usually finds that they also have specific ties of affinity or matrilateral kinship with the hosts as well.

Claims of individuals on individual 'root men.' Wives do not gain independent rights over their husband's land, but they do have a strongly recognized right to be allocated stretches of garden land which they plant and harvest. If a husband fails to provide garden strips in this way, his wife can formally complain and may leave him and return home to her own kin. A polygynist husband must be careful to divide garden strips equitably, for co-wives are jealous. Each wishes to have good land on which to grow crops for her own children and pigs, particularly as she tries to ensure that her husband conveys some of his pigs as prestations to her natal kin. In theory, as husbands see it, husbands can allocate garden strips as they please, provided they do so fairly. Divisions between co-wives' strips are often marked with red cordyline plants. These divisions remain when the garden goes into fallow. When it is recultivated, each woman may try to reclaim her old strip, particularly if its soil is fertile. The husband is then in difficulties if in the meantime he has taken another wife and wishes to give her a share of the garden.

Kinsfolk. It is when a man makes a mixed vegetable garden that he is most likely to allocate planting and harvesting rights to strips within it to kinsfolk not of his own homestead. Close affines, married sisters and their children, and matrilateral kin are those most likely to be invited to share in the use of a vegetable garden in this way. This allocation of strips does not have to be on a strictly reciprocal basis. It is advantageous for a family to obtain the use of strips in gardens planted at various times in the year, for they can thus have supplies of a range of vegetables for longer periods than if they were dependent on a single garden planted at one time by themselves.

As in the case of wives, the 'root man' grants planting and harvesting rights to his kin, but he cannot transfer any further rights over the land, for these are held by his clansmen as a whole. In particular, his lineage kin may object if he attempts to hand over his garden to a nonclansman for a longer period of time than a season and in return for a specific payment of valuables.

Women do not lose their natal clan membership at marriage. Before marriage a girl is often allocated garden strips for her use, and she has the right to continue using these strips after marriage unless they are reallocated to an incoming wife. If given a new strip after her marriage, a sister and her husband help to till and fence the whole garden. They give a present to her kin from their own section as a mark of gratitude if the garden bears well. In practice sisters maintain strips in this way only if they have married fairly close to home, which is a frequent occurrence, for there is a preference for marriage with allied, neighboring groups.

If a woman separates from her husband or leaves his place as a widow and brings her children back to her natal clan, her immediate brothers and father, if he is still alive, are likely to readily grant her the use of gardens from which to feed herself and her children. The brothers say she is returning to *elim-nga møi* 'her own land' and add that if she had been a man, she would have stayed at home anyway and thus have enjoyed full rights. If she returns to live at her brother's place, her latent rights as a group member, albeit a female one, can be activated, because she is behaving like a man by coming to live at her natal place. The maternal kin expect in this case that her children will also stay with the mother and join her group. They will be *amb-nt-mei* 'woman-bearing' members and will suffer no formal disabilities of status as such. On the other hand, they also retain an option to return to their father's group later, and his gardens may be left in fallow for them to come and use if they wish. Sooner or later, however, they should attach themselves permanently to one or the other group, and if they do so, their group membership and land rights are usually secure.

The likelihood of a widow being able to return to her natal kin with her children depends on the claims made on her by her ex-husband's subclan mates. Since they have probably helped to pay bridewealth for her, they try to retain her so that in most cases widows are in fact remarried within the clan. But the widow's own right to make a choice is also recognized. Sometimes a widow leaves against the will of her dead husband's kin. The latter may then try at least to recover her children and affiliate them with their father's group. Whether this happens or not, the children's potential land rights are not likely to be placed in jeopardy.

It is important to notice that it is only a sister's sons who have strong claims on their mother's clansmen. More distantly related kinsmen, and in-laws, have weaker claims. While a sister's son can be described as a 'ground root man' at his mother's place, his father, the sister's husband, cannot be, for he has no consanguineal tie with the 'root man' group. Whether in fact a sister's son is so described in a particular case also depends on how welcome he is as a useful settlement member at his new place of residence. I have sometimes heard one 'big-man' say that only patrifilial members are true 'root men.' He compared them to tall forest trees on which parasites (other group members) grow. Yet he also applied exactly the same metaphor to sister's sons as opposed to other categories of nonpatrifilial incomers (Strathern 1971:20).

TREES

The distinction made in the preceding section between communal and individual rights applies also to trees. Exclusive individual rights apply only to trees which are planted or are enclosed in individually held fallow areas. Unplanted forest trees are the property of all the men of the clan whose territory abuts onto the forest area in question; hence each clansman has a right to use these trees, but not to allocate their use to someone not of the 'root man' group.

The most important planted trees are casuarinas, fruit pandanus, and coffee trees. These last provide most of the individual farmer's cash income. Bamboos are also planted and owned individually and are found around homesteads and ceremonial grounds. They provide material for knives, musical instruments, water containers, and cooking utensils.

Casuarinas are valued, for they give shade, improve soil, and provide easily split timber. They seed along river banks, and men gather the seedlings to plant with crops either in gardens that they intend to return to a long fallow after use or around homesteads and ceremonial grounds. Only the individual planter holds the right to cut them down or to delegate someone to do this. Women occasionally plant casuarinas, but if so they grant the right of felling them either to their husband or to a brother. Sometimes a man grants permission to another to plant casuarinas on his garden land. One man then controls the trees, and the other works the garden land itself.

Fruit pandanus trees are planted in low-lying, fairly wet parts, especially in the Jimi Valley north of Hagen. These trees continue to bear for several years. Again, only the original planter holds the right to harvest the fruit, even if he has since left the locality to make his main gardens elsewhere.

Coffee trees have been planted in the Northern Melpa area since the 1950s. Although women do much of the weeding and harvesting work, men own the coffee trees and usually share part of the income from the berries. Almost all men keep coffee patches, but few have turned over the bulk of their gardens to coffee production, as has happened in some parts of Chimbu District (Brookfield 1968). The patches have been accommodated in pieces of land which may previously have been used for mixed vegetables and are considered fertile. Coffee growing has not yet produced severe problems for the system of subsistence agriculture. However, men are rather wary of granting permission to others to make new gardens on their land, if they suspect that the latter plan to place coffee seedlings in the garden. The usual practice is to plant the seedlings along with green vegetables and taro so that after the vegetables have been harvested the coffee remains. New plantings dropped off in the 1960s, although observation in 1970 and 1971 indicated that some planting continues.

All planted trees are subject to individual inheritance. Either a father allocates them before his death, or his sons divide them out after he has died. Patches of coffee trees are inherited in the same way as are pandanus and casuarinas.

PAST WARFARE AND CURRENT DISPUTES

Intergroup disputes. As mentioned earlier, full-scale warfare was halted throughout the Melpa area by 1945; but memories of it were still clear in 1971. Its results still show in group alignments and disputes and these occasionally give rise to intergroup conflicts which resemble muted forms of warfare. Disagreements between individual clan members over rights to clan land occur but are less significant than those that involve group interests either at the clan level or at some higher level of structure.

Although the crude overall population density in the Melpa area is not so high as it is in Chimbu (Brookfield and Brown 1963) or among the Mae Enga (Meggitt 1965), informants do sometimes speak of themselves as having fought to expand their territory.[2] Such a motive might be compounded with a wish to remove a troublesome neighboring group from one's borders or simply to take over a dwindling group's territory. Figure 1 summarizes some of the territorial consequences of disequilibrium in warfare. As a result of defeat in warfare, individual men or whole sections of groups might migrate out from their territory, either leaving it unoccupied or ceding it entirely to the enemy or sharing part of it with the successful intruders. Whether men scattered individually or migrated as groups, two major possibilities were open to them: either to be absorbed into a host group or to maintain or later recover their identity by establishing themselves on a piece of territory, whether one granted by hosts or colonized independently by themselves. In some cases, men could return to their former territory, and this has been a favored kind of move since the Australians established peace in the Highlands. If a group establishes itself in an enclave territory, obtained from a host, its men are now likely to maintain good relations with the hosts by exchanging shell valuables and pigs with them.

The degree to which refugee settlers are able to establish their own territory depends on their own numbers and on their host group's own needs for land. For example, one set of clansmen of the Minembi tribe, when defeated and driven out in an intratribal battle, were allowed to

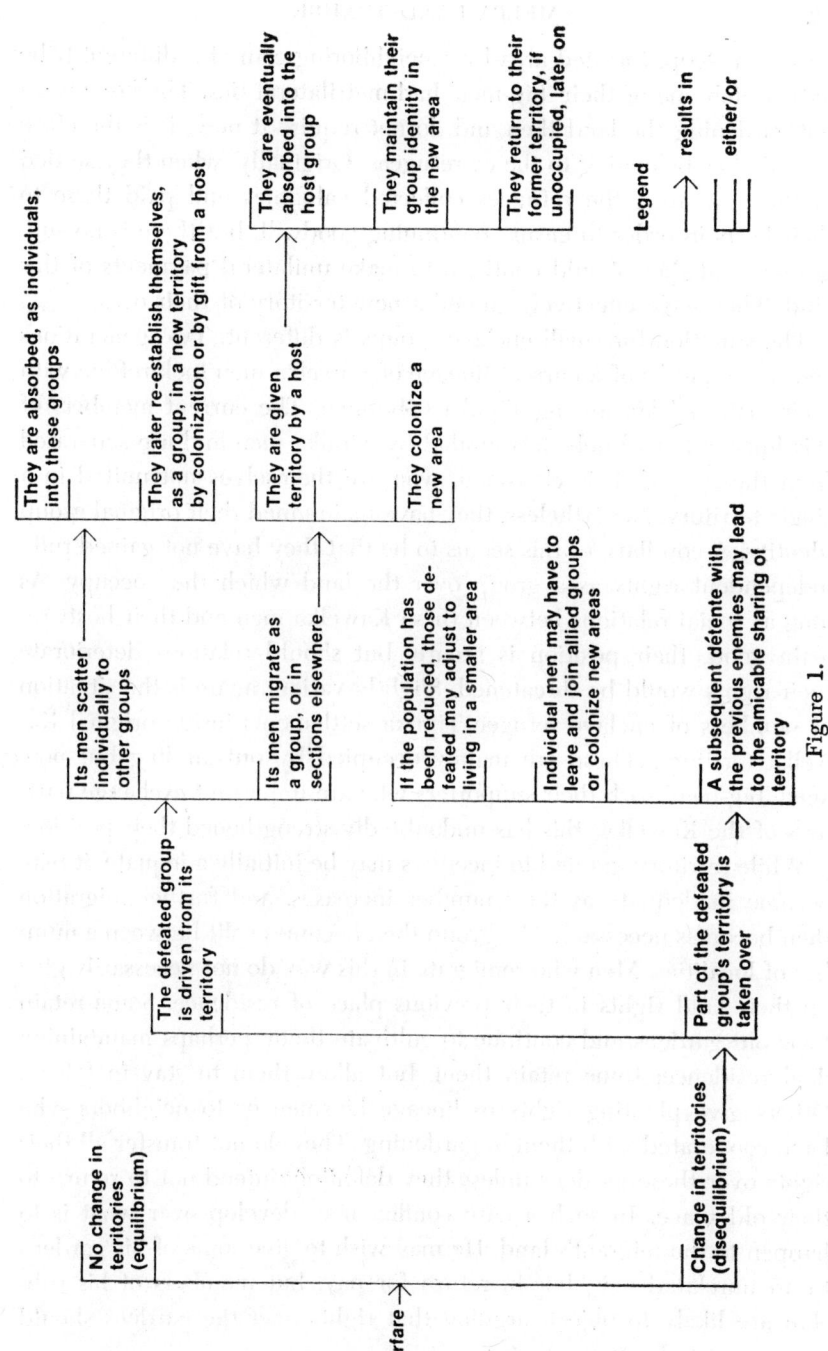

Figure 1.

occupy a steep, forested area by a neighboring clan of a different tribe with which one of their 'big-men' had matrilateral ties. The hosts were not gardening the land then and do not require it now; it is therefore regarded as belonging to the ex-refugees. Originally, when they settled in the new area, the refugees collected valuables and paid these to their hosts in order to ensure continuing goodwill, but there is no suggestion that they should continue to make unilateral payments of this kind. They have effectively gained a new territory of their own.

The situation for small enclave groups is different. Two generations ago the founders of a current lineage of Kawelka men took refuge with their maternal kin among Tipuka tribesmen. The current members of this lineage live closely surrounded by Tipuka men and are separated from the rest of their clansmen, who are themselves not united in a single territory. Nevertheless, they have maintained their original group identity. A corollary of this seems to be that they have not gained fully independent rights as a group over the land which they occupy. As long as social relations between these Kawelka men and their hosts remain good, their position is secure, but should relations deteriorate their rights would be threatened. Slightly variant again is the situation of numbers of enclave refugee Tipuka settlements inside original Kawelka territory. These are mainly occupied by outstanding but now aged 'big-men' with their supporters who are important exchange partners of the Kawelka; this has undoubtedly strengthened their position.

While territory granted to incomers may be initially adequate, it may become inadequate as their number increases, and further migration then becomes necessary. The group then becomes split between a number of localities. Men who remigrate in this way do not necessarily give up their land rights in their previous place of residence. Some retain their old gardens and continue to cultivate them, perhaps maintaining dual residence; some retain them, but allow them to stay in fallow. Others give planting rights to lineage kinsmen or to neighbors who have cooperated with them in gardening. They do not transfer all their rights over these gardens unless they definitely intend not to return to their old place. In such a case conflict may develop over what is to happen to the migrant's land. He may wish to give some of his gardens to an unrelated neighbor in return for pay, but members of his subclan are likely to object, arguing that rights over the gardens should now revert to his group mates.

The motive for new migrations is usually a wish to obtain better land for gardens, pig pastures, and, especially since the 1960s, land on which to plant coffee trees. Extraclan consanguineal and affinal ties enable individuals to move about and find new land rights for these purposes. Difficulties set in when groups encroach on each other as a result of migration and recolonization, as the following example will show.

For the past fifteen or twenty years sections of one Northern Melpa group, the Kawelka, have been recolonizing a previously held territory. They left this area as a result of warfare in the Wahgi Valley. The land in this territory had lain unoccupied at least since Europeans began to enter the Highlands in the 1930s. Their return to it was made possible by the administration's imposition of peace, and they intermarried with other groups moving back into surrounding areas. Ceremonial exchanges were begun with these groups to establish friendship, and in 1965 there was little observable friction over land rights.

However, by 1969 disputes emerged over which groups should obtain money for land alienated to the administration and for work on building new roads. Rivalry had developed between two leaders of the Kawelka and Ndika groups, complicated by the fact that the disputants belonged to two different local government councils, Dei and Hagen, respectively. A further complication was the introduction of land demarcation committees, consisting of local representatives and an administration officer. The actions of one such committee, in the disputed Kawelka-Ndika area, seem to have precipitated intense hostility over land boundaries. Representatives receive some briefing on how to handle arguments, and they are supposed to aim at obtaining agreement between the parties before they lay down a boundary marker. In this case the Kawelka and another group, the Kimka, argued that agreement had not been obtained, that the boundary markers had been laid down prematurely, and that they must therefore be removed. The administration, however, insisted that the markers remain in place.

Clearly, great care should be taken in recording and sifting evidence on land rights, especially where there is factional rivalry between groups. Further, it should be established whether markers indicate boundaries of use rights or of ownership rights to land. The reason for this is that allied groups customarily grant each other use rights over land. As a result, enclave settlements develop, and a complicated interweaving of land rights between the two groups can result. In such circumstances an attempt to lay down rigid, permanent boundaries between the two groups becomes of questionable value, quite apart from its difficulty. Even where the groups involved are not close allies, some interweaving of land rights and settlement places is likely to have occurred. The need to indicate exactly what rights are being defined by boundary markers is underlined by the fact that people in the Kawelka-Ndika case were afraid that they would suddenly be entirely dispossessed if a boundary decision went against them. It is not surprising then that they talked of either fighting for their land or of demanding heavy compensation if they should be dispossessed. Again, if dispossession is actually envisaged, it should be accompanied by consideration of the feasibility of resettlement elsewhere.

Background factors which are likely to increasingly affect Hageners' attitudes to land are the spread of cash crops and, in the Wahgi, the alienation of land for the development of tea plantations. Land alienation, in particular, may create feelings of tension and apprehension over land rights even though it removes areas from immediate dispute between local groups. The mere fact of purchase by the administration changes land from a permanent resource available to a group as a whole into a commodity convertible to cash. Since cash is desired, groups are willing to sell, but they are likely afterwards to feel ambivalent when they have spent their cash and see their previous territory being profitably developed by others.

Interpersonal disputes. Land disputes within the clan center on arguments about the nature of the rights involved in transfers and about entitlement to inheritance.

The temporary transfer of use rights to garden land between clansmen or, occasionally, men of paired clans can occur either with or without payment. Payment in the form of pigs, pearl shells, or Australian currency is made when the donor gives up a garden he values and would otherwise have cultivated. The size and type of payment depends on the relationship between the parties as well as on the size of the garden involved. Ambiguity may arise, whether payment is made or not, about the degree of permanence of the transfer. Interpersonal disputes of this kind are not common, and the only cases I know of are ones which were reported to me by lineage or clan kinsmen of the disputants themselves many months, or even years, after the events took place. However, I shall give brief accounts of four such cases in order to illustrate the main features of these disputes.

Case 1. Two men, X and Y, belonging to neighboring allied clans quarreled over a sugar-cane garden. X cultivated the garden originally. Then Y paid him a pig, a leg of pork, and two marsupials for the use of the garden. Y recultivated it, planted casuarina trees, and let it revert to fallow. When X asked for the garden back, Y said he had purchased permanent cultivation rights over it. X disagreed, saying that he had paid only for temporary rights. Y retorted that if X was going to use the garden, he must pay for the use of it. The two men then fought with sticks until Y gave in. X replanted the garden, but later Y came by night and stole from it. Challenged, Y said he had simply paid X back for removing the garden from him and now they were even. So the matter rested.

In this case, there was obviously some ambiguity about X's original transfer to Y, the sort of ambiguity which can easily arise in the absence of standardized payments and legal procedures. No mention was made to me of the clans of X and Y becoming involved. Instead, X maintained his rights only by individual forcefulness. Case 2 shows a similar pattern in relation to a dispute over inheritance.

Case 2. J cultivated a garden (figure 2). After J's death his widow remarried. Her new husband, K, claimed that he, rather than J's sons, had J's rights to the garden. The sons, G and H, did not object. However, E and F, from a subclan paired with that of J, now separately laid claim to the garden, saying J had verbally allocated it to them before his death. F claimed precedence over E in that he was E's lineage father. E would not accept this, and they fought. Finally, F gained the use of it, so that use rights were transferred between two subclans. This case shows again the importance of personal assertiveness in establishing claims to garden rights.

In cases, such as 3, where one party fails to dominate the others, clansmen or a *komiti* 'councillor's adjutant' may step in.

Case 3. Three men, C, D, and E, of the same small lineage were involved in land disputes (figure 3). First, D and E planted a garden together, but E planted coffee seedlings on a strip claimed initially by D. D threatened to fight E. A 'councillor's adjutant' failed to stop them and called in clansmen, who jointly decided the dispute by planting cordylines as boundary markers between the portions of the garden belonging to each. On another occasion, C disputed with E the use of a part of a plot previously cultivated by C's father. The clansmen again

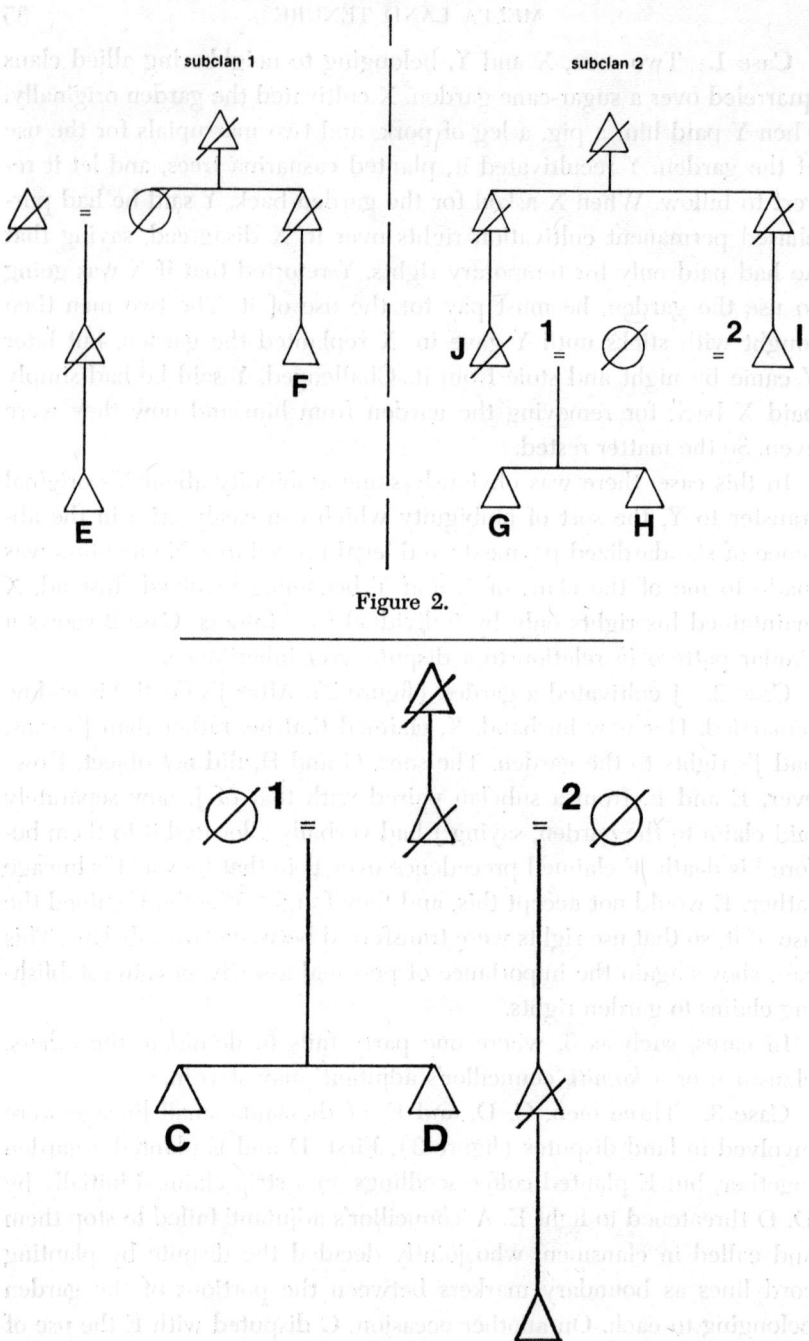

Figure 2.

Figure 3.

intervened and in this instance forbade either man to use the garden, since they would not agree to share it amicably.

Case 4. A man, D in case 3, left his main clan territory to live in an area that his group was recolonizing. He wanted to retain his gardens at his old place. Previously, he had borrowed a garden from a lineage mate, his father's sister's son's son (FZSS), a second generation nonagnate. The latter asked to resume his own cultivation rights. D refused. A 'councillor's adjutant' of his clan stepped in and decided that the garden should be divided between the two, but that D had overstepped his rights and should pay a two dollar fine to his lineage mate. In the past, 'big-men' would sometimes settle such disputes in a similar fashion.

Interpersonal disputes between clansmen are thus usually brought to settlement, either through one party dominating the other, by action of the clansmen as a body, or by decisions taken by a 'councillor's adjutant' or 'big-men.' By contrast, intergroup disputes often involve political rivalry and, for that reason, are harder to settle.

CONCLUSIONS

In this chapter I have attempted to outline the basic rules which govern the regular creation, exercise, and transmission of rights in various categories of land, planted trees, and forest resources among the Melpa speakers of highland New Guinea. The most important distinctions in kinds of rights over land are between group rights and individual rights and between the permanent cultivation rights of the 'root men,' flowing from group membership, and the temporary rights which may be transferred to others. Cultivation rights are obtained largely through kinship relations. Rights as a 'root man' can be obtained only through first cultivation or inheritance within one's group territory. Clansmen as a group retain rights of use over forest resources, cemeteries, and important ceremonial grounds, and individual clansmen cannot alienate permanent cultivation rights over garden and fallow land unless the rest of their group agree. In the case of smaller ceremonial grounds established by individual 'big-men,' the 'big-man' can himself turn the ground back to garden land if he wishes.

The stability and continuity of an individual's or a clan's rights to land depend on their ability to defend these against encroachment by others. Before 1945, when a clan could not defend its territory, there were arrangements whereby its men could be accommodated as refugees elsewhere—by either joining new groups or maintaining their old identity in a new territory. It was chiefly warfare which generated the need for such arrangements, but the results are still evident in group alignments. A factor which was as important in pre-administration times as it is today and which leads to residence changes is the search for good garden land and pig pasture. The search has been accelerated since the 1960s by the desire to obtain a cash income from one's land. Such residence changes are facilitated both by values inherent in kin relationships and by the ambitions of 'big-men,' who encourage kinsfolk to join their settlements and support them in ceremonial exchange activities.

In the Melpa system, land tenure is closely bound up with the total nexus of social relationships between individuals and groups. Accordingly, tenure rights depend on the maintenance of amicable relations and can be jeopardized by intergroup rivalries. These rivalries are exacerbated by the growth of cash cropping and the increasing alienation of land, at least in the Wahgi Valley area. Intergroup disputes have thus become a potentially serious problem. Wise solutions to this problem, however, would not involve putting an end to the total flexibility of the system by oversimplifying the existing rules or by foreclosing the possibility of processes of change in residence and group affiliation.

NOTES

1. Fieldwork was conducted, between 1964 and 1972, with the aid of grants from the Royal Anthropological Institute; the University of Cambridge; Trinity College, Cambridge; and the Australian National University. I am grateful to all these institutions for their help. I wish also to thank my wife for information on groups near Hagen township. Most of my statements relate most specifically to the Kawelka, Tipuka, and Minembi groups in the northern part of the Melpa area.
2. In the early 1960s population density was approximately 118 persons per square mile in the Hagen council area and 68 per square mile in Dei council.

3

LAND TENURE IN THE WOLEAI

William H. Alkire

INTRODUCTION

Those islands of the central Carolines in Micronesia that lie between Woleai Atoll in the west and the raised coral island of Satawal in the east are often collectively referred to as "the Woleai." Eauripik, Ifaluk, Faraulep, Elato, and Lamotrek are included. The total population of the area is approximately 1,600 individuals. Woleai Atoll itself is both the most populous, with nearly 600 residents, and the largest, even though its total land area is less than 1½ square miles.

The data for this analysis were gathered on Woleai Atoll in 1965 and Lamotrek in 1962 and 1963.[1] Minor variations in practices and especially terminology were noted between these two atolls, and undoubtedly additional variations will be found on the other islands. Nevertheless, I believe the similarities in the land tenure practices in the islands of the Woleai are greater than their differences.

The land tenure system of the Woleai is still essentially a traditional one. Even though the area has, within the memory of residents, been administered in turn by the Germans, Japanese, and Americans, no official land surveys have been made. Consequently, there are neither land registers nor land taxes although a cadastral program is currently underway in the Trust Territory which eventually will probably result in a survey and registration of land holdings in the Woleai. In addition, although there is a court on Yap which officially has jurisdiction over these outer islands, no case involving a land dispute has ever been brought before it.

Direct changes by foreigners in the tenure system have been imposed, primarily during the years of Japanese administration. But while some lands were confiscated and transferred to Japanese government and commercial interests, most of these parcels reverted to their original owners when the Japanese left Micronesia.

Indirect changes traceable to the presence of colonial powers, but not the result of their direct interference, appear to have been more long lasting. These latter changes involve parcels of land that now have importance in the copra trade. Certain previously unexploited or marginally important areas of land, that is, the ocean side of inhabited islands and the whole of uninhabited islands, now have a continuing importance for cultivation of coconuts where previously they were unimportant to the subsistence economy. The changes brought about by this, however, are mainly ones in which traditional tenure principles that previously would have been infrequently invoked are now of great importance and, consequently, frequently utilized. This is especially true of those traditional rules that permit an individual to exploit land on islands other than the one on which he normally resides.

Of direct concern in this chapter is the interrelationship of the land tenure system and the social groups of Woleai society. As Goodenough (1951) emphasized in his study of Truk, land and social groupings, primarily kin groups, are inseparably linked and thus a full analysis of the tenure system demands clear definition of such groups.

The population of the Woleai is divided among several *gailang* 'matrilineal, exogamous, nonlocalized clans, or sibs.' Each island is occupied by chiefly and nonchiefly clans, but the chiefly status of a clan on one island does not automatically indicate a like status on any other. The native explanation of chiefly status emphasizes seniority of settlement on the particular island under consideration. There are some instances where the status of a clan has changed, however, and these are reflected in changes in land holdings and/or population numbers, so seniority of settlement is not the sole, but is perhaps the most usual, explanation of status ranking at the clan level.

Table 1 lists the islands of primary concern to this chapter and notes the area and approximate 1965 population of each. The inhabited islands of Woleai Atoll are grouped according to their location on either the western or eastern lagoons, which are actually subdivisions

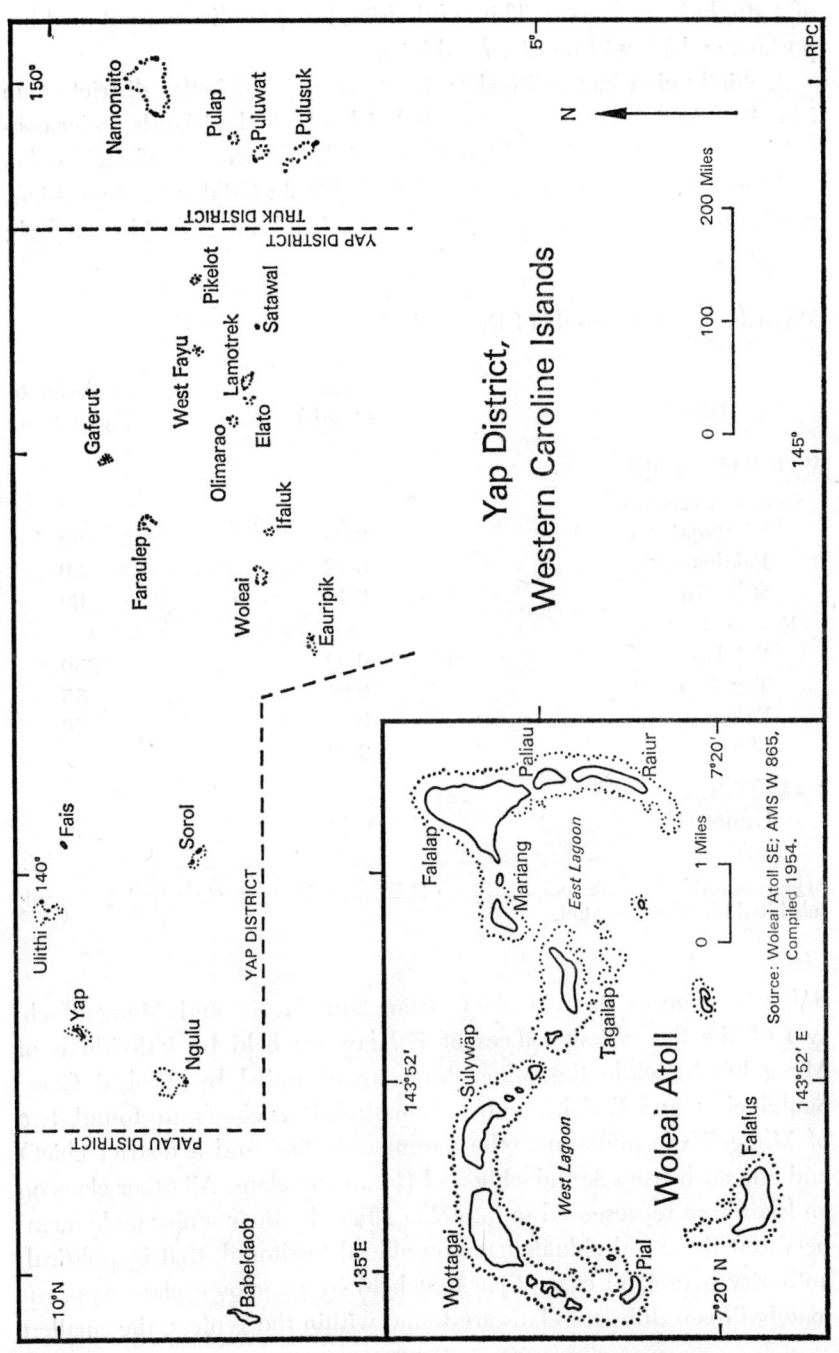

of a single large lagoon. This subdivision has a traditional political importance which will be discussed later.

A chiefly clan has political authority over a particular district of an island or, in some cases, over a whole island. Of the islands under consideration, Wottagai Island has three chiefs, one from Saufalachig clan and two from different lineages of Mongalifach; Falalus has two chiefs, one from Gailangaliwoleeya, 'Woleai Clan,' and one from Mongalifach;

TABLE 1   The Islands of the Woleai

Island	Area (sq. mi.)	Approximate Population
WOLEAI ATOLL		
Western Lagoon		
Wottagai	0.25	90
Falalus	0.12	80
Sůlywäp	0.15	60
Eastern Lagoon		
Falalap	0.43	250
Tagailap	0.06	55
Paliau	0.07	20
Mariang	0.04	a
LAMOTREK ATOLL		
Lamotrek[b]	0.24	200

[a]The few residents were temporarily on Falalap at this time. [b]Lamotrek is the only inhabited island on the atoll.

Sůlywäp chooses its two chiefs from Saufalachig and Mongalifach; two of the five chiefly offices of Falalap are held by individuals of Mongalifach, while the other three are occupied by 'Woleai Clan,' Saufalachig, and Hofalu; and on Lamotrek four chiefs are found, two of Mongalifach affiliation (the paramount chief and a district chief) and one each from Saufalachig and Hatamang clans. All other clans on an island are represented in interclan affairs by their senior male members, but these individuals have no official territorial, that is, political, authority over land other than that held by their own clan. Approximately fifteen different clans are found within the Woleai, the smallest has but a single member and the largest has more than 100 members on a single island.

NATURAL CATEGORIES OF LAND

Falu which can be glossed as 'land' is conceptually subdivided into three major types: *pi* 'sandy areas,' *nimel* 'interior land,' and *bwül* 'swamp land.'

'*Sandy areas.*' This first category is limited in importance as a resource area; it comprises beach areas bordering the lagoon and certain small uninhabited islets. The land tenure system, therefore, emphasizes the other two categories.

'*Interior land.*' This type of land is also called *chümao* 'hard land,' and on inhabited islands this is the most common and economically most important kind of land, since over half of the some 100 different varieties of locally defined plants are interior species. This includes such food crops as breadfruit, sweet potatoes, *Alocasia*, bananas, mountain apples, and arrowroot, as well as most coconut trees.

'*Swamp land.*' The amount of 'swamp land' on any island of an atoll varies, but is sufficient on most of the inhabited islands of the Woleai to support adequate acreages of *Cyrtosperma* and *Colocasia* (taro), two of the most important staples, for present populations. Falalap represents a significant exception to this generalization. Even though it is the largest island of Woleai Atoll and once had extensive 'swamp land' areas, much of this was filled in by the Japanese during World War II when they constructed an airstrip on the island. It has not been possible to reclaim this land, and, as a result, sweet potatoes are more important here than on any other island of the region.

The various lineages of an island control a cross section of these natural categories, although the parcels may not be contiguous, so that each lineage has access to all classes of productive land.

LAND USE

The natural characteristics of a piece of land delimit the agricultural use to which it can be put, but all land of one particular type is not treated identically. Some plots are more important than others. Some can be used for only certain purposes while others may be used for different purposes from time to time. Land subdivisions, boundaries, and zones are all cultural constructs. The most important of such subdivisions are those that have a political or economic reality.

The inhabited islands of Woleai are invariably divided into two or more political districts. These districts are subdivided into numerous individually named parcels in which 'interior land' parcels are distinguished from 'swamp land' plots. Boundaries are indicated by trees, large plants, paths, or some distinct feature of the land. It is unusual, however, to find that a boundary line follows a natural configuration of the land for its complete length other than those boundaries which separate particular 'swamp land' parcels from adjoining 'hard land' plots.

In the Woleai, land is set aside or allocated for the following uses: agricultural exploitation, dwelling sites, canoe and men's houses, menstrual and birth houses, auxiliary buildings, religious sites, cemeteries, and public paths. Any land which is not in one of these categories is periodically exploited for forest products; thus all land on an island is used and owned. There is no virgin land.

Agricultural parcels. 'Interior land' parcels are all generally of equal social and ceremonial importance. 'Swamp land,' however, is often ranked, whereby each island usually has one taro swamp considered more important than any other, and as such certain supernatural beliefs are associated with it. This 'swamp land' is most commonly called the *bwonnap* 'great taro swamp' and although it may in fact not be the largest, ceremonially it is considered the *fons et origo* of the taro of the island. The taboos and magic associated with taro production for the whole island, for example, are centered on this swamp above all others. Nevertheless, it is subdivided, often into very small plots, just as any other swamp on the island, and these plots are owned by particular lineages of the island.

House sites. Most dwellings border a main path which runs the length of an island one or two hundred feet inland from the lagoon shore. Every house site is either the seat of a lineage or is affiliated with another site which is. A lineage seat and its affiliated plots, whether contiguous or dispersed, comprise a *bwogot* 'estate.' Each 'estate' is referred to by the name of the ranking plot of the group. For example, one might hear that land parcel E goes with O 'estate'; in other words,

E is a part of O. This statement refers as much to the people living on the land as to the land itself. An *erao* is a 'chiefly estate' and ideally there should be but one for each district of an island. But lineages occasionally gain or lose chiefly status, and thus the term 'chiefly estate' may be associated with all of the estates of a district that are remembered as having been chiefly at one time or another.

Men's houses and canoe houses. I have grouped these two uses together because there are few remaining men's houses still standing in the Woleai; their functions have been assumed by individual canoe houses. The plots where men's houses were once found, however, are treated as though such structures were still standing or functioning, and consequently the land cannot be appropriated for any other use. Canoe houses have political functions similar to those of men's houses, but they operate at the clan level rather than the district or island levels. They are centers of activity for the men of particular clans or, occasionally, lineages if a clan is large and dispersed enough to require more than one canoe house. The women of an island avoid men's houses and also canoe houses as much as possible.

Menstrual houses. In pre-Christian times, before 1955 on most islands, each island had at least one main menstrual house situated in some shielded or remote location beside the lagoon beach. The house was used by all women even though the land on which it was found belonged to a specific lineage. These locations are still avoided by men even though on most islands the houses are no longer used.

Spirit houses. Particularly important spirits may be associated with or may frequent certain areas of an island. A medium for a particular spirit may thus construct a spirit house at the location in which offerings are left. In 1965 there were two spirit houses on Falalus, one on Wottagai, and a recently abandoned one on Sůlywäp. These sites are respected and in some cases avoided even by recent converts to Christianity who minimize the importance of traditional spirits. The sites, even where abandoned, have not been converted to other uses.

TYPES OF RIGHTS

Sawei rights. Control or ownership of land in the Woleai exists at several levels of the socio-political system. In the context of the interisland *sawei* 'overseas exchange system' is the Yapese belief that particular islands or parts of islands belong to certain Yapese kin groups or "overlords." The active aspects of this system, that is, the tribute payments by outer islands, such as the Woleai, to the Yapese, and certain counter-presentations by Yapese, ceased many years ago. However, there is still a feeling on the part of these Yapese that the outer islands belong to them, and this feeling is centered on the land rather than the people.

Case 1. In 1962 one Yapese informant from Gagil district stated, "I don't care about the outer islanders, but I do resent the loss of my land." Among other Yapese, resentment over their loss was manifested in grumblings about not receiving a share of the rents paid to Ulithians by the U.S. Coast Guard for the land occupied by a loran station. Traditional sanctions were even alluded to. A story widely circulated on Yap at that time held that a Yapese weather magician had brought a typhoon down on Ulithi on one occasion and caused lightning to hit a Ulithian canoe on another as punishment for not sharing these rents.

These rights, from the outer islanders' point of view, were only important on those rare occasions when a Yapese visited one of the outer islands. At such a time, the Yapese was taken in by his *sawei* partner, housed, and fed for as long as his visit lasted. The outer islanders saw the sawei system as primarily a socio-political and religious system which had an adaptive value in insuring survival in times of crisis. With the advent of direct colonial control the system gradually lost its importance to the outer islanders and is now largely inactive.

Chiefly clan rights. At Woleai Atoll each inhabited island is divided into either two or three districts, and each district is represented by a chief. Lamotrek is divided into three districts, each with a chief; there is also a paramount chief with authority over the whole atoll.

District chiefs are supposedly ranked according to their clan's seniority of settlement on the island. Each chief has political authority over the residents of his district regardless of their clan affiliation. On Woleai Atoll, where there is no paramount chief, in the days when the *sawei* system was active, the chief of Olimara district (also called Nigapalam district) on Wottagai Island had the authority to reach decisions relevant to the *sawei* for the whole atoll, but this position did not, it seems, give him similar status in local affairs.

It is usual for the chiefs of an island to reach collective decisions in island-wide affairs and, as in other systems of this type, it often happens that particular chiefs because of characteristics of personality often wield greater authority than that appropriate to their actual rank. A chief has the authority to organize and initiate district- or island-wide activities and ceremonies, and the responsibility to maintain peace and quiet. It is a chief who decides, for example, when communal fishing expeditions should occur, when village paths are to be cleaned, when a particular ceremony should take place, how long a funeral taboo must last. If someone under his authority breaks the peace or violates a restriction, he can impose sanctions on the individuals concerned or on the whole population. The following three cases are examples of situations where a chief can legitimately impose sanctions.

Case 2. Two men who were members of a drinking group in the northern district of Lamotrek got into an argument one evening that resulted in shouting and a scuffle. The next morning the chief of the district imposed a month-long drinking prohibition on the two men.

Case 3. The paramount chief of Lamotrek, who happened to be a woman, thought the men of the island were drinking and arguing too much and consequently threatened to have all the taps on the coconut palms removed, thus stopping palm wine production on the island. Most of the men disliked the decision, but none disputed her right to make it.

Case 4. One young man from Falalus who was attending school on Ulithi Atoll violated a traditional restriction when he began an affair with a Ulithian girl. The chiefs of Falalus heard of his behavior. When the three young men who were attending school on Ulithi returned to Falalus for summer vacation, the chiefs called a meeting of all men of the island. The matter was discussed at length, and the chiefs then decided to tell all three boys that if they did not promise to behave, they would be prohibited from returning to school. Collective reprimands such as this are common, for they serve to diffuse criticism from a single individual to a group since direct person-to-person confrontations are frowned on in the Woleai. Additionally, in this case, threat of collective punishment would encourage the other Falalus students to help in disciplining the delinquent while all were away on Ulithi.

As far as authority over land is concerned, at no time have chiefs had true eminent domain over land. They cannot expropriate land or adjudicate land disputes. If their own clan is involved in a dispute, the chief's authority is the same as that of any other clan head. The chiefly clan of a district normally controls the majority of the land of the area. However, there is no clan that owns all the land in any one district, although it is held that this was sometimes the case in the distant past. A chiefly clan, however, has two symbolic prerogatives associated with the land and its products in the particular district concerned, namely, *malumei* 'first fruits' and *fät* 'chiefly shares.'

'First fruits' are presented to a chief at the beginning of the breadfruit season by all landholding groups within his district. These fruits are redistributed by him to district residents or in some cases to all residents of the island. A 'chiefly share' is a supplementary share of fish, turtle, or other meat given to a chief when an animal is butchered and distributed. This share is usually passed on by him to a homestead of his district with which he has some type of consanguineal or affinal tie.

Since a chief has responsibility for communal ceremonies he, or his personal appointee, takes special interest in communal structures. In traditional times the men's house was the most important communal building. Today the chief makes decisions about such structures as the school, dispensary, storehouse, and cistern, if such exist.

Case 5. The chiefs and residents of Wottagai agreed to erect a new schoolhouse with materials provided by the American administration. A, the chief of Olimara district, the highest ranking on the island, agreed to donate a site for the building. The administration's education officer from Yap and the two other Wottagai chiefs thought the site ideal since it was centrally located. Before construction began, however, A changed her mind and withdrew the offer. The other chiefs and most of the residents were disappointed but could do nothing about it. Finally B, the chief of the western district, agreed that a portion of his lineage land could be used. When I discussed the matter with A, she was unwilling to go into detail concerning the reasons for changing her mind, but she left the impression that she was afraid that other demands would be made on her land if she agreed to this one. Even though she was a chief, she felt she was in a precarious position since she was the sole direct survivor of her lineage and subclan in the district, her heir being an adopted child about eight years old.

Tenure rights in the Woleai include rights over reefs and lagoons. At Lamotrek and Woleai atolls these are rights that rest with chiefly clans and subclans. At Lamotrek, different sections of the reef and lagoon are under the control of chiefs from Mongalifach, Saufalachig, and Hatamang clans. An additional senior subclan of Mongalifach, the highest-ranking clan of the island, controls a portion of the reef and lagoon, and informants state that this particular subclan is one from which chiefs were previously selected.

A similar situation is found at Woleai Atoll. Sections of the reef and lagoon are divided among the various chiefs of the islands, but intra-atoll political organization has resulted in a more complex division of rights. Here there is a socio-political system called the *chülifeimag* that unites the different districts and clans of islands at opposing ends of the lagoon in a reciprocal exchange system (Alkire 1970). This system can be referred to as the 'intra-atoll exchange system.' In these instances a clan from an eastern district which controls any portion of the reef shares this control with a clan from the west which is united with it in the 'intra-atoll exchange system,' and vice versa (see table 2).

TABLE 2 Intra-atoll Exchange System

Western Lagoon	(is tied to)	Eastern Lagoon
Nigapalam district, Wottagai		Paliau Island
Tabwogap district, Wottagai		Raiur Island and Lülipelig district, Falalap
Falalus Island		Iur district, Falalap
Sülywäp Island		Ifang district, Falalap

Case 6. Because of the 'intra-atoll exchange system,' Woleai clan of Falalaus has a right to exploit that part of the eastern reef of the atoll that is directly under the control of the chief of Woleai clan of Iur district on Falalap Island. The Iur district Woleai clan chief could give sections of the reef to some other clan if he wished, as long as he gained permission from the other senior members of his clan; but he would have to tell Falalus residents about the transfer so they could appropriately restrict their fishing.

The whole 'intra-atoll exchange system' seems intimately tied to reef and lagoon ownership. Pïgül district of Wottagai is the one major district of the atoll not involved in the 'intra-atoll exchange system,' and the chief of this district does not control any reef or lagoon areas.

Chiefly control of a reef area not only means that the chief can pass these rights on to another clan as outlined above, but that he can restrict or prohibit fishing in these areas. Only members of the particular chiefly clan are permitted to place fish traps on the reef. Anyone, however, is free to fish the area with spears or hook and line. Net drives on the reef are also restricted since they are communal affairs initiated and organized by a chief. The chief can close the area to all types of fishing for the duration of a funeral ceremony, which may last for several months, when someone from his clan dies.

Small uninhabited islets within an atoll, or neighboring atolls that have never been inhabited or subdivided into separate plots, may be exploited by all residents of any nearby island or atoll. The chiefs have a right to control this exploitation through imposition of taboos. The chief as a political head is given a percentage of the profits from any commercial exploitation of the area. The Lamotrek paramount chief, for example, can collect a percentage of copra profits from exploitation of uninhabited Pigalot Island. In addition, today, as in traditional times before copra was commercially valuable, this paramount chief expects a share of all turtles taken from the island.

Ordinary clan rights. Basic and effective control of land begins at the clan level. Ultimate title to land is expressed in clan terms, that is, land is said to belong to Sauwel clan, Hofalu clan, or some other clan. A visitor to an island who has no close kin there can expect food and shelter from any clanmate on the island. And the limits of simple transfer of parcels of land are marked by clan boundaries. This means that if no more closely related kin group, as described in the sections to follow, makes claim to particular parcels at the death of a former holder-exploiter, then common clan membership is enough to establish a legitimate claim. Cases of this type are not too common, however. They occur only when the sole surviving member of a clan in a particular district dies.

Case 7. C is a Carolinian woman who was born and raised on Saipan. Her great-grandmother moved to that island during the 1800s after a series of typhoons devastated two islands at Lamotrek Atoll that even today remain uninhabited. In the mid-1950s C visited Lamotrek and was convinced by the chief of the northern district that she should remain on Lamotrek and reside on common clan land that was not being worked at the time because of a shortage of manpower. Her claim to the land was based merely on common clan membership with the extinct lineage of the land.

This type of situation occurs because land continues to be identified with and to belong to particular clans until it is formally given to another clan.

Case 8. An important piece of land on Lamotrek is called Saur clan land even though no Saur people survive on the island. Today Hofalu clan members work the land because one of their members was married a generation ago to a Saur man. If any Saur members should move to Lamotrek from any other island where the clan survives, they would have a right to claim this land.

In most cases the clan itself is a group whose origin seems closely associated with particular places. The people of Woleai do not emphasize a folk etymology when discussing clan names, but of the clans present in the atoll the majority are named after places, such as 'People of the North,' 'Clan of Woleai,' or 'People of the Small Island.' A minority emphasize supposed attributes of their members, such as 'Pandanus Eaters' and 'Straight People.' There is only one clan on Woleai which is named after a person—Gailangalifelu, the 'Clan of Telafelu,' the first part of his name having been dropped in the clan name.

Certain clans (Mongalifach, Saufalachig, and Sauwel among them) are found widely distributed throughout the central and western Carolines, and they usually hold important political positions on most islands. Since wide distribution often reflects age, and since political position in the Carolines is held to indicate time of settlement, these clans are probably the ones brought to Woleai by early arrivals. However, their actual islands of origin are generally unknown to present-day members.

Other clans with more restricted distribution are known to have emerged quite recently, and their places of origin are clearly reflected in their names. Gailangaliwoleeya, for example, supposedly arose after a war between Ifaluk and Woleai. Before that war, Falalap was divided between Saufalachig and Hofalu clans, but the war killed all the people of Falalus and many of the residents of Iur district on Falalap. Those individuals who resettled Iur district took the name 'Clan of Woleai' (Gailangaliwoleeya) and later some of these individuals moved to Falalus.

Location, residence, and the importance of land are further emphasized in the cases of Saoifang and Lugufalu clans and the relationships these two groups have with Saufalachig. The relationship is one which occasionally develops between landed and landless groups whereby a landless clan may have a *hagula* 'understanding' with the landed and politically dominant clan of a particular district. Under this system the low-ranking group, probably of recent origin or arrival on the island, is obligated to follow the directives of the higher-ranking group. In return for this the former receives certain rights to land.

Case 9. On Wottagai Island, Saoifang clan has an "understanding" with Saufalachig, one of the chiefly clans of that island. Informants stated that some time ago a branch of Saoifang asked permission of Saufalachig to leave the district and move to the middle district of the island where Mongalifach clan had offered them land. This permission was granted; the lineage took up its new residence and changed its name to Lugufalu 'Middle of the Island,' thus forming a new clan having an 'understanding' with Mongalifach. The fact that permission from Saufalachig was needed seems to indicate that these individuals were not residents of longstanding on the island.

Subclan rights. Subclans are groupings of closely related, perhaps genealogically traceable, lineages of a clan. Conversely then, the lineages of different subclans, even though found on the same island, usually cannot trace a relationship any more exact than common clan name. It seems likely that such subclans often are descended from core lineages which originated on different islands and arrived at Woleai at different times. Subclan distinctions affect land transfers in the following way.

Individuals of the same subclan are identified as the legitimate heirs of the lands occupied or worked by that subclan even if the permanent residence of such individuals is on another island outside the atoll. The land passes to another subclan only if the original subclan of ownership becomes extinct on the atoll and surviving members of other lineages of the same subclan which may be found on another island are unwilling to move to assume stewardship of the land in question. During the course of fieldwork, both on Woleai and Lamotrek, I noted several instances where sole surviving members of subclans took precautions to assure orderly transfer of land holdings when they died. In most instances the solution was to adopt a child who would carry on the lineage.

Case 10. On Lamotrek, D, a Sauwel woman, chose as her heir the adopted daughter of her deceased brother, who had married and then died on Ulithi Atoll some 300 miles away, rather than any other Sauwel resident of Lamotrek. She stated that all other Sauwel people on the island were members of different and distant subclans. Control of the land in question had passed according to numbers (1) through (5) in figure 4 and will pass to (6) when D dies.

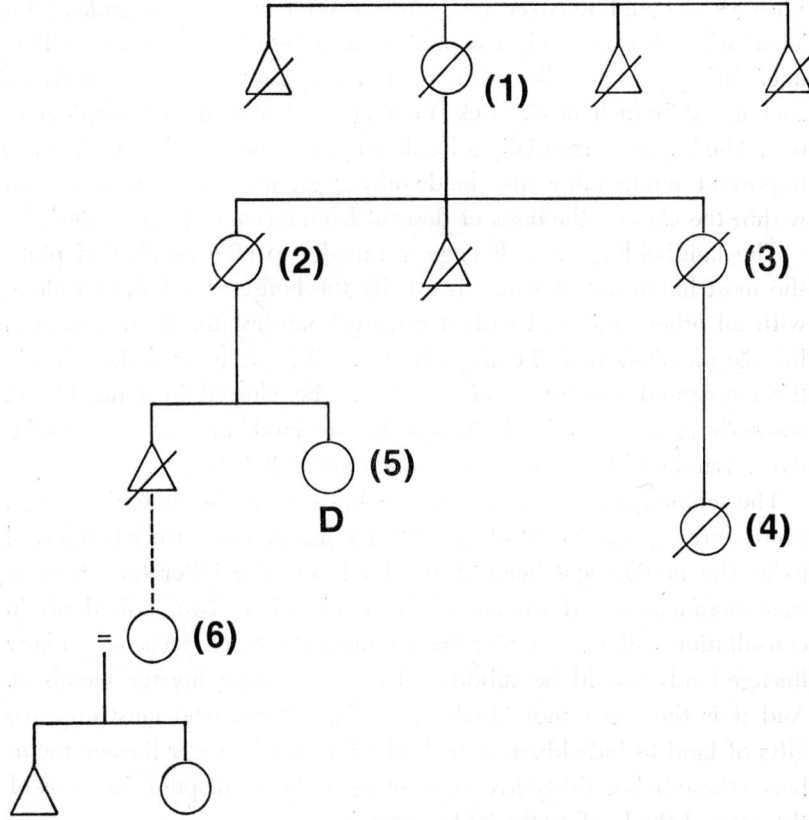

Figure 4. Control over the land of this lineage has passed according to the sequence of numbers. D (5) is the present 'old woman of the land,' and 6 has been designated as her heir. Crossed symbols indicate deceased members and the dashed line an adoptive relationship.

The reality of subclan distinctions is apparent in another case from Lamotrek.

Case 11. E, the paramount chief of Lamotrek, is the last surviving member of a Mongalifach subclan. She has adopted a daughter who will inherit subclan lands when E dies, but it is not clear who will assume the paramount chieftainship. The general opinion is that a subclan member on a neighboring island would have a right to this position if he moves to Lamotrek. If he should do this, he will also assume joint control of the lands of the subclan along with E's adopted daughter.

Lineage rights. Most lands in the Woleai are actually controlled by lineages. I could uncover no word in Wolean, such as *gailang* for 'clan,' which is exclusively accepted as meaning either 'subclan' or 'lineage.' Informants usually made reference to such groups with words such as *ral* 'branch' or *ira* 'stick,' making an identification through analogy. The lineage, essentially a localized group, nevertheless is the most important landholding and landworking group. And each is ranked within the clan on the basis of descent from senior or junior sisters.

The landholdings of a lineage are made up of a number of plots, the most important of which is usually the house site. This plot along with all others affiliated with it constitute an 'estate.' If one refers to lineage members with the above term *ral*, it is rarely used alone but in the compound *ranubwogotai* which can be glossed in a number of ways—'branch of my land,' 'people of my land,' or merely 'my relatives.' Land and kinship in this context are indivisible.

The senior man and woman of the lineage are the individuals who exercise the greatest control over lineage lands. The former is referred to as the *malibwogot* 'man of the land' and the latter the *chabwut tugofaielibwogot* 'old woman of the land.' These two individuals in consultation with other senior lineage members reach decisions on how lineage lands should be subdivided for use among lineage members. And it is these two individuals, above all others, who must approve gifts of land to individuals outside the lineage. Younger lineage members (those below thirty-five years of age) do not dispute decisions of the 'man of the land' or the 'old woman.'

Land under the stewardship of a particular lineage may be subdivided for use among the sisters of the eldest generation of the lineage. If the landholdings are quite dispersed, one of these sisters and the members of her descent line probably will establish an independent household near the land she actually works. Such a group, however, is still referred to as part of the mother 'estate.' It is possible, of course, that this kind of dispersion may lead to true fission if the separation is of long standing and the respective lineages continue to grow in membership. It is more likely, however, that at the death of the lineage head the younger sister will succeed, or at the death of the younger sister her descent line holdings will be reabsorbed by the lineage for redistribution. Succession to the position of 'man of the land' is also usually from elder to younger brother with preference given to the elder descent line—that line that is descended from the eldest sister in the highest-remembered ascending generation.

In the Woleai, although land is inherited matrilineally, it is believed that every lineage needs a strong 'man of the land' to protect lineage rights. In two cases already cited, cases 5 and 10, the women involved stated their fears about losing lineage land in the same way, namely, because they had no man to take care of the land.

The 'man of the land' is thus overseer and guardian of all lineage land, including any land received as gifts by other lineage members. Gifts of land are usually made by an individual to another individual. The donor, however, must obtain lineage permission to give land away; likewise, the recipient does not expect to retain individual rights over it, rather the land is incorporated into his lineage holdings. One 'man of the land' phrased it this way, "If [his sister's son] is given some land he should inform me and I will become 'man of the land' over it." Another 'man of the land' disputed the universality of this rule, however. He stated he had rights to certain land parcels and that these rights were not shared by all others in his lineage. These were the parcels he had received from his mother and which she had received from her father. He stated that other members of his mother's descent line share these rights. This type of fragmentation of land rights seems to involve taro 'swamp land' more often than 'interior land.' This situation probably arises because of the nature of taro-land exploitation. Taro, unlike most 'hard land' crops, requires constant care and this is usually the responsibility of the woman who received the land as a gift. If help is needed, she obtains it from her daughters. If her lineage 'man of the land' is strong, the land may be incorporated into general lineage holdings.

Rights in father's matrilineage. Even though the Woleai inheritance system is fundamentally a matrilineal one, an individual does have some rights in the lands of his father's matrilineage.

Case 12. G was a Lamotrek man who married a Trukese woman

and consequently went to that island to live. He died there about fifteen years ago. Several men from Lamotrek sailed to Truk in 1960 and while there approached H, who was G's son, and invited him to Lamotrek, as they felt he should visit the island of his father. In 1961 H did visit Lamotrek and took up residence with his father's matrilineage.

All individuals can, if they choose, make certain hospitality demands of their father's lineage.

Case 13. J was a young man from Lamotrek who had been away at school on Yap for a year. In the summer of 1963 he came to Lamotrek for a two-month vacation and returned to his own lineage homestead. During the course of his vacation, he often visited the lineage land of his father and obtained food there. The 'old woman' of this homestead said J had a right to do this because his father was from that land. In this case, too, the father had died several years earlier.

Individual rights. On only one occasion did I encounter a situation where land was said to belong to an individual, and this was the result of an unusual pioneering situation. All of the islands of the Woleai are small and have probably been inhabited for several hundred years. There is virtually no land on any inhabited island which is not claimed by one or another lineage. In only this one instance did I observe a situation which might be termed pioneering of unclaimed land.

Case 14. K was a man from the western district of Wottagai Island. A small islet lay on the reef southwest of Wottagai and on a sandspit at one end of this islet K was regularly planting coconuts. Several people said that if the coconuts survived, more sand would accumulate and the islet would grow larger. The land reclaimed in this manner would belong to K.

Reclaiming or claiming land by planting coconuts may once have been common. It is possible in the Woleai tenure system to distinguish between the owners of land and the owners of trees which grow on that land. Nevertheless, where a large number of trees in a single stand are involved, claims may be made to the land itself. Consequently, anyone who permits another to plant trees on his land must make clear to all concerned that no transfer of land rights is meant.

Case 15. L belonged to Hatamang clan and was the son of M, a man from Fairucheg, a Mongalifach clan 'estate.' L planted several coconut trees on a portion of Fairucheg land and thereafter Hatamang clan claimed ownership of this plot. The senior members of Fairucheg denied that any permanent transfer of ownership had taken place and would only reluctantly admit that Hatamang gained use rights to the land for the purpose of planting trees; they insisted that the land still belonged to Mongalifach clan.

Whereas individual control over land is rare, individual ownership of trees, both coconut and breadfruit, is common. Not all coconut trees are individually owned; many, if not most, are exploited by lineage members who have rights to the land on which they are found. However, many trees in or near the village, and many exceptionally fruitful trees, are owned by individuals. Trees tapped for palm toddy are always individually owned.

Individual ownership of this type may originate in one of three ways. A man may plant his own tree. Since ownership of trees may be completely separated from ownership of the land upon which they grow, it is easy for a man to defend his claim. A man might also gain individual control of a lineage tree by approaching his 'man of the land' and asking for exclusive exploitation rights; he might do this if he wishes to tap the tree for toddy. However, lineage trees used for copra production, a collective activity, are not usually individually owned. Finally, one may obtain individual control of a tree as the result of a gift. Coconut and breadfruit trees are often given away or exchanged.

Case 16. Approximately twenty trees on Hapilamagol 'estate' lands have been given away. N, a former 'man of the land' of the lineage who died several years ago, gave a tree to his daughter and one to his son's wife. O, another man of the lineage who died fifteen years ago, gave a tree to his son's wife. P, a younger brother of the current 'man of the land,' gave a tree to his wife. Q, the current 'man of the land,' has given away ten trees: one to his son; two to his wife, one of which she has since given to someone else; one to a woman who composed a song for him; one to another woman who rendered him medical aid; one to his mother's brother's son's son; two to a man who married a girl from his lineage; one to a woman who adopted a daughter of a man from this 'estate'; and one to a man who did carpenter work for Q. Q also gave a tree to his sister's son's wife at the request of his sister's son when this woman bore her first child. P, a younger man of the 'estate,' exchanged trees with another man to formalize their friendship.

This case indicates the range of reasons for giving trees away, but it is not meant to indicate the frequency of certain types of gifts. I do not have statistics that are complete enough, for example, to determine whether males or females give or receive such gifts more frequently.

Summary. A continuum of unrestricted to more restricted rights over land in the Woleai might be outlined as follows:

1. *Sawei* rights were held by certain Yapese which entitled them to tribute from the residents of land they controlled and food and lodging if they should ever visit the lands.

2. Islets that have never been inhabited and, consequently have never been subdivided, are claimed and worked by all the residents of nearby inhabited islands. This ownership may be symbolically affirmed through the person of the paramount chief, if such exists, wherein all residents are free to take subsistence food from the islet, but all have to pay a tax to the chief for turtle hunting or intensive commercial exploitation for personal profit. The population would expect the chief to use such taxes for public benefit.

3. Reef and lagoon areas within an inhabited atoll are claimed by the chiefly clans of the atoll, but are casually fished and exploited by all residents. Intensive exploitation, that is, by traps and net drives, can be done only by members of the chiefly clan or by others with the permission of the chief. This permission would probably be given routinely to district residents. A chief has a right to close off these areas to all kinds of fishing on certain specified occasions such as the duration of a funeral taboo.

4. Clan membership gives one a general right to subsistence exploitation when visiting another island: This is perhaps best termed a hospitality right. However, clan members who are co-resident on the same island do not automatically have rights in each other's lands. Rights of intensive exploitation usually are limited to the lineage. Lineage members share rights of residence, subsistence exploitation, commercial use and rights to subdivide and dispose of land. One's seniority in the lineage is a measure of one's voice in the above matters, consequently, the 'man of the land' and the 'old woman of the land' have the most authority. Intensively exploited areas, especially taro plots, may be divided among descent lines of a lineage (comprising a woman and her adult daughters) but these lands are reapportioned from time to time as a result of marriages, births, and deaths.

5. Individual rights to real property seem limited to particular trees. Coconut trees within and near the village, trees which are especially

fruitful, and breadfruit trees may be owned by individuals. Individual ownership is restricted to a type of property which itself is single, specific, and intensively exploited. Small intensively exploited taro plots are the only parcels of land that closely approach individual ownership because of the number of restrictions imposed on their use.

TYPES OF TRANSFER

The above discussion of rights over land has made reference to several different types of land transfers. These are itemized more completely in this section.

Transfer of rights from one generation to another primarily occurs within the matrilineage. An individual born into a lineage gains rights similar to those of all other members. His voice in lineage affairs increases with age. When the oldest lineage male dies, the 'man of the land,' his younger brother, or the next senior male inherits the position. Lineage land does not actually change hands, but, rather, there is a change in the headship of the on-going landholding group.

Where transfer of land involves a change in the group which has authority over it, one is usually not talking about inheritance, but some other type of transfer which sees the land passed from one clan to another or at the minimum from one subclan to another. All types of land may be given away, and there are a variety of reasons which justify such gifts. The two cases that follow refer only to taro land, but similar cases could be cited for other types as well.

Case 17. Four taro plots that belong to Hapilamagol 'estate' have been given away. The first was given to S, the wife of the 'man of the land' of the 'estate'; the second was given to T, the wife of a younger man in the lineage; the third to U, who adopted a child from the lineage; and the final plot to the wife of a former 'man of the land' of the lineage.

Case 18. Lechib is another northern 'estate' on Lamotrek. Several persons of this lineage have received taro plots as gifts. Palimach plot was received by V from her husband; W was given Setiap plot when she adopted a child from another lineage; Maison plot was incorporated into lineage holdings when X, a man of Lechib, received it as a gift from his wife's lineage; and, finally, Peilugulugul plot was given to Y by her husband.

It should be made clear that gifts of land and trees are not the complete transfer of all rights. Rather, the donors retain a residual right to reclaim the land and the recipient group recognizes this right symbolically by presenting certain gifts to the former on all significant ceremonial occasions, namely, first-fruits ceremonies (when the donors are members of a chiefly lineage), first pregnancy ceremonies, deaths, construction and repair of the donor group's houses, or when a senior member of the donor group makes an important interisland voyage. Collectively these gifts are sometimes termed *palewan* 'answer' or 'response,' but more often the name of the gift reflects the type of transfer involved, that is, *chülübwogot* 'in return for ordinary land'; *chülübwül* 'in return for taro land'; and *chülümai* or *chülünü* 'in return for transfer of rights over a breadfruit tree' or 'coconut palm,' respectively. The 'response' takes the form of woven skirts and loincloths (for most ceremonies), or sennit twine (when houses are repaired). If the recipient lineage fails to make this gift, the donor can taboo the land that was given by placing a *machang* 'coconut frond taboo' sign on it. The recipient removes this by making a *muimuimachang* 'redeeming gift'; if he fails to do this, the donor reclaims the land or tree involved.

Land and tree transfers of this type, then, are essentially transfers of use rights, even though they may extend for such an indefinite period that they might be considered permanent. Informants did not completely agree about the conditions under which the land could be reclaimed other than by failure to present a 'response.' Some said that if the donor lineage should once again need the land, perhaps because it had grown large, it could exercise its residual right and ask for the land back. This would probably not happen during the lifetime of either the original donor or recipient, when it is most likely that many parties would be aware of the conditions that had stimulated the gift. In actual fact my data indicate that few pieces of land once given away are ever reclaimed. Community sentiments probably inhibit any attempts to reclaim such plots as the reputation of the donor lineage would suffer. A donor lineage then has at least a theoretical right of reclaiming, but it does not retain any continuing exploitation rights while the land is held by the recipient lineage.

Short-term use rights, lasting for only a few years or a generation, are linguistically differentiated from the above. Here it is stated that the recipient lineage works the land but that the donor lineage still owns it. Although my information is not clear on this point, I believe that in this situation it is possible for the donor lineage to continue exploitation of the land. The five most common types of these land gifts are to a spouse, to one's children, in return for a favor, as part of an adoption process, and on the occasion of some marriages.

Gift to a spouse. A person obtains lineage approval to give land to his spouse. This type of gift may be made to a spouse who has few holdings of his own on the island, and thus it often involves individuals who have moved to the island at marriage. Disputes over the intended permanence of this type of gift appear to be common after the original donor dies, but it is usual for the transfer to be in effect as long as the recipient is alive and resides on or exploits the holdings.

Case 19. Z was a Woleai clan woman from Falalus who married a Mongalifach man from Wottagai. Instead of following the usual matrilocal residence pattern, the couple took up residence on Wottagai because the husband's lineage was small and short of personnel. As a gesture of appreciation Z was given some Mongalifach land on Wottagai, and this is now called Woleai clan land.

Case 20. AA was a Hatamang clan man of Lamotrek. After his marriage to a Saufalachig woman, he continued to live on his own lineage land. Shortly before his death, he told his wife and children that they should remain on the land after he died. They did so and the land is now called Saufalachig land. 'Response' is given to the appropriate Hatamang lineage.

Gift to one's children. As case 20 suggests, a man may not always make clear whether his gift of land is meant exclusively for his wife or for her and his children. If he expressly makes it to his wife, she in turn, following matrilineal principles, will pass it on to her children. It is more common, however, for a man to make land gifts directly to his children, bypassing his wife and perhaps any children she might have after his death.

I term land gifts to children "patrilateral," for the link is a male one between two matrilineages—the matrilineage of the man from whose members he must obtain permission to make the gift and the matrilineage of the children who most likely will amalgamate it with other lineage holdings.

Case 21. BB, a Saufalachig clan man, was 'man of the land' of his lineage. He gave a piece of land to his son, CC. CC told his sisters of the gift and the land was incorporated into his matrilineage holdings.

CC stated that if everyone in his lineage should die, this land would revert to the Saufalachig lineage of his father.

The next case suggests that land disputes may arise when the limitations of the transferred rights are not made clear to all parties or when there is an attempt by one side in the transaction to gain or retain rights not usually associated with the gift.

Case 22. Leomar is an 'estate' in the southern district of Lamotrek which belongs to Sauwel clan. DD and her sister live on the land, but their brother who was 'man of the land' died some years ago. The son of the younger sister, a man of about twenty-five, is now 'man of the land.' Because of his age, he is not considered a knowledgeable or forceful leader. EE, a very senior woman of Saufalachig clan who is 'old woman of the land' for a lineage farther south on the island, was told by her father, a Sauwel man, that she could take food from certain Leomar landholdings. FF, the 'man of the land' of the Saufalachig lineage, claims that EE's father gave the lands to the lineage. EE herself only claims she has a right to take food from the land.

If a man tells his children they can take food from his land, there is always a possibility this may be interpreted as a full gift. A patrilateral gift to one's children can involve other complexities as well, as in the following case where an adoptive link is involved.

Case 23. GG, a Sauwel clan man, was adopted by a Hatamang clan woman. Before GG died he gave some land to his own children to which he had rights because of the adoption. His children then made 'response' presentations to Hatamang.

Malicha. This is 'a gift of land made to someone who has rendered a great favor.'

Case 24. HH fell from a coconut tree and was seriously injured. JJ was sought out as a skilled masseur able to care for such cases. His treatment proved successful, and, upon recovery, HH gave a piece of land to JJ.

Case 25. KK's daughter was gravely ill. LL, a woman whose ability at concocting medicines was well known, was asked to prescribe and treat the girl. When the girl recovered, KK gave a piece of land to LL.

Sulitupul. This is 'a gift of land made by the parents of a child to a couple who adopt the child.' The gift probably is meant to symbolically acknowledge the fact that the child gains the right to inherit land from his adoptive group.

Case 26. MM, a Mongalifach clan man, asked the 'man of the land' of his lineage to give a piece of land to NN, a woman who had adopted his daughter. MM probably made this request because his wife was from another island and therefore her lineage was not able to make a gift to NN.

Gon. This is 'a gift of land that is made to a man who gives his daughter to another clan for the purpose of marriage.'

Case 27. Two or three generations ago, OO, a Woleai clan man of Wottagai, gave his daughter in marriage to a Saufalachig clan man. OO was then told by the members of this Saufalachig lineage that he could remain on and work a particular piece of Saufalachig land. This type of transaction is not common and probably occurs in the case of widowers who are resident on their wife's island as a result of a matrilocal marriage but were originally from another island.

Patterns of transfer. In itemizing the types of transfers, the impression may have been given that changes in tenure are infrequent and that the system is rather rigid. This is not the case and land redistribution generally occurs when necessary to maintain a balance between the size of social groups and the land needed to support them. The formal rules are meant to provide for a hierarchy of claims and a minimum of disputes. However, they do not eliminate disputes altogether as it seems always possible for rival claimants to make reference to a different rule in order to legitimize a claim. Land disputes, then, are common in the Woleai and are rarely permanently settled. Rather, they remain latent, perhaps for a generation or two, until activated whenever a particular claimant group feels its chances of succeeding are good.

The small populations of the islands of the region, fragmented as they are into clans and lineages, are subject to rapid demographic changes. Rules permit land to be transferred to another clan when the controlling group begins to die out. Alternatively, other rules permit a clan to be artificially perpetuated and enlarged so that land does not have to be given away. This may entail adoption or some other less formal kind of common residence. The rules of land tenure are rules of adaptation suited to a small population on a small land area, which is subject to disruptions and natural disasters. A great number of the changes in present-day landholdings in the Woleai can be traced either to the highly destructive typhoon of 1907 or to other less severe but more recent ones.

Since interclan transfers of land require continued 'response' presentations, it is relatively easy to compare present with past holdings for any one clan and in this way to determine how common land redistribution actually is. The tables that follow are meant to do this for Wottagai and Falalus islands. Original holdings in these charts refer to an undefined time in the past which may vary from clan to clan but probably refers to the time when the clan first became established on the island concerned.

TABLE 3 Wottagai Island Landholdings

Clan	Present Holdings	Original Holdings
NIGAPALAM DISTRICT		
Mongalifach[a]	17	5
Woleai Clan[b]	15	23
Sauwel	0	3
Saufalachig	7	8
TABWOGAP DISTRICT		
Saufalachig[a]	34	47
Woleai Clan	8	1
Hofalu	4	0
Mongalifach	2	0
PIGUL DISTRICT		
Mongalifach[a]	44	44
Hofalu[c]	15	25
Saufalachig	11	4
Lugufalu	13	6
Saoifang	3	8
Woleai Clan	2	1

[a]Present chiefly clan of the district. [b]Previous chiefly clan of the district. [c]Said to have once been chiefly.

These figures suggest a close relationship between chiefly status and the amount of land held. Further, table 5 indicates that political status and landholdings are related to total population numbers.

TABLE 4 Falalus Island Landholdings

Clan	Present Holdings	Original Holdings
TABWOGUTAG DISTRICT		
Woleai Clan[a]	43	37
Sauwel	7	19
Mongalifach	5	1
Hofalu	5	1
Mailibwel	2	4
TABWOGUTU DISTRICT		
Mongalifach[a]	23	5
Sauwel[b]	15	49
Hofalu	15	3
Woleai Clan	6	5
Mailibwel	3	0

[a]Present chiefly clan of the district. [b]Previous chiefly clan of the district.

TABLE 5 Population, by Clans, of Wottagai and Falalus

Clan	Wottagai	Falalus
Mongalifach	18	11
Saufalachig	17	0
Sauwel	9	6
Hofalu	17	15
Woleai Clan	12	38
Lugufalu	6	0
Bwùl Clan	1	0
Saoifang	5	0
Mailibwel	0	2
Unaffiliated	1	0
Unknown	2	2

I have indicated previously that kin groups and the land they control are so closely interlinked that in many cases it is difficult to distinguish between the two. This is most clearly seen in the case of the 'estate,' that is, the seat of a lineage. Anyone who is permitted to take up permanent residence on a particular 'estate' is incorporated into its kin group and thus is subjected to the same rights and obligations as if he had a true genealogical relationship. This most commonly affects regulation of marriages, for such an individual is no longer permitted to marry into the family of the land. Permanent residence in this context does not refer to someone who is living on the homestead as the result of a matrilocal marriage for, obviously, he has married into the group. His residence is temporary, however, in the sense that it will persist only as long as the marriage. If the marriage terminates for any reason, the man moves back to his own 'estate.'

Case 28. In 1963 on Satawal I noted a group of Lugufalu clansmen whose parents and grandparents had left Woleai Atoll after the 1907 typhoon. These individuals were living on an 'estate' which belonged to a Gatoliar clan lineage and, as a result, on Satawal these two groups were not permitted to intermarry. Informants stated, however, that they may possibly intermarry in the future when their relationship is no longer close. This may refer to such a time when the Lugufalu homestead somehow breaks away from Gatoliar control. These restrictions do not apply to Lugufalu and Gatoliar individuals on other islands.

Case 29. In Tabwogap district of Wottagai, Saufalachig is the chiefly clan. The man who presently occupies the office of chief, however, is a Woleai clan man who, as the result of a gift of land two or three generations ago, is now considered a member of this Saufalachig lineage. The chieftainship has not been transferred to Woleai clan, but, rather, both are eligible to hold it for they are all of one 'estate.' At this particular time the Woleai clan man is the most senior individual of the homestead and thus was selected as chief by the combined lineage.

I have discussed elsewhere a similar situation that prevailed on Lamotrek Island, where a lineage of Mongalifach clan was absorbed by Hatamang clan, and thus had access to the chieftainship of this latter group (Alkire 1965). In this instance, however, because of the resettlement, the Mongalifach group lost its rights to a chieftainship that was tied to its former place of residence. In all of these cases, intermarriage is prohibited between the lineages of the different clans involved because common residence and stewardship over land are closely identified with common kin group membership. In none of these cases, however, would these individuals deny their true biological clan affiliation.

MODERN TRANSFORMATIONS

Colonial rule in the central Caroline atolls has had little permanent effect on land tenure. The biggest single event which affected indigenous patterns was World War II. Between 1898 and 1945, during the German and Japanese periods of administration, at various times the government bought or confiscated certain parcels of land for either commercial or military purposes. Most of these holdings, however, have since been returned to their original owners. Commercially the central Carolines have offered little to colonial regimes and changes have been far fewer here than in the comparatively richer volcanic islands of the chain. There is no evidence that either regime actually changed any indigenous rules of tenure.

Military activities during the last half of World War II had typhoonlike effects on some areas of the Woleai. Falalap, Tagailap, Sùlywäp, and Wottagai at Woleai Atoll and, to a lesser extent, Lamotrek were all occupied by Japanese troops. On Falalap large blocks of land were taken over by the military in order to construct an airfield. At the height of war activity at Woleai Atoll, the native population was first removed from Falalap, Tagailap, Wottagai, and Sùlywäp to Falalus and Ifaluk. Then, toward the end of the war, when Falalap was heavily bombed, Falalus was also abandoned for Ifaluk. Only ten or fifteen natives remained on the atoll, taking refuge on Pial, a small islet, normally uninhabited. These individuals refused to leave, as they felt someone had to remain behind to establish a claim to the atoll in the postwar period.

As soon after the war as possible, the Woleaians returned from Ifaluk. Individuals from Wottagai, Sùlywäp, and Falalus immediately moved back to their home islands, which were little disturbed. Since the exile had been of short duration, there was little difficulty in reestablishing claims to previously held land. Residents of Falalap, on the other hand, found their island devastated and they were initially forced to take up residence with relatives on one of the other islands. They remained dispersed for several years until replanting schemes resulted in the recovery of their own island. Many natural markers from the prewar period had been destroyed, so boundary lines had to be reestablished through common consent of the lineage heads concerned. It is probable that some of the parcels thus marked off are not identical to the original ones, but I have no evidence that, as a result, land disputes on Falalap are any more common than on the other islands of the atoll.

Even though the U.S. administration returned all of the land of the atoll to the Woleaians at the end of the war, there is still a fear in the minds of some of the islanders that the Americans may someday attempt to reclaim land originally expropriated by the Japanese as government land. There are plots of land on the atoll devoted to public uses related to the American administration or to Catholic missions, namely, schools, dispensaries, and Catholic churches. Invariably the Woleaians feel that the land occupied by these structures still belongs to the clans of original ownership, and it is only through the generosity of these clans that the foreigners are permitted to use it.

The legal code adopted by the U.S. administration for the Trust Territory allows land disputes to be heard in the district court on Yap. As far as I am aware, however, no such dispute has ever been taken there by Woleaians or other outer islanders. In part this is because most outer islanders have a distrust of the Yapese and what they consider Yapese laws, and in part there is a fear that the publicity generated might result in additional claims by other individuals or the government itself.

With the increasing importance of copra as a commercial crop, disputes over previously unimportant or unused pieces of land in the Woleai have increased. These are settled in traditional ways, that is, by a compromise agreement between the parties in which one side temporarily backs down in favor of the other when it appears the dispute is going to result in some form of open conflict which would attract the attention of a chief. Similar disputes probably occurred in precontact times when the population was much larger, and most land was consequently of value for subsistence purposes. It seems likely that disputes were settled in similar ways at that time. A new aspect to the disputes that is probably related to the commercial importance of copra, however, is the interisland nature of some land claims. Individuals quite frequently invoke certain rights to land on islands other than the one on which they reside in order to exploit additional copra. These claims make frequent reference to patrilateral, adoptive, or gift rights.

NOTE

1. The fieldwork upon which this analysis is based was supported by research grant GS-506 from the National Science Foundation and research grant M-5125 from the National Institute of Mental Health of the U.S. Public Health Service. I gratefully acknowledge the support of both these institutions.

    I wish to thank Henry Lundsgaarde, Andrew Strathern, Michael Lieber, and Judith Huntsman for their helpful comments on an earlier draft of this chapter.

4

LAND TENURE ON KAPINGAMARANGI

Michael D. Lieber

INTRODUCTION

For the people of Kapingamarangi Atoll, no other single concern seems to be as omnipresent and as anxiety-provoking as their concern over land.[1] No other single concern generates the intensity of interest and emotion as does land. People may insult one another, but the insults will be forgiven; tempers sometimes flare and end in fist fights, but others will intervene, and the opponents will apologize and forget the incident; marriages break up, but the wounds heal. But a land dispute is never forgotten, nor do the opponents forgive each other, nor is the matter ever really settled, even when the litigants are long deceased.

The importance of land to the Kapingamarangi people is evident not only in the intensity of social relations involving land but also in the manner in which considerations of land seem to permeate social relations on the atoll. The range of relationships involving land as a consideration encompasses far more than simply matters of inheritance and litigation. Land is either an explicit or implicit consideration in such relations as marriage, adoption, funerals, the building and repair of houses, birthday feasts, welcoming feasts, canoe making, residence, the organization of certain holiday celebrations, and the structure of the work week.

It is tempting to try to explain the importance of land on the atoll in terms of its ecology. After all, the total land area of Kapingamarangi is less than one-half square mile, and the island supports a rapidly

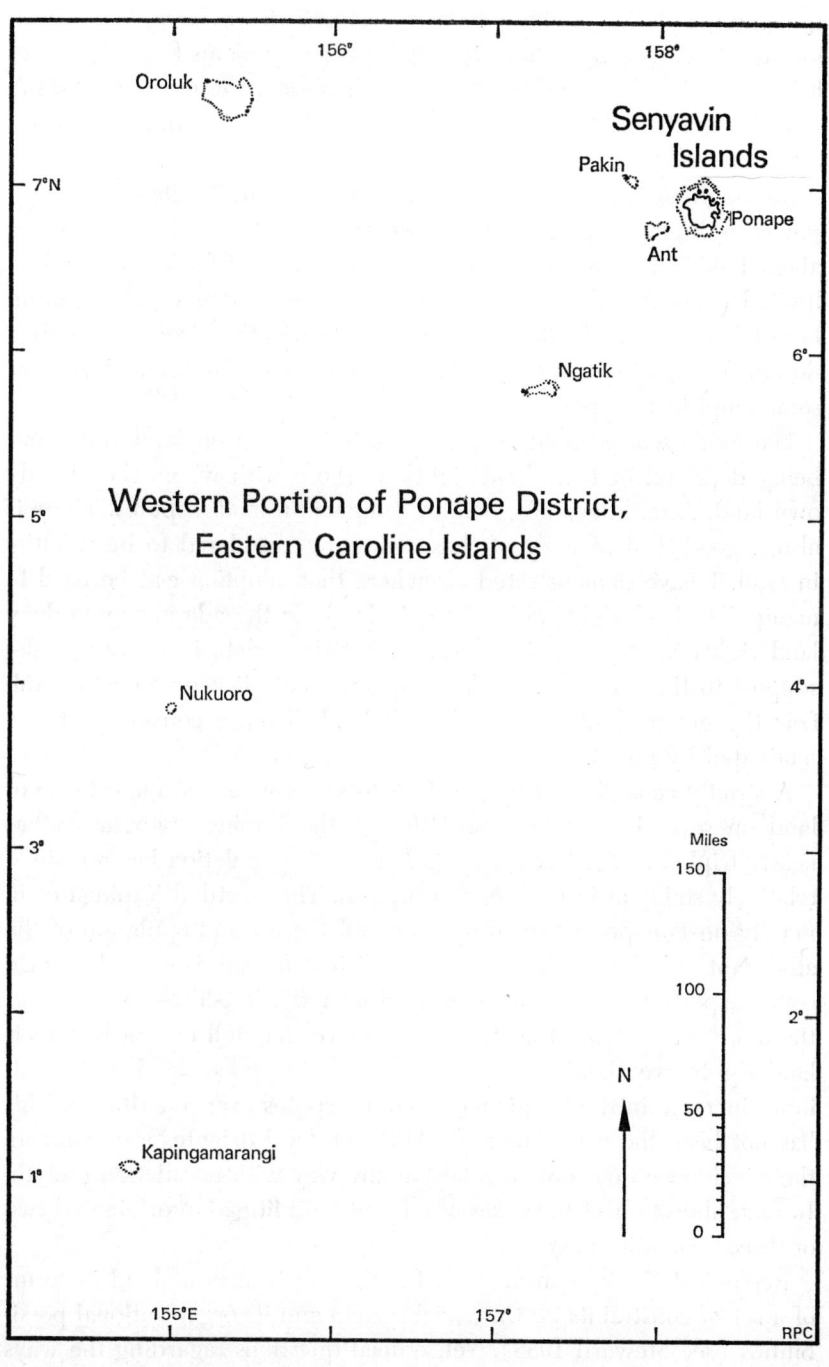

growing population of about 400 people. Staple foods have always been locally grown coconuts, taro, breadfruit, and pandanus fruit. Access to fish, the major source of protein, depends on land resources for fishing gear. Naturally, land is of central concern to the Kapingamarangi (hereafter referred to as the Kapinga).

Although such an ecological argument has validity, its explanatory power is limited. An ecological argument can explain the anxieties about land in two ways: (1) the constant threat of food shortage in a limited universe and (2) real or imagined threats from a growing number of land users. The first argument is empirically false: the Kapinga do not fear food shortages. The second argument, however, does have some empirical support.

People do worry about others trying to "steal" their land and about being deprived of their land rights by those with whom they jointly own land. Accusations of greed are common in land disputes. There is also a good deal of envy of those who are considered to be wealthy in land. I have demonstrated elsewhere that adoption can be used to manipulate land rights either to gain land for the adopter or to deny land rights to others (Lieber 1970). Yet these data lend only partial support to the ecological explanation since not all people on the atoll fear the greed of others, nor are all land disputes considered to be motivated by greed.

A strictly ecological argument fails to account for the importance of land on several other counts. Although the Kapinga population has nearly tripled in the last fifty years, the atoll population has remained relatively stable at just under 400 persons. The resettled Kapinga community on Ponape has steadily drawn off the excess population of the atoll. Not only has atoll land been sufficient for subsistence, but local copra exports have steadily increased over the last fifteen years. Furthermore, considering that those who leave the atoll do not lose their land rights, we should expect that population pressure should result in an increase in the frequency of land disputes over inheritance. This has not been the case, however. Although land disputes are common, their incidence does not correlate in any way with population growth. In fact, almost all of the cases of current land litigation originated two or three generations ago.

Ecological theory can account for the importance of land in terms of a set of constraints on the social system and its organizational possibilities (see Steward 1955). Yet, crucial questions regarding the ways in which land is perceived by people, how such perceptions structure their behavior in social relations, and how such social relations are organized are not answered by an ecological account. An ecological theory cannot predict, for example, that land would be defined so that it is part of the meaning of kinship, as it is on Kapingamarangi.

When we talk about land as an energy resource, we are involved in an analysis of energy transfers, food chains, and the like. This tells us little about the social relations that comprise land as property, however. What is needed for a complete account of the importance of land on the atoll is an analytical framework that encompasses ecological and social relations. Such a framework is that of information theory or cybernetics. The response of a human community to its environment is, after all, based on the information that the community has about its environment. This information is a transform of the sense data provided by the environment. The relationship between the total environment and the information a community has about it is the relationship of territory to map (see Bateson 1972:448 ff.). Individuals and groups never deal with a total environment, but with only parts of it at any given time. What parts are dealt with, how they are dealt with, and when they are dealt with is dependent in large measure on the map that structures people's perceptions of it. The relationship between the environment and the human community forms the context of which the adaptive responses of the members of the community are a part. Nested within this context is another set of relations that we can designate as property.

Hohfeld defined property as a set of complementary social relationships with regard to an object, and I follow his definition here (Hohfeld 1919:27). When I talk about land as property, I am talking about a set of social relationships regarding the possession, use, and conveyance of land. This set of social relationships is also a context of actions and utterances, that is, the responses of people to each other as regards land. It is the exchange of information, or messages, between people that constitutes the context of their actions, according to Bateson (1972: 276). Characteristic of any context is its structure—that set of rules which specifies how to put together the information constituting the context. Thus, when we deal with the rules of possession, use, and conveyance of land, that is, the rules of land tenure, we are specifying the structure of the social context that I have labeled property.

The task in this chapter, then, is to specify the nature of the information that comprises each level of context and to demonstrate the constraints that this information places on the perceptions and actions of people on Kapingamarangi as regards land. Specifically, I propose to demonstrate that land is of such central importance in the thought and action of the Kapinga because, as a symbol, it embodies sets of propositions by which the Kapinga define both themselves and their interpersonal relationships. What land symbolizes (the information encoded on the symbol) is propositions about what people are, what kinship is and is not, what responsibility is, and what wealth is. The rules that specify the rights people have over land, how the rights are acquired and disposed of, and how the rights are to be exercised are logical ramifications of these propositions. The rules spell out the implications of these propositions in concrete, relational terms. Moreover, land also symbolizes the higher order relationship between people and environment which is the wider context of these propositions about human relationships. Thus, into a small semantic space is packed a large body of information which is fundamental to the way the Kapinga define and organize themselves.[2]

The arguments presented in this chapter will be developed in the following sequence: (1) a description of the atoll environment, the Kapinga view of it, and the ways in which they exploit it; (2) a cultural account of the relationship between kinship and land; (3) the kinds of rights, duties, and disabilities that pertain to land; (4) how these rights, duties, and disabilities are distributed and exercised; and (5) the kinds of constraints which enforce the rules of land tenure.

THE ATOLL ENVIRONMENT

Kapingamarangi is an atoll located at 1°4' north latitude and 154°46' east longitude. Its inhabitants are Polynesian in physical type, language, and culture. The atoll is an egg-shaped reef with thirty-one flat islets perched on the reef's eastern edge, and it occupies 0.42 square miles of land area. The soil is sandy, and the humus layer is relatively thin (Niering 1956:2).

Because of its relatively thin soil, the atoll produces only ninety-eight different species of plants (Wiens 1962). Another factor limiting plant productivity is the availability of fresh groundwater, whose only source is rainfall. The annual average rainfall is about 108 inches (Emory 1965:8). Although coconut and pandanus trees, two of the four major food plants, are able to grow in the absence of groundwater, breadfruit trees and taro, the other two plant staples, cannot. Breadfruit grows on only eighteen of the islets—those which are large enough to support groundwater lenses. Taro (*Cyrtosperma*) grows only on the five largest islets. The coconut, breadfruit, and pandanus trees provide, in addition to food, leaves for plaiting mats, wood for house and canoe construction, husk for sennit cord, and fuel. Other trees, such as hibiscus, supply wood for craft work.

Other than land resources, the lagoon and sea provide the major source of protein in the diet. The Kapinga have developed many kinds of techniques for catching shellfish, eels, and lagoon, reef, and deep sea fish. These techniques include netting with hand nets and coir nets, pole and line fishing, trapping in nets and basket traps, spear fishing, and communal surrounds (Buck 1950). The Kapinga are known throughout the Ponape district of the Trust Territory as skilled fishermen. Yet it should be emphasized that the means for success in fishing still depend on land resources. Fishing gear from canoes to lines and hooks derive either from local wood or from hardware purchased with the proceeds from copra sales. It is land resources that enable the Kapinga to exploit the lagoon and ocean resources.

Land provides not only subsistence but also living space. The population is distributed mainly on two large islets in the east central portion of the reef with a few families scattered over three smaller islets near the two main ones. Each of the two major islets is subdivided into named homesteads and residence compounds. Each homestead contains dwelling houses and various kinds of work houses. From one to three nuclear families may dwell on a homestead, each family occupying its own dwelling house.

Atoll inhabitants have always made their living almost entirely from local resources. Although there are several salaried employees of the Trust Territory—teachers and co-op managers—these people also subsist mainly on atoll resources.[3] Kapinga clearly recognize the importance of their atoll habitat. But having had occasional experience of living on high islands since the 1920s, most of them also recognize its limitations.

Kapinga conceptually divide the environment into the ocean, the lagoon, the atoll, and intermediate areas along the edge of the reef. Included within the atoll are islets, soil on the islets, plants, animals, and people. They make a distinction between soil and land that is very similar to our own. Soil is the object seen as a set of physical attributes while land is the object seen as the subject of property. Land is further distinguished as wet land and dry land. Wet land is the swamp in which taro grows and will be referred to hereafter as taro plots. Dry land is the land on which trees, bushes, and other kinds of plants grow and will be referred to hereafter as land. The kinds of labor required to maintain taro plots and land are quite different. Land can be planted, weeded, and cleared of undergrowth periodically and casually by any number of people. Taro plots must be tended continually; they must be weeded, pruned, and fertilized with decaying vegetation. One further distinction is made with regard to land: land used for homesteads is distinguished from land used for plantations. The kinds of distinctions that Kapinga make between taro plots and land and among different kinds of land correspond to distinctions among the kinds of rights and duties which people have regarding them.

KINSHIP AND LAND

Property is a set of relationships between people regarding some object, in this case, real property, or land. A major part of these relationships are the rights, duties, privileges, and disabilities that stipulate how people are to behave with regard to land. These rights, duties, privileges, and disabilities are stated norms of behavior. The position taken here is that for the Kapinga these rights and duties form part of a larger, more inclusive set of cultural propositions—the propositions which define kinship. The norms of kinship relationships, the kinds of behavior expected among kinsmen, and thus the rights and duties with regard to land follow from this more abstract and more inclusive system of symbols.

The essence of kinship to the Kapinga is sharing and continuity. The Kapinga believe that conception is a process by which biological substance is transmitted to new human beings. Not only is biological substance transmitted through conception, but propensities for certain kinds of behavior are also transmitted, such as forensic skill, sorcery, and theft. In other words, for the Kapinga, phenotypic traits and behavioral dispositions form a unitary construct which we can label life substance. A child thus shares some life substance with each of his biological parents, and children of the same parents share life substance with each other. Therefore a person's life substance is continuous with that of his parents and their parents, his children and their children, his siblings and their children, and so on. Conception serves to maintain this continuity. To be one's kinsman is to share life substance with him. But sharing and continuity do not ramify endlessly. One shares life substance with all those he recognizes as ancestors and with all of their descendants, but at the same time many of those with whom he shares life have life substance which is unlike his own and which he does not share. As the degree of life substance which is discontinuous with his own outweighs that which is continuous, the feeling of sharing approaches negligibility. One important manifestation of continuity and discontinuity is the behavior of the individuals involved. If one does not behave as a kinsman should, then in all probability he is not a kinsman. Proper kinship behavior, which is naturally shared among kinsmen, is a message as to the kind of relationships obtaining among them.

One naturally shares with kinsmen. In the first instance, what is shared is life substance: biological substance and propensities for behavior. Sharing these things, it follows that kinsmen would naturally share other kinds of things such as goods, labor, knowledge, children, and love. As an object of sharing, land sustains life substance. Children are fed from the land by their parents, and aged parents are fed from the land by their children. Siblings are fed from the land by one another. Land is shared not only by the living, but also with the dead. People are buried in the land on which they lived. Thus within the land and that which composes the land are the physical remains of the life substance which one shares with his ancestors and other relatives. There is a physical continuity between people and land. As people share descent from a common ancestor, they also share a physical continuity between themselves and the land in which the ancestor is buried.

Land is part of life substance. Since kinship is sharing of and continuity of life substance, any two or more persons who consider themselves kinsmen must necessarily share land. The manner in which land is shared is expressed explicitly in the norms of behavior regarding the possession, use, and transfer of land. It follows that any social relationship involving land is a transaction between kinsmen or has implications of consanguineal kinship. The implicit ideas defining kinship are manifested in the rights and duties regarding land.

As stated earlier, there is a contrast between rights and duties with respect to land and those regarding taro plots. The contrast is based on the kinds of labor required to maintain them and on their productive uses. As the amount of land given over to taro comprises only about 3 percent of total land area of the atoll, primarily rights and duties with regard to land (and only secondarily those of taro plots) will be discussed.

There are three kinds of land rights on the atoll, which I arbitrarily label ownership, usufruct, and disability. Although the Kapinga themselves do not have any words which correspond exactly to these analytical categories, they articulate their notions of possession and land use in such a way that one can infer that distinct conceptualizations of different rights and duties do in fact exist. The categories will be described in two ways: (1) as a set of contrasting ideas in Kapinga usage and (2) as a set of stated rules, the set being used to define the category.

Ownership rights to land include the rights of continual use of the land for any and all purposes for which the land can be used, including planting, clearing, harvesting, house construction, residence, and conversion of land to taro plots and vice versa.[4] Ownership ideally also includes the right to convey one's rights to anyone whom one chooses.[5] The right of conveyance includes the right to name the recipients of ownership rights and the power to appoint an interim guardian to control the use of the land for the recipients, as in the case where the recipients are very young children. Implicit in this right is the more general right to create privileges of use to persons at the owner's discretion. The owner has the right to divide the land into sections before conveyance or to stipulate that the land not be divided. Ownership also includes the right to deny access to the land to anyone who has no rights to the land. For example, he may deny an individual right-of-way over his land.

Ownership also involves duties toward certain categories of people. These include the duty to permit people who hold usufruct rights the occasional use of his land for specified purposes. Before the advent of Christianity, owners had the duty not to cut down breadfruit trees without the prior permission of the chief and chief priest. In the case in which ownership is shared jointly one has the duty to consult with others, especially the steward of the owning group prior to or subsequent to use of the land. One also has the duty to consult with co-owners when a change of status of the land, such as land division or succession to the stewardship, is contemplated. This corresponds with one's right to be consulted by co-owners who contemplate such changes. Ownership also involves the duty to contribute products of one's land for communal work projects and for ceremonial occasions in which the descendants of a former owner of one's land are specifically involved (Lieber 1968:94–97).

Usufruct involves the right of occasional use of a plot of land to which one does not hold ownership rights. The contrast between ownership and usufruct is expressed by Kapinga in phrases such as "I eat from my land" as opposed to the statement "I can go out of hunger to his land." The distinctions in the phrases are those of one's own or another's possession and of continual or occasional access. This latter phrase connotes special need, which is occasional by definition.

Use rights include use of the land for some but not necessarily all purposes for which it can be used. Certainly, use for all purposes implies continuous access while usufruct involves only occasional access. A usufruct holder also has the right to convey his usufruct to his children but to no one else. A usufruct holder cannot convey ownership rights over the land to which he has the usufruct. If he is a guardian of a land parcel, he can convey the ownership rights to heirs designated by the owner, but he cannot decide to whom the parcel is to be conveyed. Usufruct involves the duty to obtain permission of the owner before using the land and to comply with any restrictions the owner might impose regarding use. Usufruct also involves the duty not to interfere with the owner's exercise of his own rights and the duty not to damage the owner's land.

A disability to a plot of land is phrased in Kapinga as follows: "One cannot go to that land." As indicated, a disability involves having no rights whatever to use or to enter onto a plot of land. One might have a right-of-way over a plot, but this is really a privilege which can be revoked by the owner, although difficult to enforce on outer islets. A disability involves the duty not to enter the plot or to take any fruits as well as the duty not to interfere with the owner's exercise of his rights.

There are two categories of rights and duties with regard to taro plots—ownership and disability. Ownership of a taro plot is phrased in the same way as ownership of land—"my taro plot." Ownership of a taro plot, which is individual, unencumbered ownership, involves the right of continual use for any and all purposes for which it may be used. This use includes planting of taro, banana, or lime trees; clearing; and harvesting. Ownership also involves the right to convey ownership rights over the taro plot to others, the power of designating a guardian to care for the plot if the recipient is a young child or disabled, the right to exclude any nonowner from the plot, and the right to allow others the privilege of using it. The only duty the owner has is that of occasionally contributing taro to others on certain occasions. These occasions include communal work projects in which workers are fed by the community through food assessments and ceremonial occasions involving an ancestor who was a former owner of the plot. In the latter case the taro would be contributed in the ancestor's name or as an acknowledgment of common descent with others besides the current owner.[6]

The contrast of rights and duties regarding land and taro plots corresponds to the kinds of labor required to maintain each. A parcel of land requires only occasional care, usually periodic clearing of undergrowth once or twice a year. Since anyone can do this, a man can send his son. A taro plot requires constant care, and women spend many hours each week pulling weeds, cutting leaves, and fertilizing the swamp with compost. Coconut trees replenish their own fruit quickly on the same tree, while taro does not. One coconut tree will produce fruit over a thirty-year period, but when taro is pulled up, it will not renew itself. Neglect of a taro plot will quickly destroy a crop, while this is not the case with coconut and breadfruit plantations. With individual, unencumbered ownership, responsibility for care of a taro plot rests squarely on its owner. At the same time, demands on an owner for taro by another is considered unreasonable because of the labor required to produce it. However, this does not mean that people do not share taro, for once it is cooked it is freely shared.[7]

That there are three categories of rights and duties regarding land implies that there are social relations between three categories of persons—owners, usufruct holders, and those with disabilities only. Relationships among people holding the kinds of rights and duties we have abstracted are conceived of and are subsumed under categories of kinsmen. This conception follows from the principle regarding transactions involving land. Since all people who share rights in land are also kinsmen, categories of rights correspond to categories of kinsmen. The relationship between an owner and a usufruct holder is expressed as that between a parent and a child since the owner is feeding the usufruct holder.

ORGANIZATION OF RIGHTS AND DUTIES

Ownership rights to land are acquired either by gift or inheritance, usually the latter. The Kapinga state that a person can give or will his land to anyone whom he chooses. In point of fact, land is usually willed to one's natural or adopted children. The land of a person dying without natural or adopted heirs reverts to his siblings, but people usually provide themselves with heirs by adoption if necessary.

Land can be owned by individuals or by corporate groups. Kapinga, however, prefer to own their land as individuals rather than as members of corporate groups because of the relative freedom associated with individual tenure. The tendency until the post-World War II period was for parents to divide their landholdings into separate parcels for each child. The trend toward individual tenure has been reversed over the past twenty-five years by two factors.

First, the Kapinga population has nearly tripled since 1919. Ponape has been able to draw off the excess population thus far, but Kapinga living off the atoll do not lose their land rights. So, although Kapinga on Ponape or other islands are not using atoll land for subsistence to any great extent, they must still be considered for inheritance.

Second, one result of population growth and the tendency to divide land for individual inheritance has been an increasing fragmentation of land parcels. For example, the number of land plots increased from 244 in 1947 to 339 in 1966, an increase of 39 percent. Obviously, the average size of a plot has decreased accordingly. Because of the increase in the number of heirs and the decrease in the amount of land available for inheritance, a marked trend toward corporate inheritance has appeared.[8] For example, 52 percent of the total land plots in 1947 were individually owned. By 1966, individually held plots had decreased to 33 percent. The total number of individual owners as well as their relative numbers has also significantly decreased.[9]

Corporate ownership is the result of a person willing land to his children to hold as a group. The members of that group can divide the land if they so choose, but if they feel that the parcel of land is too small, as is often the case at present, they are reluctant to divide the land.

Each sibling set has a male and a female leader, usually the eldest male and female (Lieber 1970:160). A male leader, hereafter referred to as a steward, is responsible for the welfare of all the members of the descent group. He is charged with the control and care of corporate property, the responsibility for the care of unmarried siblings, and provisioning of feasts and work parties on behalf of his siblings and their children. The female steward occupies the ancestral house of the group on the residence site owned by the group. She is responsible for supervising women's work for any feast or work party in the group's behalf.

The same organization characterizes sibling groups and descent groups. The only differences are that the descent group includes not only the apical siblings but also their children and grandchildren and that the steward of the apical sibling set is also steward for the whole descent group. The most important part of a steward's role is management of the group's land. With many people using the land, he must coordinate its use carefully to insure that each member will be adequately provided for and that group feasts are planned well enough in advance so that they can be sufficiently provisioned. Thus, group members must notify the steward prior to using land so he can tell which section of which plot to use. In this way the steward can keep track of which sections of land are being depleted and can maintain conservative use of group resources. The steward rotates the sections of land used for copra making, and he also rotates the personnel making copra so that group members get their fair share of cash income from copra. Succession to the male steward's position passes first to his oldest living male sibling and then to his oldest son. If, for example, a steward, X, has two younger brothers and two sons, succession to his position will go first to the elder of his two siblings. At the latter's death, X's youngest male sibling would assume the stewardship, and at his death, the eldest son of the original steward (X) would succeed to the position. The succession to the female steward's position passes, at her death, first to the next eldest female sibling. If the female steward has no living female siblings, her position is assumed by the eldest daughter of the male steward of the sibling group.

As long as a descent group maintains its corporate ownership of land, it maintains its integrity as an ongoing social entity. Most such groups are from two to four generations in genealogical depth. When group size seems too large to coordinate land use properly, the tendency has been for the group to divide its land. The land is divided in such a way that a separate parcel of land is given to each member of the apical sibling set. If any of the siblings are dead, the parcel is given to his children in his name. If a sibling group divides its land, then each of the siblings becomes an individual owner. If a large descent group divides its land, then several new descent groups emerge from the division. Figure 5 illustrates the foregoing.

Although descent groups own land (including plantation land and homesteads) as a group, they are never co-resident units. This is because postmarital residence is uxorilocal, and group members are thus scattered over different homesteads. For that matter, the frequency of adoption, fosterage, and emigration to Ponape usually prevents sibling sets from being co-resident at any time. A person who is living with his spouse's family usually uses his spouse's land for subsistence, but he also uses his own land for copra occasionally. However, one is not considered to have any rights over a spouse's land.

Individual and corporate ownership of land contrast in several ways. The individual owner can use his land whenever and however he pleases. He can will or give his land to whomever he pleases, and he can create the privilege of use in others as he pleases. He can also allow usufruct holders to exercise their rights without consulting anyone else about it. Where land is corporately owned, joint owners are not free to use the land as they please. Since several people are using the land, each must accommodate his usage to the needs of the other group members. Each must consult the steward prior to or subsequent to use. A joint owner can will his ownership rights to his children, but, unlike an individual owner, he cannot alienate the land at his pleasure. Any change in the status of the land must be decided on by all of the group's members.

If joint owners are unhappy with the steward's management, they can demand a land division or replace him. Such an instance occurred in 1966 when a steward had on several occasions promised one of the descent group members an opportunity to make copra and then reneged each time. The disgruntled member demanded a land division. At a membership meeting, it was decided to replace the steward rather than divide the land. A joint owner can neither deny nor grant a usufruct holder permission to exercise his rights; only the steward may do that. The steward is not entirely free to grant or deny the exercise of usufruct, however. If other owners object strongly to his decisions, they

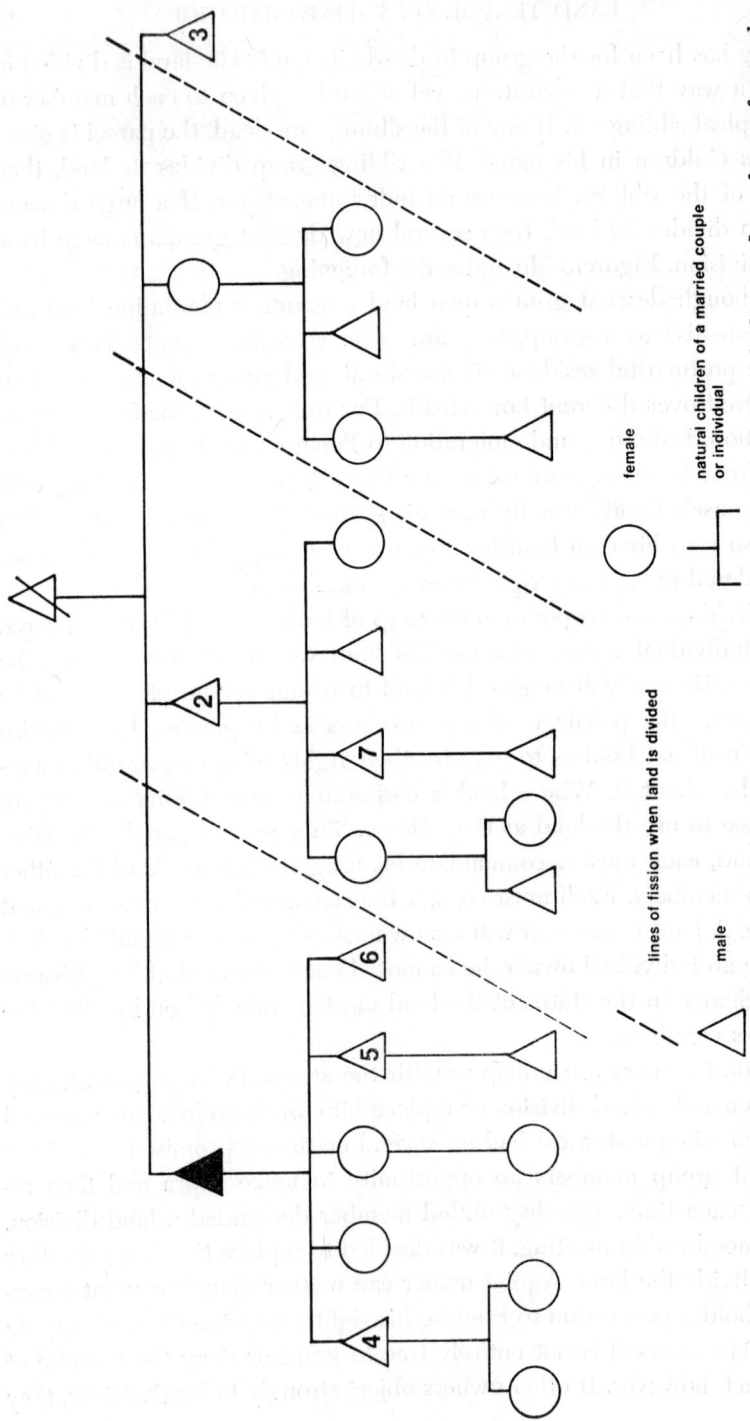

Figure 5. A descent group which is a landowning corporation. The present steward is indicated by shading, and numbers refer to the order of succession to the stewardship.

can force him to reverse them. Two such cases were described by informants.

Exclusive of ownership rights, a Kapinga ideally has use rights to the land of anyone with whom he shares descent from a recognized common ancestor, provided that the owner has inherited land from that ancestor. Since descent is traced through both males and females and land is inherited through males and females, it is likely that any individual to whose land another has a usufruct will also have a usufruct to at least one plot of the other's land.

Kapinga wedding feasts provide a unique opportunity to test the extent to which this ideal is realized because of the way the feasts are organized. All descendants of an ancestor of each parent of the couple are invited to participate in the feast preparations. Thus, there are four descent groups participating, each working at the ancestral house where that ancestor was buried.

By collecting the names of all participants in a wedding feast who work as a single group, it should be possible to establish that all or most of the participants have some kind of ownership or usufruct rights to one another's lands. In fact, at five wedding feasts where such data were recorded during 1965 and 1966, it was established that the majority of the participants shared ownership or usufruct rights with most of the people in the descent group with which they worked. In no case, however, did every participant share rights with every other participant in the group. In other words, within a single descent group working at a wedding feast, we should, ideally, expect completely reciprocal sharing of use rights among members. What was found, in fact, was a tendency toward complete reciprocal sharing. What has occurred to produce this deviation from the ideal has been a gradual attenuation of use rights among the descendants of the sibling set in the fourth generation. The deviation is part of a more or less regular process of attenuation of kinship ties and of use rights which depend on those ties.

Individuals learn about their use rights in two ways. First, one learns about one's use rights as a child by accompanying parents on trips to land plots for harvesting or other purposes. Through repeated trips, a child quickly learns which land plots belong to his parents. When a child accompanies his parents to unfamiliar land plots, the parents will explain the use right and the child's connection with the owner of the land. Second, part of every person's last will and testament to his children is a recounting of the history of his own land, including the people to whom usufruct duties are owed and usufruct rights which his children have to other plots of land. People to whom one's heirs owe usufruct duties are the heirs' 'children.' People over whose land one's heirs have use rights are the heirs' 'fathers' or 'mothers.'

One exercises his usufruct by asking an owner's permission to use his land for a specific purpose such as collecting coconuts or breadfruit. The owner may not categorically refuse such a request. To do so would be tantamount to denying kinship with the usufruct holder, and few people are willing to risk rupturing a social relationship in this way. If the owner is using the land for the same purpose at the time of the request and would incur a shortage by granting the request, he may deny permission for that reason and ask the usufruct holder to delay use. If the owner has already promised another the use of his land, he may deny one's request only temporarily on those grounds.

There are several kinds of constraints on both owners and usufruct holders regarding the exercise of use rights. On the owner's part, consistent denials for whatever reasons will result in strained relations with the kinsmen involved. The owner might be gossiped about and would suffer a loss of prestige among both his own kin and the community in general. Being overly generous is also detrimental to an owner, economically and socially. He would be considered foolish to allow himself to be put into the position of incurring a shortage through overindulgence of his generosity. Kapinga see this as showing off.

For a usufruct holder, attempts to exercise use rights too frequently could easily subject him to malicious gossip as a sycophant. Overexercise of his use rights puts him publicly in a position of dependency, for one always exercises his use rights as a 'child' with respect to 'parent.' Thus, even if permission continues to be granted by owners, overexercise of use rights will eventually threaten one's status as a responsible adult. On the other hand, failure to exercise one's use rights can be taken by an owner to mean that the usufruct holder does not care about him, does not need him, or does not "love" him. One case was cited by informants in which a landowner became concerned when certain kinsmen never exercised their use rights over their land, although these people had showed up to help with work projects in the past. The landowner adopted a child from one of the kinsmen concerned as a way of reminding them of their relationship with her.

The frequency and extent to which people recognize and exercise their usufruct depends on the genealogical and social distance between owners and usufruct holders. The very existence of usufruct depends on the recognized existence of a kinship relationship between owners and usufruct holders. The degree of genealogical relatedness at which people still recognize a kinship tie is quite variable from person to person and even with one person from one time or social context to another. As the feeling of kinship diminishes between any two people, the less likely it is that either will recognize or exercise use rights to the other's land. The reluctance to recognize attenuating rights was expressed by informants during questioning in two ways: (1) An informant would list the plots to which he had usufruct, then belatedly list another saying, "But I never go to that plot"; (2) reluctance to utilize a use right was most often expressed by an informant saying, "I am afraid to go there." One is never afraid to ask a relative for something; one does not fear an exchange with people he considers to be his kinsmen.

Attenuation of a use right is the result of the attenuation of kinship ties. Attenuation might be marked in several ways. For example, if one's parents never exercised a certain use right, then it is unlikely that one's children will exercise it either even if they know of the right. Another effective way to attenuate a use right is to neglect to inform one's children of its existence. This can work equally for an owner or a usufruct holder. In either case, the usufruct is effectively attenuated.

DISTRIBUTION OF LAND RIGHTS

All Kapinga inherit ownership and use rights through each of their parents and sometimes through their adopters (Lieber 1970:167). Individuals always inherit ownership rights to more than one plot of land, and there are several possibilities as to what kinds of rights one gets in the total parcel of which he may be said to be an owner.

For example, one inherits ownership rights over at least two homestead sites and usually more than two since each parent has rights in at least two. Since homesteads are rarely divided in inheritance, ownership rights in them are corporate rights.

With regard to plantation land one might inherit plots to hold as an individual owner from one or both parents. One might inherit individual ownership of one or more plots from one parent and corporate ownership rights over other plots from the other parent. One might also inherit corporate rights from both parents. These latter two possibilities occur frequently at present as land comes increasingly under corporate ownership. Suppose, for example, that a sibling set inherits parcels of land from each of their parents with instructions to hold all of them corporately as a descent group. In this case, the land of two individual owners is pooled to form the estate of one group. Suppose, on the other hand, that a sibling set inherits each of its parents' corporate memberships in land-owning descent groups. Then each of the siblings is a member of at least two and possibly four or more such groups, that is, the father's father's, father's mother's, mother's father's, and mother's mother's groups.

Each individual usually receives at least one taro plot from each parent and often one or more from each adopter as well. The number of taro plots per person received in inheritance averages just over three. The range of the number inherited by a single person varies between one and twelve. As in the case with land, owners of taro plots include not only atoll residents but also Kapinga on Ponape and other islands. The taro plots of emigrants are left with relatives, usually siblings or children, to care for. The expansion of taro acreage has generally followed the expansion of the population, large new pits having been dug just after World War II. The taro acreage is slowly expanding at present as small groups of people cooperate in the heavy labor of digging and filling new pits. There are well over eight hundred separate plots of taro at present, and the number increases not only through expansion of taro acreage but also through division of plots in inheritance. Like land, taro plots are becoming highly fragmented.

Each individual inherits ownership rights to several parcels of land, including at least two residence sites, at least two parcels of plantation land, and at least two taro plots. Besides this, each individual also inherits use rights to several other parcels of land. An individual's tracts of land and taro plots are rarely, if ever, contiguous, nor are they usually localized on one islet. For example, an individual might own four tracts of land on four different islets, residence sites on two islets, taro plots on yet another islet or two, and usufruct to tracts on yet other islets. Such scattering of rights means that the individual must travel from islet to islet in order to plant, clear, or harvest. Although this requires more time and effort than it would if tracts were all localized in one area, it does lend an ecological advantage. Given the unequal distribution of groundwater, the scattering of plots generally assures individuals of access to the full range of plant life that the atoll produces. For instance, there is no one on the atoll who does not have ownership rights to at least one plot of land containing breadfruit trees. If all the individual's land were concentrated on one islet, there would be people who did not have access to such plants as breadfruit. Usufruct further extends an individual's access to plants he might need.

It is clear that individuals have a multiplicity of options regarding rights to various plots of land. In any situation in which land is to be used, individuals must select from among several sets of rights the particular set which will be useful for a particular purpose. Selection is never a random process. There are several principles determining choices of which set of rights an individual might exercise.

First, choice will be influenced by what kind of land resource is needed. If one needs coconuts, he will utilize rights to those plots where they are in plentiful supply. If breadfruit is needed, one will obviously utilize those rights to tracts containing breadfruit stands. If an individual needs a breadfruit tree to make a canoe and has no mature breadfruit tree on two tracts he owns as an individual, he might well invoke corporate ownership rights to get the tree, rights which he might not normally exercise.

Second, individuals tend to exercise their ownership rights to those plots over which they have the most direct control. The case is clear for individual owners of land plots; these people tend to use their own plots to the exclusion of other corporate rights they might have except in cases of unusual need. People holding only corporate rights tend to exercise rights in the corporation in which they are most closely related to the steward. For example, if one is a member of a corporation in which his mother's brother is the steward and of another in which his brother is the steward, he would tend to restrict the exercise of his rights to the latter.

Third, exercise of one's rights depends to a great extent on the kind of social relationships one has with his kinsmen, especially in the case of corporate ownership rights and use rights. Let us take the case of corporate ownership first. Although most Kapinga will state that they are related equally to both their mother's and their father's kin, no Kapinga in fact ever feels equally close to both. One's most solidary relationships, socially and emotionally, are always with the people with whom one resided through childhood. Thus, if one's childhood was spent on his maternal grandfather's homestead, he will be most closely affiliated socially with the latter's family. This solidarity will be expressed by his visiting patterns, gifts of food, and his participation in ceremonial activities. He would also tend to exercise his land rights most frequently in a corporation of his maternal grandfather's descent group. Adoption, since it can affect a child's early residence, can also influence one's primary loyalties and the exercise of one's land rights (Lieber 1970:162). For example, one young man has several sets of ownership rights that include a tract which he owns individually, several parcels in his maternal grandfather's descent group, and others in his maternal grandmother's descent group. The plots he actually uses most frequently are those belonging to his adoptive father. The social and emotional ties between these two men determine the younger man's selection of land rights to the exclusion of other considerations.

Solidary social relationships are important determinants of the exercise of usufruct. The extent to which usufruct is recognized depends to some degree on genealogical distance between usufruct holders and owners, but genealogical distance is never an absolute criterion in any sense. Among 144 informants from whom a list of use rights were obtained, there was a good deal of variability in the maximum genealogical distance between owners and usufruct holders, ranging from siblings to fourth and fifth cousins. The majority of informants claimed usufruct to lands of at least second cousins. The lists ranged in length from one or two parcels of usufruct land per informant to over a dozen parcels. Part of the variability is related to age differences. Older informants know more about land rights than did younger ones. Extremely land-poor informants tend to recognize and claim more usufruct plots than those who are not land-poor. Members of several large and traditionally prominent families of former secular chiefs and high priests tended to recognize reciprocal usufruct to more land plots among a wider range of relatives than did other families. This illustrates the interest of these family members in maintaining solidary ties. Not only do they recognize many land ties, but these families also engage in a good deal of intrafamily adoption which, like recognizing and exercising usufruct, is always a message about the kinship relationship between adopters and natural parents of the adoptees (see Lieber 1970:186–189).

The frequency and extent to which usufruct is exercised depends also on the social distance between owners and usufruct holders. Siblings tend to exercise usufruct to each other's lands more frequently and for more purposes than do other categories of kinsmen. One would not hesitate to ask a sibling for permission to collect coconuts for copra or for a breadfruit tree for a canoe. One would hardly seek permission from a second or third cousin to use his land for the same purposes unless, as is sometimes the case, one has very close ties with these relatives. In this latter case, exercise of usufruct does as much to maintain the solidarity of the kinship relationship as does the giving of gifts or sharing of work.

There is another consideration which affects particularly the frequency with which usufruct is exercised—the relative positions of the owner and the usufruct holder and the connotations of responsibility and prestige in their relationship. The positions of owner and usufruct holder in the actual exercise of usufruct are those of 'parent' and 'child' respectively: the 'parent' is 'feeding' his 'child.' This manner of conceptualizing the relationship conveys two very important kinds of messages. The first is that kinsmen ought to take care of and be generous toward each other—by feeding one's child, one sustains him. The second is about the relative responsibilities of the parties to the relationship. A parent is responsible for his child, while a child is supposed to obey his parent. This is an asymmetric relationship with responsibility clearly on the side of the parent-owner.

What is so important about this is that the most important rewards the atoll society confers upon individuals, those of esteem and prestige, are acquired only in proportion to the responsibility which people are able to assume for the welfare of others. One gains no prestige, and in fact one may lose prestige, by being dependent on others. It is for this reason that people are reluctant to exercise their use rights to the land of anyone except those to whom they are socially close. It is also for this reason that people prefer to inherit land parcels as individuals whenever possible. Situations of frequent and obvious dependency are threatening to people's public images and to their own self-esteem. For this reason, usufruct tends not to be utilized with great frequency by anyone. Even people with relatively little land avoid exercise of usufruct unless it is absolutely necessary or unless they are willing to accept the loss of prestige which is concomitant with such use.[10]

Even when a person owns land as a member of a descent group, the fact that he must consult the steward before using the land places him in a position of dependency. A steward who makes this dependency situation too obvious through high-handed behavior faces the possibility of losing his position and the prestige that accrues from it.

The owner's position is both independent and superordinate in the asymmetrical relationship. He is supposed to demonstrate the generosity and responsibility characteristic of the good person. He gains prestige in such a relationship; this is why usufruct permission is rarely denied to usufruct holders. The more dependents one has, the more obvious it is that one is well off and able to be generous. Generosity, which is much emphasized in Kapinga thinking and social behavior, is a communication about one's self: that one is prestigious and good in cultural terms and superordinating in social terms.

It is in the context of responsibility that we are able to understand the concept of wealth and why wealth should be measured only in land. The literal meaning of the Kapinga term for wealth is 'many people full of food.' Wealth means a set of social relations between a person and many others for whom he is responsible and over whom he is superordinate.

Having a good deal of land assures one of a responsible position among one's kinsmen and in the community for three reasons. First, having a good deal of land virtually assures one of having everything he needs in terms of food and goods; therefore, one need never exercise his use rights. Second, it assures that one will have many dependents among one's kin since the more land one has the more kinsmen who will hold usufruct to this land and to whom one is potentially superordinate. Third, having a great deal of land enables one to command the labor and services of others such as house builders, canoe makers, and carpenters who can be provided with large quantities of food in exchange for their services. In precontact days, men with much land could hire members of their men's houses to fish or even to fight for them in exchange for a large feast.

There are other ways by which one can acquire responsibility, but none which involves one in relationships that have the permanence and solidarity of the kin relations presupposed by land. Even the former position of high priest, probably the most powerful position on the atoll before contact, involved only occasional superordinacy, and the priest could be forced to abdicate his office while a landowner cannot be disenfranchised no matter how he behaves. It is the kinds of social relationships made possible by landownership that is the basis for the concept of wealth.

CONSTRAINTS ENFORCING LAND TENURE RULES

The kinds of contraints supporting the Kapinga land tenure system are inherent in their social relationships. Opprobrium of one's kin and community and the threat of possibly rupturing important relationships have served to maintain appropriate behavior among joint owners and among owners and usufruct holders. Gains or losses in social prestige motivate owners and stewards to act in a fair and generous manner. But as is true of any social system, the kinds of informal sanctions within the social system never wholly suffice to maintain its operation without some serious disputes.[11]

Land disputes involve either blood kin as protagonists or are the result of some prior transaction among blood kin. They involve ownership rights only, and there is usually no question about whether either party has a right to use the land.[12] Given the motivations for wanting land, we can expect land greed to influence people's behavior to some extent. Given the population explosion and the limited amount of land, we can expect an increasing anxiety over providing inheritance for children. Since people tend to exercise their ownership rights selectively, their ownership status in corporate groups whose land they do not use tends to become ambiguous over two or more generations, possibly resulting in exclusion from a share in land divisions. The position of guardian is sometimes abused; the guardian wills the land held in trust to his own children rather than to the rightful heirs. Parents sometimes give different oral versions of their wills to different children, creating confusion a generation later.[13] Land which is willed to a non-kinsman, most often a stepchild, is always likely to be the basis of a dispute one or two generations later as the lineal descendants or kin of the former owner try to reclaim the land of their family. Adoptees are sometimes denied their inheritance by the natural children of the adopter. Stinginess or obtuseness of a steward is sometimes the basis for demanding a land division.

Before the introduction of a native court, land disputes were settled in three ways: (1) The protagonists cut off further social relationships. (2) An alternative was verbal battle or physical combat between individuals. In this case, either one of the protagonists would exclude the other from the land, or other people would intervene and mediate the dispute until the protagonists were pacified and agreed on a compromise. This course was usually followed when the protagonists were close kin, and the dispute had not been of long standing. (3) Sometimes there was recourse to brute force—whole families fighting pitched battles over a piece of land or a man hiring members of his men's house to intimidate an opponent in a dispute. In the early twentieth century, one man used firearms to intimidate his own siblings into abandoning land which they jointly owned.

By about 1921 or 1922, a resident Japanese trader, who had been pressured by the Kapinga to settle land disputes, inaugurated a land court, presided over by the chief and his assistant. Claimants would notify the chief of their dispute, and the chief would call a meeting of the entire community to hear their arguments. After these were presented, the chief would poll the assembled adults to elicit any further information having a bearing on the case and to determine whether or not there was a consensus of opinion. The chief and his assistant, who recorded the proceedings, conferred privately, and the chief would announce his decision. The chief often, but not always, followed the consensus of the meeting. Litigants rarely, if ever, asked for disenfranchisement of one owner in favor of another; the plaintiff's claim was usually that the land should be divided between himself and the defendant. The chief's decisions usually ordered the land divided or admonished an owner or steward to be fair lest he suffer subsequent division of his land. Such decisions were always accompanied by paternal attempts to reconcile the disputants. In the case of disputed taro plots, decisions either awarded the plot to one of the litigants or awarded half the plot to each. The authority of the chief before 1956 (when a democratic regime replaced the chieftainship) was such that his decisions were not questioned.

After the death of the last traditional chief in 1955, land disputes began to be tried by the Trust Territory High Court. The laws by which the court decides land disputes are based on American real property law, though the Trust Territory code states that "native custom" should be followed. As a result, the kinds of questions the court asks and the kinds of assumptions it makes about evidence presented are quite different from the kinds of assumptions that Kapinga make and the kinds of evidence that are relevant to their disputes.

The Kapinga have come to realize this, and it has opened a veritable Pandora's box. Disputes that were settled thirty or forty years ago by the chief have been and are being revived in the hope of getting a second chance to acquire more land or to remedy what are considered to be past injustices. The present-day claimants realize that they have an advantage in having an outsider hear the case since the latter does not know the Kapinga land tenure system. Plaintiffs gather witnesses before the hearings and coach them, hoping to present a united front before the American judge or Ponapean master appointed to hear the case.

Judges have, on the whole, assumed that landownership was perfect ownership in fee simple absolute.[14] Their decisions therefore leave one litigant with total ownership rights and the other litigant with no rights. By pressing his claim, the present-day plaintiff risks only usufruct in attempting ownership rights. Disputes often begin with a person demanding a land division in order to get what he feels is his rightful share of a corporately owned plot to which he has been denied use by a steward. By the time the case goes through a local, preliminary hearing (by elected local judges) and then to the Trust Territory court, the plaintiff is demanding the whole parcel. By this time, enough bitterness has been generated that demands have hardened, protagonists' arguments have been pruned of embarrassing or compromising details, and it is difficult to tell which argument has more validity. With an ever-increasing number of disputes and the court's lack of recognition of anything other than perfect ownership, the Kapinga are for the first time facing the possibility, and in some cases the fact, of total disenfranchisement. Younger men may see this implication clearly; most people do not.

It would be a grave error, both from a theoretical and an empirical standpoint, to view sanctions as merely enforcing rights and duties with regard to land. Land for the Kapinga is a set of relations among human beings, a part of what kinsmen share, and a part of that which makes them kinsmen. Thus sanctions must be seen as a set of messages to persons about their behavior. More precisely, the message is that perceptions of the situation that give rise to the dispute are wrong perceptions. This is why the informal but powerful sanction of gossip networks is the initial and often the ultimate sanction in cases of dispute. Claims and counterclaims are made through one's immediate household and kin, who not only spread the word through their kin and friends but also have the opportunity to intervene before the dispute reaches the point of litigation.

Since consanguineal kinsmen are so often the antagonists, litigation is tantamount to the disruption of kinship relations. Even if the protagonists are willing to take this step, often some of their kinsmen (especially older people) are not willing to permit it. The sanction of gossip, that is, the public condemnation of behavior, is activated not only in disputes, but, more importantly, it operates in those situations which might give rise to a dispute, such as a denial by a steward of a joint owner's right to use a plot of land. It has already been pointed out that this same sanction also functions with respect to behavior regarding land which does not and cannot lead to a dispute, such as overgenerosity and stinginess in extending use rights.

This emphasizes the essential point that what we are dealing with are social relationships as culturally defined by the Kapinga, not simply economic relations set within a kinship idiom (cf. Leach 1961). It is significant in this context that in every case where a land dispute has reached the stage of litigation, the dispute is of long standing, usually of at least two decades, and the social relationships among the litigants had long ago deteriorated to the point of hostility and bitterness toward people who consider themselves as nonkinsmen.[15] Thus litigation is not an automatic or inevitable result of a land dispute.

There are yet other social activities acting as correctives to disruption of social ties in land disputes. One of these is adoption, which is practiced exclusively among kinsmen and which always serves to remind people of their kinship ties (Lieber 1970). Another such corrective is the periodic reminder of ceremonies such as wedding feasts, births, first birthday feasts for children, funerals, and work parties for the repair of ancestral houses. Kinsmen who might be contemplating litigation are likely to find themselves working together in a feast preparation in which an atmosphere of solidarity precludes the hostile feelings. Sanctions and ceremony can therefore be seen to be intimately interrelated as forms of communication acting in this context as a means of self-correction within a system of culturally defined relations among people.

CONCLUSION

It has been demonstrated that land as a symbol encodes information about social relationships on Kapingamarangi Atoll. Land serves to specify the nature of kinship relations, of personal responsibility, and of wealth. These relations are spelled out in terms of the rules of landownership, use, and conveyance. To the extent that land is defined in terms of kinship, it serves to specify the content of those relationships. Land also symbolizes the relationship of the human community to its environment. Within this symbol is encoded information about a series of relationships, or contexts, which are hierarchically ordered.

That relations involving land are characterized by emotional intensity and anxiety is not surprising considering what land means. It is not the threat of starvation or disenfranchisement that evokes anxiety, but rather it is the nature of interpersonal relations and people's positions in those relations that are the source of anxiety. Yet it is also the case that relationships regarding land evoke feelings of cooperativeness and security. This is not surprising since land symbolizes the solidarity and sharing that is kinship. As a tangible symbol of kinship relations, it follows that land would be a focal consideration in many, if not most, relationships among kinsmen as it enters into activities, such as wedding feasts, in which kinsmen participate either as a source of food or as a means of identifying potential participants. This is what accounts for the range of relationships in which land is a consideration.

It is the informational content of the Kapinga conception of land that accounts for the variety of relationships and the intensity of emotion associated with it in social relationships. It is one of those particularly crucial, or core, symbols which serve to order the physical and social universe that the Kapinga inhabit.

NOTES

1. This chapter is based on thirteen months' field research on Ponape and Kapingamarangi sponsored by the Pacific Displaced Communities Project directed by Homer Barnett. I wish to thank Henry Lundsgaarde, Vern Carroll, Martin Silverman, William Alkire, and Andrew Strathern for their help in the preparation of this chapter.
2. This idea is not original with me but has been developed in my thinking through conversations with Vern Carroll and Martin Silverman.
3. Money from salaries as well as that from copra sales is spent mostly on

utensils and hardware or luxury foods, such as flour and rice, used mostly for feasts.

4. Taro plots are created by digging a pit to the groundwater level (about six to eight feet below the ground surface on the highest part of the islet) and depositing dead leaves and other organic material. Once a swamp is created, taro is planted. The taro plot can be converted into dry land by filling it with dirt or by simply abandoning it and letting it fill naturally.

5. This would seem to contradict the principle stated above concerning transactions involving land as being among kinsmen or having implications of consanguineal kinship. In fact, by stating that a person may give or will land to whomever he chooses, the possibility is left open to disinherit one's children and other kin. Giving or willing land to a non-kinsmen is usually considered to be an act of disinheritance by the Kapinga except when the recipient is a stepchild. Obviously, disinheritance has implications concerning consanguineal kinship. It is a message to one's kin.

6. These occasions include wedding feasts and whenever the thatching of ancestral houses occurs (see Lieber 1968:94–98).

7. There is an interesting parallel to this in the Kapinga colony on Ponape. Fish are sold for cash by Kapinga living there, and in many instances fish sales are the sole source of cash for the fisherman's family. It is considered unreasonable to ask someone for raw fish, the equivalent of money on Ponape. Cooked fish, food, is freely shared with others.

8. My source for the 1947 figures is Kenneth Emory's field notes, which he kindly allowed me to copy and use.

9. A very few residence sites were owned by individuals one or two generations ago, as shown in 1910 census figures (Eilers 1934) and those of Emory (1965) from 1947. One case of virilocal residence involved a man whose family shares ownership rights over a residence site with a nonrelative through a complicated series of adoptions and land exchanges (see Lieber 1968:370–373). He lives there in order to maintain his siblings' interests.

10. It is instructive to point out a case dating from 1954, when homesteads were being offered to Kapinga who would emigrate to Ponape to get them. When one prominent man suggested that they be given first to land-poor families, he was criticized bitterly by many, especially those who were land-poor. No one wanted to admit that they were poor, and they resented the suggestion that they be made to degrade themselves by publicly claiming homestead land on the basis of their poverty.

11. For an extended discussion of Kapinga land disputes, see Lieber 1968: 230–301.

12. Obviously one can only dispute land to which one has a recognizable claim. This means that each of the protagonists must have had at least a use right to the disputed land. Thus, either the protagonists are kinsmen or each must have gotten his claim through some prior transaction, such as disinheritance, among kinsmen.

13. Wills are now recorded in writing by the chief magistrate and the secretary of the elected island council.

14. This conclusion was reached on the basis of study of transcripts of court cases and decisions by High Court judges on the cases. The cases are on file at the district courthouse on Ponape.
15. Therefore, land litigation can be seen to be one of the few permissible forms by which people can act out their aggressions.

5

LANDHOLDING ON NAMU ATOLL, MARSHALL ISLANDS

Nancy J. Pollock

INTRODUCTION

The population of Namu Atoll in the Marshall Islands is able to maintain equable access to limited land and subsistence resources by flexibility in allocating land rights. This chapter discusses the way in which this is managed and describes in detail the various social and ecological opportunities that enable the Namu people to make the most advantageous use of the limited amount of land on which they must survive.[1]

Namu, in the Ralik or western chain of the Marshall Islands, is located thirty-five miles southwest of Kwajalein Atoll and some twenty miles north of the most northerly point of Ailinglapalap Atoll. The 1968 population of 620 lives on only four islets: Namu Namu, Majkin, Mae, and Leuen. At any time the total population may be about 5 percent more or less as school children, young adult laborers, or sick people go to Majuro or Ebeye, the urban centers of the Marshall Islands. Namu Atoll, lying on a northwest-southeast axis, has a lagoon thirty-five miles long and, at its broadest point, fifteen miles wide (see map). The total land area, which consists of fifty-one separate islets that vary considerably in size, is 2.42 square miles (Bryan 1965:13). The atoll is divided into 128 permanently separate and individually named land parcels. On the four populated Namu islets approximately two-thirds of all land parcels are used as residence sites. The remainder of the land parcels are used only as work sites for making copra. Thus 40

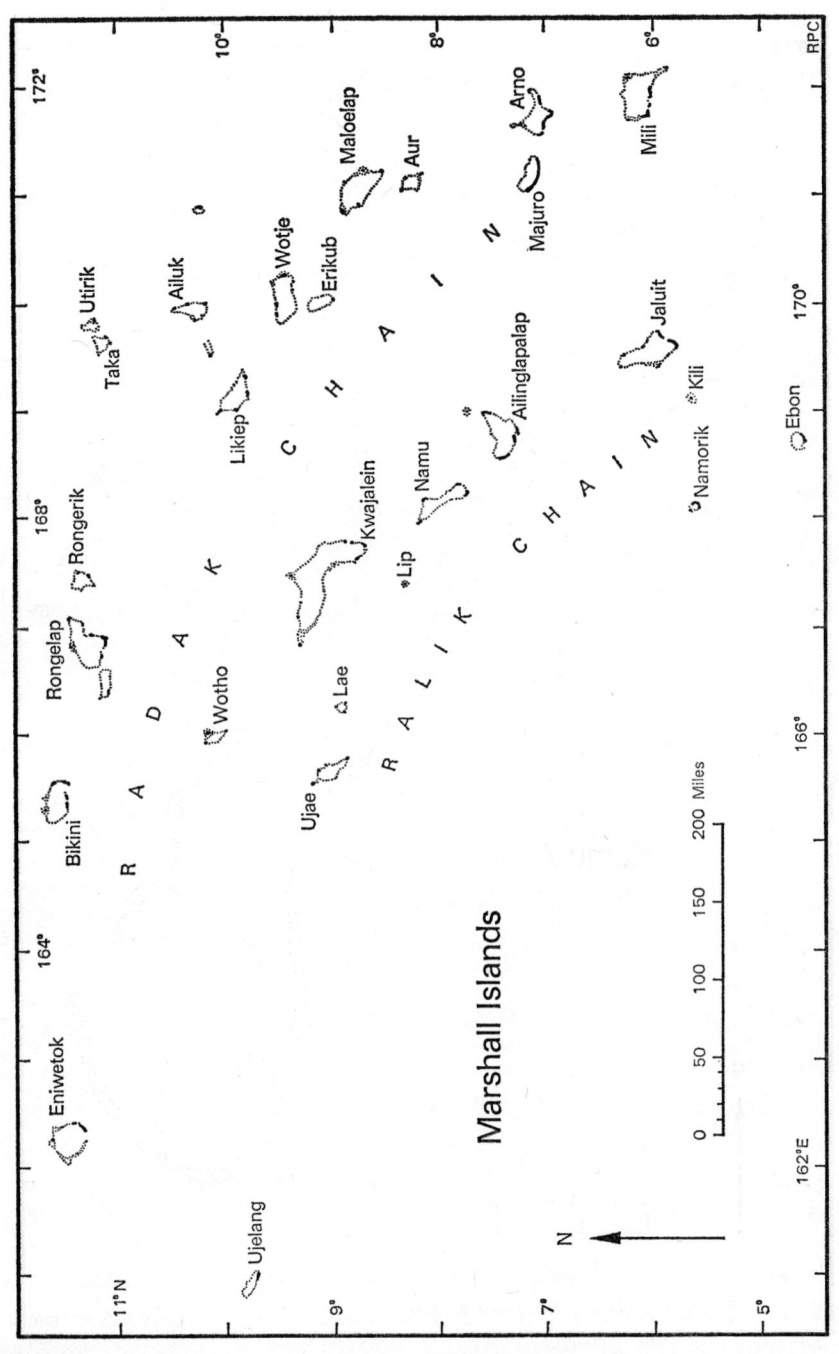

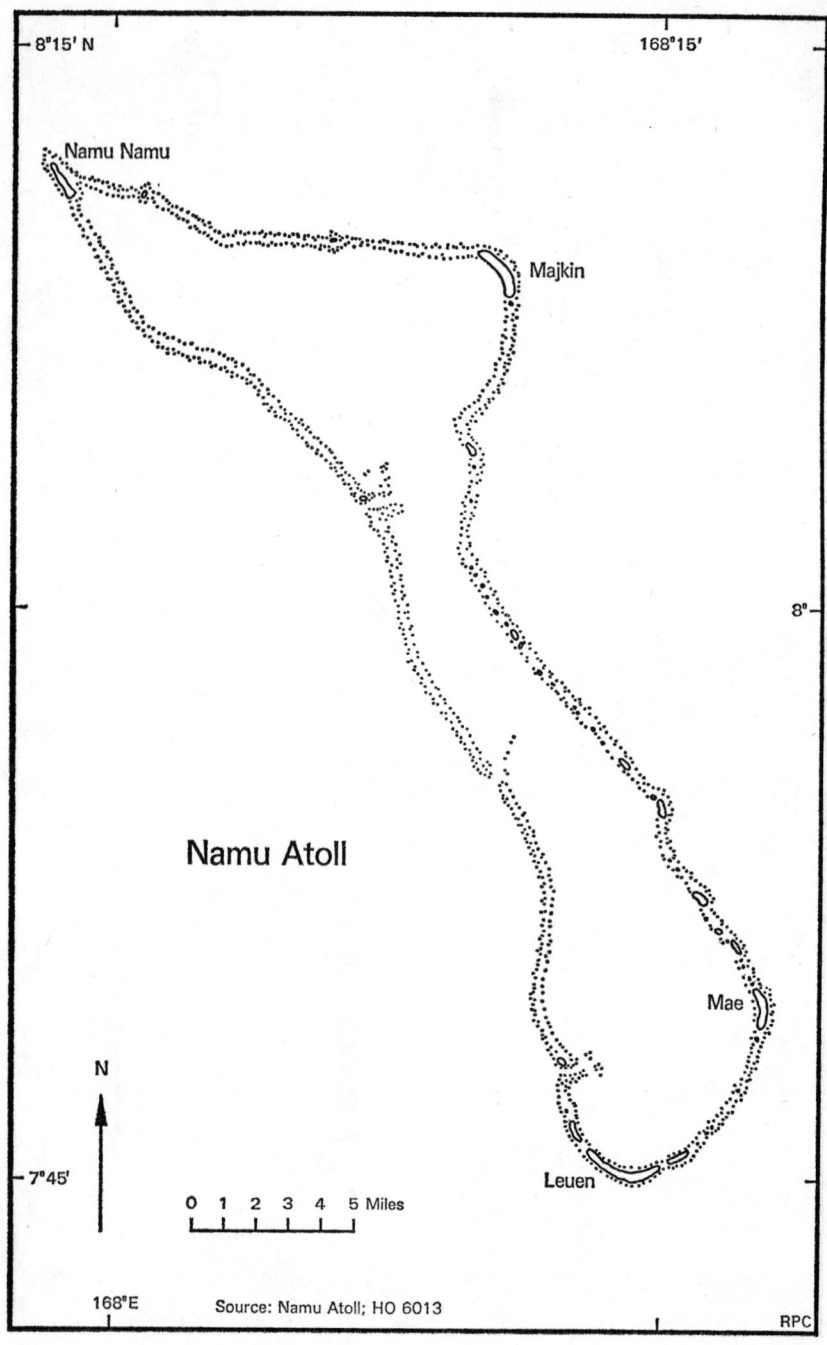

(30 percent) of the total 128 plots on the atoll are residence sites, and 88 (70 percent) are work sites. Land is the basis of support for all Namu residents, apart from seven teachers and a health aide who are salaried government employees. Access to land is thus of prime importance.

The principal argument of this chapter is that the Namu social system can be characterized as flexible because it offers four major ways to gain rights to use land and because an individual may choose which right or rights he may invoke.[2] Moreover these options are not mutually exclusive. There is also a fifth option which derives from environmental conditions rather than from the social system as such.

The first two options arise from the fact that both marriage and postmarital residence are entirely a matter of individual choice. A third option allows an individual access to land both by inheritance rights transmitted by his consanguineal relatives and by assumption of the rights of his affines. As a fourth option an individual may supplement his subsistence income derived from residence sites by invoking his rights to prepare copra at various work sites. Further flexibility in the system originates from the environment. Land is used mainly for arboriculture rather than horticulture or agriculture. The main products are coconuts, breadfruit, and pandanus. Since these fruits only need to be harvested when needed for consumption, several different sets of individuals, who share equal access rights to the land, can exercise use rights in quick succession to one another.

It must be stressed that included in the general category of land use rights is the right to benefit economically from the products of land. Given a number of alternative kinds of rights to land, a Namu individual may select where and when he will use land and for what purposes. The individual is restricted neither by residence nor by unilineal descent affiliation to a limited number of parcels of land. Nor is he required to wait until someone else has planted and harvested his crop in order to use the land. Land is still owned by paramount chiefs who retain the right to appoint new users. Use rights confer harvesting privileges and may also allow a tenant to build, dig water wells, or plant trees and plants.

A child born into a named clan of his mother retains his membership in it throughout life. He is raised among the lineage mates of his mother and of his father, and he moves frequently between their respective households and works both sets of residence sites and work sites. Because he learns that ties are slightly stronger to persons of his mother's lineage than to his father's, he has a greater incentive to live among his mother's people. He differentiates his rights to work different plots of land according to the parent from whom he receives them; he distinguishes between *lamoren* 'land belonging to his matrilineage' and *ninnin* 'other than matrilineal rights.'[3] His matrilineal rights are held concurrently with other members of his matrilineage, but his non-matrilineal land rights, inherited perhaps from his father, father's father, father's mother, and mother's father, are held with various other kin groups. An individual thus obtains his land rights from several overlapping kin groups.

Furthermore, in marriage an individual has considerable freedom in selecting a partner. Marriage within the atoll population and marriage with a cross-cousin are considered ideal. Neither form is prescribed (Pollock, Laloulel, and Morton 1972). A marital union, which may be broken without penalty by either party, conveys the right to use the partner's land. For the duration of their marriage the couple thus doubles their available options for land use.

Postmarital residence may be established at any site to which either party has rights. The period of residence at any given site is rather short—it is common for couples and their children to move two or three times during the year. Because of this, it is possible to consider residence and lineage membership as independent variables.

Ecological factors add an important dimension to the analysis of land use. If the people of Namu are to benefit appreciably from a social system that allows them maximum access to small amounts of land, then that land must produce a crop which yields a quick return from short-term labor input. On Namu coconuts are such a crop. The coconut palm requires minimal care for the forty years of its productive life, and its fruits can be harvested at short intervals. A person can, in the space of two or three months, produce copra on two or three noncontiguous plots. Another man who holds similar rights may follow shortly thereafter and repeat the procedure.[4] The land thus supports as many people as may make use of it. The coconut palm is one of the few crops that lends itself to this form of continuous harvesting. Despite any irregularity of its exploitation it will provide a return, though the yield can be increased if the area under the tree is cleaned regularly.[5] Similarly, the breadfruit and pandanus trees, both sources of dietary staples, produce fruit with minimal attention.

PRINCIPLES OF LAND TENURE

The system of rights and duties that determine how land can be acquired, held, and disposed of by individuals and groups is an important consideration in the study of the principles of land tenure on Namu. After this has been described, two social principles—kinship ties and status differences—that intersect with Namu land rights will be examined.

Land is held as distinct parcels, each of which the Marshallese refer to as a *wato*. This is a general term for a parcel of land that in most cases runs from the ocean side of an islet to the lagoon side. Larger islets may be divided into many parcels (from fourteen to eighteen on Namu) whereas a very small islet may comprise a single parcel. A land parcel may range in size from 9 acres to less than 1 acre, but the average size is about 3.7 acres (Mason 1947). Boundaries are marked either by planting a red-leafed shrub, *Cordyline,* or by making slashes at shoulder height on coconut trees near the main pathway. Each parcel is individually named, referred to by its name, and seldom if ever subdivided. Evidence of consolidation of several small parcels is found on Namu. The consolidated parcel is known by one name although the names of the former divisions are not entirely forgotten. Three nonproductive islets on Namu Atoll are not designated as plots.

Some land parcels are less useful than others. Land fertility is affected by variable soil conditions and relative exposure to prevailing winds and salt spray. Thus, a parcel that is somewhat protected from the full force of the predominating trade winds is more likely to have breadfruit trees growing closer to the ocean shore than one that is exposed to the full force of those winds.

Residence sites are distinguishable from other areas by the clusters of buildings located along the lagoon shore. These sites are surrounded by a greater abundance of breadfruit, pandanus, papaya, and banana plants than is found on noninhabited areas. A residence area is in continuous use by those who have rights to live there and is separate from all other residence areas. Small white pieces of broken coral cover the general living area between the buildings and improve the drainage and neatness of the site.

Although kinship groups in the Marshalls, as elsewhere, serve many different purposes, this analysis will focus on kinship groups on Namu that control the allocation of property rights. The dominant form of group membership in the Marshalls is that based on descent through women.

The largest unit is the *jowi* 'clan' which is a named, nonlocalized exogamous group consisting of all descendants of females who can trace a common relationship from an eponymous ancestor. But all clans are not necessarily to be found on all the inhabited atolls. Mason, for example, refers to a hierarchy of clans elsewhere in the Marshalls that was not found on Namu (Mason 1947:67).

Each clan may include several distinct *bwij* 'lineages.' These lineages consist of a living group of siblings and their matrilineal ancestors and descendants. Each lineage owes its discreteness to fission between an ancestral female and her sisters, perhaps over a land dispute or as a result of the group size. The senior lineage may be distinguished from the junior lineage and from other intervening lineages (DeBrum and Rutz 1968:13).

Although the finer terminological distinctions within a lineage were seldom made explicit on Namu, it became obvious from land tenure histories that once a sister and her descendants formed a landholding group separate from that of her sisters and their descendants, the newly formed lineages divided the landholding rights so that each held distinct rights from the other lineage groups (figure 6). Linking the different lineages bearing the same clan name proved impossible, especially for the two larger clans within which eight or ten lineage groups were recorded (see Pollock 1970: appendix A). Most of the members of a lineage tend to be resident on their atoll of birth because of the high percentage of marriages endogamous to the atoll. But informants also stated that membership is not withdrawn if an individual lives away from the atoll (Pollock, Laloulel, and Morton 1972). Clan and lineage rights belong to an individual in perpetuity.

Land inherited through the matrilineage bears much of the emotive significance of "the fatherland" or "land of my birth" to Western societies. Although a lineage, unlike a clan, has no distinctive name there is a tendency on Namu to use the name of the long-established house site which has served several generations of the lineage in the sense of "people of X who have a right to use the well-developed resources at X." It can thus be inferred that a lineage is a much more localized form of the descent group than is the clan. While the clan has greater overall persistence, the lineage reflects the generation-by-generation

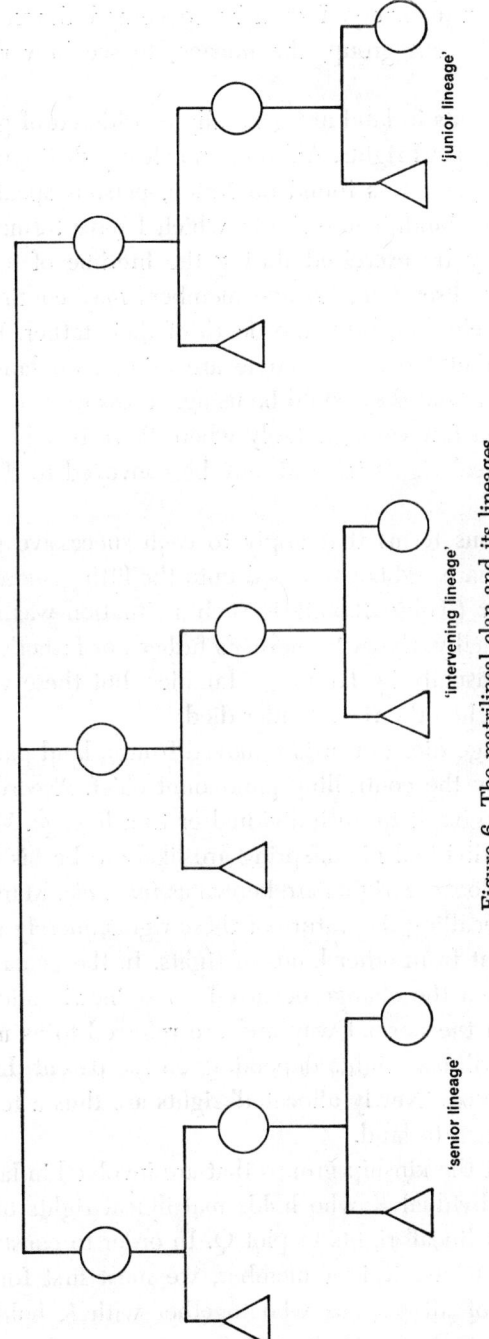

Figure 6. The matrilineal clan and its lineages.

dynamics of Namu society. I shall be concerned almost entirely with the localized descent group, the lineage, to see how rights in land operate.

Matrilineal rights in land are generally considered of greater importance than other land rights. Although no clearly distinguishable patrilineal descent group was found on Namu, persons speak of rights to use their father's land. These rights, which I have termed 'other than matrilineal,' may be exercised during the lifetime of an individual's father. At their discretion, lineage members may continue to extend these rights to children after the death of their father. If the lineage members feel that too many people are using their land or that the users have other land they could be using, access to those plots may be terminated. In a few cases, notably where there is only one male offspring, matrilineal rights in land may be conveyed to the man's children.

Tobin mentions terms that apply to each successive generation of children who share rights continued unto the fifth generation from the original transfer (Tobin 1958:20). Such a situation was not found on Namu. Occasionally, rights to mother's father's or father's father's land were claimed, usually by land-poor families, but these were likely to be terminated when the right holder died.

When a lineage dies out or is removed from a land parcel, the land is reallocated by the controlling paramount chief. According to informants, he may give it to an individual or to a lineage. Where the recipient is an individual his offspring are likely to be his beneficiaries. These 'newly allocated' rights are known as *imon aje*. Many informants had difficulty recalling the nature of these rights, merely remembering them as different from other kinds of rights. In the generation following that in which the change occurred, these 'newly allocated' rights are inherited in the normal way and are referred to as matrilineal or 'other than matrilineal' rights depending on the parent through whom they were received. 'Newly allocated' rights are thus a tertiary means of obtaining access to land.

Let us look at the kinship groups that are involved in land use starting from an individual K who holds matrilineal rights to plot P and 'other than matrilineal' rights to plot Q. In order to construct the kinship groups of which K is a member, we must first form Group 1, which consists of all persons who together with K hold matrilineal rights to land parcel P. For Group 2 we must take K together with all persons holding 'other than matrilineal' rights to parcel Q; these are likely to be persons from anywhere within K's cognatic stock. Whether or not K passes these Group 2 rights on to his children determines the continuity of his section of this group. Groups 3, 4, and so on would consist of K and others with whom he shares rights to parcels T, S, and so on whether matrilineal or 'other than matrilineal.'

Since rights held by Group 2 have been obtained from relatives of those in Group 1, but through a diversity of relationships, we may see both a unilineal and a nonunilineal principle governing the use rights on parcels P and Q. At the same time, K shares access to parcel P not only with his matrilineal kin but also with those who have 'other than matrilineal' rights to P. K may be a member of one, two, or more different kin groups in regard to one land parcel. His access rights to other parcels may place him in other groups that coincide with or are additional to those for parcel P. We thus have two or more kinds of kinship groups operating with respect to several specific parcels of land. Furthermore, on one parcel a kinship group may share rights to plot P with another kinship group operating on a different principle. The group with matrilineal rights is considered to have higher priority of access.

Residence is a specialized form of land use and falls under the same options described above. A residence site is one that is in regular use and has several permanent buildings on it as well as some land that is used as a basis of support for the residents. There is normally only one residence site per land parcel on Namu (two exceptions were found where wealthy sons have built small separate houses on their fathers' land). An individual may live on a residence site to which he has matrilineal rights, 'other than matrilineal' rights, or to which he has been assigned 'newly allocated' rights. Since residence within the atoll is highly mobile, most Namu people exercise several of these rights during the course of one year. Most commonly the nuclear family moves as a unit in order either to join relatives (usually siblings of the husband or wife) or to work copra on a nearby plot that is not a residence site. Residence in a household entails fully sharing the responsibilities of providing for and cooking for the entire group of residents. The core of the residential group is usually a set of siblings together with their affines and offspring and one or both parents. But other more distant relatives may join the household if they have matrilineal or 'other than matrilineal' rights to do so. A household is thus composed of all co-residents on one plot at one particular point in time.

Rights in land are differentially assigned to status levels. Three operate on Namu: the commoners, alternatively known as those who work the land; the *alab* 'manager' of a particular set of land parcels and head of a group of workers; and a paramount chief.[6] The paramount chief is in ultimate control of all land parcels held under his jurisdiction, although he delegates some authority to the 'manager'; the commoner worker must obey the wishes of the 'manager' and the paramount chief. Technically speaking, all members of the three status levels have worker rights to specific land parcels, but the status of 'manager' or paramount chief overlies these and gives the individual holding that status certain economic and political authority over others. Thus, worker status applies to everyone at all times, while 'manager' status or paramount chief status is more restricted.

For each plot there is one 'manager' together with many workers under him. Several 'managers' are responsible to one paramount chief. According to Dr. Tobin, there are fourteen paramount chiefs throughout the Marshalls; only four of these have jurisdiction over land on Namu Atoll.

The paramount chief is the only person with power to alienate or reassign rights to a particular land parcel. He controls use rights to it and may appoint a new 'manager' and new workers. He receives the taxes from all copra made on it and should also receive first fruits from that plot.[7] If these duties are fulfilled, he should not obstruct the use of that parcel. He should bestow small favors upon his diligent workers, such as a plate of varied foods when they come to visit him and, very occasionally, a loan for some capital expense or the gift of small items such as fishhooks and cigarettes. Moreover, he should contribute to the life crisis celebrations of each of his workers and should pay their medical expenses if hospitalization is required in the urban centers of Ebeye or Majuro. Overall, his judgment must be sought in all disputes and problems concerning the land.

The 'manager' is the caretaker of lineage rights to certain land parcels and thus has important controlling authority over those parcels to which his status pertains. He coordinates the activities of those workers who have use rights to those parcels. In respect of each parcel, one person holds the status of 'manager'; each 'manager' generally controls several parcels. He may manage these parcels for one or several paramount chiefs.

The relationship between the 'manager' and the paramount chief is one of liege to lord. The 'manager' holds the position in the name of his siblings and other lineage members in regard to specific named land parcels at the paramount chief's favor in reward for particular services performed (see Tobin 1958:26–62 for details of the varied means of original acquisition of land). He is thus the leader of a particular group in respect to particular pieces of land and must represent the interests and welfare of many persons to the appropriate paramount chief and convey the latter's wishes to the people.

The link between a 'manager' and the workers on the land is one of kinship. Informants detailed the genealogical links between themselves and their 'manager,' though some had difficulty tracing the exact nature of remote kin connections. In general, the senior living member of a matrilineage holds the status of 'manager.' He is thus the leader of the lineage group and the 'manager' of the plots belonging to that group. When he dies, the status passes to his next youngest sibling and so on through one sibling set from one mother. When the youngest of a sibling set dies, the status of 'manager' passes to the oldest child of the oldest woman of that sibling set.

For all persons holding 'other than matrilineal' rights to a particular parcel of land, a kin link also binds them to the 'manager' of that parcel. The 'manager' may be the oldest living member of an individual's father's matrilineage, or the kin link may be traced to his father's father's lineage or to his mother's father's lineage. However, the principle of a kin link between 'manager' and worker still pertains. When a 'manager' of 'other than matrilineal' rights dies, the rights may in turn pass to his siblings, and from his youngest sibling it should pass to the oldest son of the oldest male of that sibling set.

In the case of 'newly allocated' rights the paramount chief simultaneously reallocates land parcels and appoints a 'manager' of them. The conferral of this status is in time passed on to heirs. Thus 'newly allocated' rights become fused with either matrilineal or 'other than matrilineal' rights, and the same principle of succession to the 'manager' status in regard to them applies.

In his capacity as head of a land-using group, the 'manager' should be consulted before any worker uses a parcel for the purpose of making copra. He should collect the taxes from the copra that is made and carry a portion of it to the paramount chief for that parcel. The 'manager' may retain a proportion of these taxes to meet expenses of the kinship group, such as the biannual assessment for church support and a gift from the group to the paramount chief. He should also see that all land, both residence and work sites, is kept cleared and that seed nuts or cuttings of productive trees are planted to assure continued productivity. If land is not properly looked after and productivity drops, then a paramount chief may reprimand the 'manager' and exhort him to put that land in order. If the 'manager' fails to comply, then he and his kin group may in theory be removed from that land by the paramount chief.

A 'manager' must also see that all his workers present personally some of the produce of their land to the paramount chief when he is in residence and sends for it. In addition he must insure that first fruits from his plots reach the paramount chief and that special gifts are presented at Christmastime. He is also custodian for the cemetery that belongs to his kinship group and must give his approval when a person is to be buried there. He is likely also to be head of the household in which he lives if it is on his group's land. In the dual role of household head and land manager, he is the representative to the community council and the atoll council.[8] To these latter two bodies he is in one sense representing the landholding interests of his kinsmen, but in a second sense he is representing their interests as co-residents in the community. He is their designated delegate to this political body by virtue of his position of assigned leadership.

In return for these duties duly fulfilled, the 'manager' and the group of workers whom he represents have the right to security of tenure and freedom to live on the land and exploit the resources as needed.

Kiste, who worked on Kili Island, has raised the distinction between 'manager' of the lineage and 'manager' of the land. The former, he says, is one who holds his status by virtue of his position in the lineage, that is, as the senior living member of that lineage, regardless of whether or not it has land. A 'manager' of the land, as Kiste contrasts them, is one who holds his status by virtue of his position as 'manager' of the lineage with the added factor that the lineage is the landholding unit (Kiste 1968:164). The Namu people do not recognize this distinction since their 'managers' are all in charge of some plots of land, either residential or work sites. Thus every 'manager' of a lineage is also a 'manager' of the land.

A 'manager' appointed to lands that are categorized as 'newly acquired' may choose to pass this to his own children instead of his sister's children, thereby bypassing his matrilineage. In the next generation the sibling group that inherited the 'newly acquired' land must decide whether this plot will become the property of their matrilineage or whether it will be inherited by children of both brothers and sisters, that is, as 'other than matrilineal.' Whatever system applies to the land rights themselves also applies to the title of 'manager' of those plots.

On a given plot a close genealogical tie binds the 'manager' on matrilineal land to the other workers who are his kinsmen, but in the case of the 'manager' on 'other than matrilineal' land the genealogical link with his workers may be more remotely defined. Moreover, there is likely to be more than one lineage group, all holding worker rights to the same plots and each with its own set of genealogical ties to the 'manager' of that plot. Since the common denominator of these two categories of 'manager' is land management, it would seem to be more accurate to analyze the two categories of management in terms of their basis in different principles of land usage than to say one category is associated with land and the other is not (Kiste 1968:164).

Each worker has certain rights and obligations in regard to land which he has inherited either through his matrilineage or through other kin ties. He has the right to work the land, to reside on it, to obtain a livelihood from it, and also to pass those same rights on to the next generation. His obligations are to keep the land productive, pay the copra taxes, and meet other levies required of him in his status as a landholder.

A worker has a third kind of right to land in addition to the inherited matrilineal and 'other than matrilineal' rights discussed above. When a man marries, he acquires use rights to his wife's parcels, and, similarly, a wife has use rights to her husband's parcels. There is no specific term for these rights, which are good only for the duration of the marriage and terminate on the separation of a couple or on the death of a partner. These rights carry the same kind of obligations as the matrilineal and 'other than matrilineal' rights with regard to paying taxes on copra produced, keeping the plot cleared, and seeking the 'manager's' permission to work that plot. But the duty to pay first fruits and food gifts to the paramount chief from this plot should be met by those with direct rights to the land with their spouses helping where necessary.

The principles behind the marriage contract are also important for full understanding of how land rights are transmitted. Marriage is most frequently based on consensual cohabitation and usually is not formalized in church until many years after a couple has started living together openly; and perhaps not even then.[9] Thus the regulations binding a married couple are loose and easily set aside. Principles regulating selection of a spouse include marrying outside one's named clan, finding a partner who is within ten years of one's own age, and finding one who is wherever possible a cross-cousin (on either the mother's or father's side). Regulations binding a married couple are variable, and the liaison may be temporary or permanent. Thus children receive permanently their matrilineal rights from their mother, but the 'other than matrilineal' rights from the father may be withdrawn if he is no longer acting in capacity of father to them. The latter rights only last for as long as the marital relationship is maintained, much like the rights of spouses.

We have thus seen the principles by which access to land is regulated on Namu. The division into separate land parcels gives a number of discrete units which are more easily manipulated than large pieces of land when a kinship group splits. Moreover, access to land may be inherited through either parent, as either matrilineal or 'other than matrilineal,' or it may be acquired from the paramount chief as 'newly allocated' rights, thereby providing alternative mechanisms for the land-poor to increase their rights. Furthermore, an affine is privileged to exercise any of his spouse's rights for the duration of their marriage. With endogamy and cross-cousin marriage preferred, this may place double claims on some land parcels, and it results in as widespread a use of land as is needed within the atoll. Control of all these rights is distributed among three status levels: ultimate power rests with the paramount chief but is delegated to the 'manager,' who is responsible for enforcing the obligations of the workers. Consanguineal ties form the major bond between land users. To this may be attributed the relatively conflict-free attitude necessary if there is to be maximum access to the small amounts of land.[10]

LAND USE

The following data pertain only to Namu Atoll where direct observations were made. They are fairly representative of other parts of the

Marshalls inasmuch as brief visits to other atolls have borne out these findings.

While the system of landholding was not the major focus of my research, specific information was needed to ascertain how much land each individual could use for subsistence purposes and the nature of his social rights and duties resulting therefrom. Thus the following data were derived from asking adults living on Namu, "What are the names of the land parcels to which you have rights?" In answer to this question, many people asked whether information was wanted about just the parcels on which they can live (their residence sites) or also the parcels on which they can work. The distinction between residence land and work land is the important one that governs how land is used. In further questioning it was ascertained whether the right was matrilineal or 'other than matrilineal' as well as the nature of the genealogical link between the respondent and 'manager' for each of his parcels.

It is evident from table 6 that, for the most part, the holdings of paramount chiefs tend to cluster on three or four islets. It is also clear from table 6 that one particular paramount chief controls most land

TABLE 6 Plots by Islet and Controlling Iroij on Namu Atoll

Islet	Albert	Kabua	Lejolan	Nemaro	Total
Namu Namu	7	2	18	1	28
Majkin	2	0	16	0	18
Mae	0	6	0	10	16
Leuen	8	2	16	0	26
Other*	7	0	29	4	40
TOTAL	24	10	79	15	128
%	18	8	62	12	100

*The remaining small islets, most of which lie on the southeastern reef.

on Namu Atoll, and it follows that he has the allegiance of a major segment of the population.

This paramount chief is the one who visits the atoll with considerable regularity. In fact he considers it to be one of his homes, a traditional family seat. He has houses on all three major islets in the atoll, even one on Mae, where he is not in control of any land. He has also built less elaborate houses on two of the smaller islets. One of these, Eo, is now used as a place of permanent residence by the workers appointed to take care of the place while the paramount chief is away. The houses on Namu and Majkin are substantial and in keeping with his prestigious position. They are located on land over which he has control, and he expects the workers on these plots to maintain the houses in good repair and clean the surrounding area. These workers may not use his houses for their own purposes but are the source of his household labor force while he is in residence there.

The other three paramount chiefs rarely visit Namu but either send representatives occasionally to collect copra taxes or send word that the taxes should be sent to Ebeye or Majuro by way of a trusted individual. These other paramount chiefs are more casual in seeing that customary obligations are met.

The particularly active paramount chief, by virtue of his frequent visits to Namu Atoll and his constant vigilance and exhortation to his workers to keep their plots clean, maintains productivity at a higher level than it would be if he did not visit. He orders copra to be made on parcels which have not been recently exploited and thus encourages increase in copra production. To assist in this task, he provides the all-important gasoline for the outboard engines on the boats needed to get to distant islets. He is unrelenting in his attempts to keep the main islets neat, and he bicycles down the main path on a tour of inspection each day while in residence. As a result, many visitors remark on the unique orderliness of Namu island.

Several land disputes are ongoing although they are not very actively pursued. In due time the paramount chiefs may settle these disputes. Two major land disputes which flared up in 1968 from old dissatisfactions are briefly described in the following cases.

Case 1. The border between Mwenkio and Kabinbwil residence sites on Majkin has long been contested between these two neighboring groups. Borders on Namu are indefinite at best. As a general rule, Marshallese prefer to leave it this way, hence their suspicion and distrust of anyone mapping land—each side suspecting that the other may gain by default. In this case, access to the well, which is an important source of water for a household, was in question. The Mwenkio people had sunk the well, but apparently most of it fell in Kabinbwil territory. This well site had been disputed several times in the past, but because it is no light undertaking to dig such a well, Mwenkio people had preferred to let the question ride and continued to use their well. The Kabinbwil people had their own well in the middle of their land. However, as a result of several minor irritations between the neighbors, a 17-year-old schoolgirl was urged, it was claimed, to contaminate the disputed well, effectively putting it out of use. Her punishment became a subject of much community discussion. The community council wanted to fine her $100 and "imprison" her for three months (i.e., weed the village roads), but the paramount chief decreed that she should be banished from Majkin, fined fifteen dollars, and put to work on the roads in Mae. At that point the land dispute fell into the background, and it became a case of antisocial behavior. The well has been filled in and cannot be used; so far a new one has not been dug.

Case 2. The 'manager' living on La Donak, Namu Namu, died suddenly of peritonitis, leaving a widow and three adopted children living on this parcel. This widow claimed that she had a piece of paper validated by the headman of Namu Namu[8] stating that she was to have full rights to both La Donak and Jabilo-ai rak, also her husband's land, and she was, moreover, to be 'manager' of both plots. The man's matrilineage consisted of some twelve adult women resident within Namu Atoll and a brother then living on Ebeye, Kwajalein Atoll. The whole kinship group was furious at what they termed trickery. Those women who had been living with their families at La Donak when their brother became sick moved to Eonemaj, Majkin, the only other lineage residence site close by. Meanwhile, the widow worked the copra on the two sites and pocketed the 'manager's' taxes. She also killed off and ate all the chickens and pigs on the residence site.

There was much public and private discussion of the case. The general consensus seemed to be that things were not right, but that the paramount chief would know the right steps to take and that they must wait for his settlement of the case. By December 1968, eight months had elapsed at which time the paramount chief discussed the case with both sides and convinced the widow to move out. The end of the case was marked by a public breakfast between the widow and the recently returned adult male of the offended lineage and the paramount chief. At this time the disputants shook hands, and the case was marked as settled. The woman moved to her own matrilineage land, an unusually small plot of land which happened to be next door to La Donak. Namu informants stated that only the paramount chief could know the best way to settle such land disputes so that both parties would abide by the decision, although atoll council members can be effective up to a point.

The power of a paramount chief to redistribute land in cases in which a lineage dies out or in which a land right is tenuous has been exercised on some eight parcels in the recent past. In one case, the paramount chief's most recent wife's father, a man from Lae Atoll, was given four work sites among the small islets and a residence plot on Namu Namu. In another case, a man on Majkin had not been allowed by his two older brothers to work his copra lands but had worked faithfully for his paramount chief for some twenty years. That chief rewarded him by making him worker on a parcel on Majkin which was then converted into a residence site. The parcel had been given to that paramount chief in payment for a past favor. However, the worker did not receive full rights to the land, but rather was told he must work the copra regularly and might be allowed to keep the cash from the sale of some of it, depending on how the paramount chief felt. The rest of the cash from copra was to go to the chief. On those occasions when the paramount chief did not allow the worker to keep the cash, he would give him some rice, flour, tea, and sugar as basic supplies. Thus the worker is beholden to his chief, and it is none too clear what will happen to these rights when either chief or worker dies.

The exercise of the paramount chief's power over land on Namu is very much a matter of individual personalities. One chief exercises his rights and duties very extensively while the other three are less active. The picture of land use on Namu must reflect this situation.

All of the 128 plots on Namu Atoll fall under the jurisdiction of one of the twenty-six 'managers'—each 'manager' has an average of five plots apiece. He may hold these plots under different paramount chiefs.

Each plot has at least one 'manager.' Some of these 'managers' hold their status by virtue of their matrilineal land. The others hold the status on different plots of land because of 'other than matrilineal' rights. Moreover, one 'manager' may control some of his plots because of matrilineal rights and the others because of 'other than matrilineal' rights. Except for two 'managers' who were recently given their rights, all 'managers' have inherited title either through their matrilineage or from a person outside their matrilineage.

The 'manager' title to a particular plot may be reported as pertaining to two persons, one male and the other female. The male is supposed to carry out all the responsibilities of the position, while the female is the main link in succession to the title of that position. These persons are usually the oldest brother and oldest sister in a kinship group, or mother's brother and oldest sister where the mother is dead. A woman may make the decisions and attend meetings of 'managers' if no man is available to do so. When asked whether the man or the woman is more important, respondents indicated that each is, in his or her own sphere. However, the woman is the key link in the system and the man "just works for her."

If the person holding status as a 'manager' is senile, sick, or nonresident on Namu Atoll, a distinction is made between the person with the status of 'manager' and the person working in that capacity. However, it is the rightful 'manager,' whether or not he is on Namu, who gets the copra shares. The substitute 'manager' must collect these each time copra is made and hand the total sum over to the real 'manager' whenever he sees him. The latter may tell the former to keep all or a certain proportion of this money, depending on his disposition.

There is no confusion in people's minds between the de jure and de facto powers of persons holding 'manager' status. It cannot, however, be conclusively asserted that the status is assigned to a particular category of persons, for as we have seen this distinction is circumstantial.

'Managers' on residence plots have greater responsibilities than 'managers' on work sites. If a male 'manager' is living on lineage land, he holds the position of household head as long as he resides in that household. (Not all households on Namu are headed by 'managers.') Combining the roles of 'manager' and household head confers a dual set of responsibilities which include presenting a selection of the best foods of his plots to the paramount chief when the latter is in residence. On Majkin the 'managers' or their representatives regularly presented their tribute from the households for which they had jurisdiction on Sunday mornings when the paramount chief was in residence.

The Namu Atoll council and the local community councils are made up mainly of 'managers.' Here these men are representing not only the interests of a landholding group with rights to a particular parcel but also the interests of the household in which the 'manager' resides. In either case, the 'manager' acts as spokesman for the interests of a group of kinsmen and conversely is the whipping boy when reprimands are given by the paramount chief. Informants stated that the 'manager' should only speak on behalf of the group that he represents after they have met and agreed which course of action is felt to be suitable, but this is not always practical.

The 'manager' on a work site must be consulted each time copra is made on a parcel under his control. He is the one to whom a man will go when he wishes to exercise his right to work one of these plots. That 'manager' will help to decide which of two kinsmen should work a particular plot if both wish to work it at the same time. But if one individual assists another to make copra on a particular plot, the manner in which the proceeds are divided is a personal matter between those two alone.

The prescribed copra taxes for both residence and work sites are collected regularly. Tax collecting is made easier by a system of bookkeeping in which the 'manager' of each parcel keeps a book for each parcel under his jurisdiction. Each time copra is made on that plot a ticket from this book is filled out with the name of the producer, the total weight of copra sold, and the cash price. Then the ticket is signed by the purchasing agent on board ship at the time copra is sold. These tickets are then presented to the paramount chief to indicate how much tax is owed to him. Each time a 'manager' presents his workers' taxes to the most influential paramount chief he must pay an additional five dollars. Out of copra taxes the 'manager' must also pay the semiannual church tax, which is the major source of support for the church minister. This assessment ranges from $1.50 to $5.00 every six months per inhabited household. Occasional other levies made against households and lineage groups are met by the 'managers' out of group funds.

All workers on Namu have access to one or more plots, and all plots of land have one or more persons with workers' rights to it. The basic land-utilizing unit is a married couple. They can select from either the husband's or wife's matrilineal or 'other than matrilineal' rights to several separate plots at any given point in time. Throughout their married life, a couple makes repeated decisions about selection of residence site and selection of parcels on which to make copra. These two decisions are only indirectly interrelated. A couple may be in residence on a plot, but not make copra other than that needed to support the household for three or four months or longer. When they do decide to make copra for themselves, they may live on a residence plot to which the husband has rights and work a work site to which the wife has rights or vice versa or some other combination of their total rights. All options are open to them.

Every individual on Namu has rights to take up residence on one of his land parcels. Each parcel is a potential residence site and therefore potentially a locus of one household. What makes a residence site? It must be near other residence sites. It must provide access to freshwater, that is, the Ghyben-Herzberg lens. This lens is large enough to provide sufficient freshwater only on larger islets. Thus residence sites tend to be clustered on one of the four major islets on Namu, but not all plots on these islets are used as residence sites. At the extremities of an islet the freshwater lens tends to be too thin, and thus the water is always brackish.

A residence plot is similar to all other plots in that it runs from the lagoon to the ocean side of an islet. The house structures and general living area are usually located about fifty yards or more in from the lagoon shore alongside the road that runs the length of the inhabited islets. All buildings of one household are clustered together. The total ground area around them is covered with small white pieces of coral. Around the house site are a variety of useful trees, shade trees, and occasionally some ornamental plants. In particular, pandanus, papaya, and banana plants are located near dwellings. Breadfruit trees may also be found around the house site. The taro pits are located near the middle of the plots on which they are found because that plant needs fresh water.

Rights to residence sites may be to an individual's own matrilineal or 'other than matrilineal' land, or they may be through an affine in the case of a spouse marrying in from another atoll. Marriage is approximately 80 percent endogamous to Namu Atoll (see Pollock, Laloulel, and Morton 1972). Where both partners are from Namu there is no dominant pattern in choice of residence site.

As of March and April 1968, more couples on Majkin were living on residence sites to which the man had rights than on Namu Namu, where a slight balance favored couples residing on sites to which the woman had rights.[11] On Majkin two families were living neolocally— the Congregational minister whose location is rotated throughout the Marshalls every two years and the health aide who lives on public property. Only one family on Namu Namu, the assistant minister's, lived neolocally.

Marshallese frequently change residence sites within the atoll and even live outside the atoll if they have rights to residence sites, perhaps through a spouse, from another atoll. The unit that moves most frequently is the nuclear family—husband, wife, and offspring including adopted children. If some of the offspring are in their teens or older, they may not follow their parents but rather stay with extended kin, especially if they are of school age and prefer to stay within access to a particular school. Such movements of nuclear families may occur two or three times a year or a family may not move for two or three years. There are a variety of factors influencing a decision to move. The most important reasons given for a move, in relative order of importance and frequency, include filial obligations, public affairs, copra production, and pregnancy.

Of the forty couples on Majkin only six (15 percent) made no moves or trips together during 1968. Many trips were made by one partner alone, usually for the purpose of attending public affairs such as atoll council business, teaching duties, carrying medicine or attending the sick, or for religious observances. The moves that resulted from filial obligations were made by sons or daughters to visit a sick mother or father or, more rarely, to carry out a task for the mother or father such as helping to build a house. Desire to be with one's siblings or to help them in illness also resulted in some moves.

Duration of the trips varied, and only those that lasted longer than a month can be classified as a change in residence for a couple.

Copra-making trips may last anywhere from five days to six weeks depending on how often that site has been worked, how many sites can be combined in one trip, and how the couple balances the discomforts of living on a work site against their need for, potentially, several hundred dollars.

When any couple moves, they decide whether to live with the husband's kin or the wife's kin. Among the factors they consider are the size of existing membership of the households of their respective kinsmen, the amount of sleeping space available in each, which household is within easy access of several work sites, proximity to a health aide or a Marshallese midwife (if the wife is pregnant), compatability with others members of the household, and proximity to school (if children are concerned). Informants stated that when a young couple first begins to live together, they should live with the girl's kin so that the girl's mother and classificatory mothers can help her through her first pregnancy, but this is not rigidly adhered to. Of five cases where the couple began living together for the first time during 1968, four of the couples lived with the girl's family initially. But two of these moved at least twice before the end of the year, living with his kin and then with hers again for varying periods. Such wandering about is the characteristic pattern of residence, for mobility between several residence sites continues throughout the lifetime of a couple.

This mobility is an important feature in the flexibility of the social system that enables population and resources to be kept in balance. Taking up residence gives a couple rights to use the products of the land surrounding the house and also obligates them to the household established on that residence site. Its resources are the basis of both subsistence and cash economy for all persons joining the household and sharing the same facilities.

However, the combination of families sharing any one residence site is constantly changing. A household group at any one time is composed of several nuclear families linked by consanguineal ties. These draw together in one household kinsmen who share direct co-residence rights. Most frequently, a household forms around a set of siblings and their spouses and their children. The average size of a household is fifteen persons, composed of perhaps as many as three nuclear families.

A household links together those who have a right to live there by serving as a concrete symbol of their relationship to each other. Over time it is in constant use by several of these persons and their families.

Those who live together in one household also share rights to work and gather the produce of the plot on which that household is situated. It is generally agreed that produce from residential locations is to be used for everyday living purposes. The breadfruit and pandanus are either cooked for meals or cooked and given away. The coconut trees are multipurpose. Any copra that is made on a residence plot is sold, and the money earned is used to buy food for whoever resides in that household. All members of a household work together to produce the copra on a residence plot; the proceeds are considered to belong to the residence unit as a whole. Both consanguines who share direct rights to the plot and affines of those consanguines are expected to work together toward the support of the household in which they reside.

In addition, affines must also assist in the support of any residence unit with which they have close consanguineal ties if the residence unit is located on the same islet as the one on which they are living.

This applies particularly to siblings. If a man is living on his wife's residence plot but his siblings or classificatory parents have a residence plot on the same islet, he must work not only to support his household of residence but also to support his kinsmen, especially if the latter household is short of men to do male work.

The resources of a residence plot are thus in constant use as long as people reside there. The coconut trees planted by earlier residents yield a crop of nuts the year round. Certain trees are selected for drinking nuts while the rest of the nuts are allowed to fall in their natural cycle and are used either in the preparation of food or are dried to make copra and then sold. Copra is made about once a month on a residence plot or more often if news is received of the expected imminent arrival of a ship. Every time copra is made the land is cleared, undergrowth is cut back, and leaves and trash are burned. The constant working of residence plots means that these are clean—too clean to allow humus to develop—and their products are used to a maximum. Continuity of use is due to the fact that people are regularly present and a ready supply of labor is available to keep the land at maximum productivity. But this productivity is not maintained by any particular group; rather it is the constantly fluctuating group of household members under their 'manager' that works a residence plot. In direct contrast is the type of unit that uses a work site.

The main use of work sites is to produce copra, and 70 percent of the total number of plots on Namu Atoll are used almost solely for this purpose. Most of the work sites are small islets lying on the southeast reef so that a boat is needed to reach them from the three main islets. The people now depend greatly on launches with outboard engines so that gas shortages have become major deterrents to making copra on these work sites. Although four sailing canoes were reoutfitted and made seaworthy during 1968, they were not available much of the time and needed constant repair. Transportation problems are therefore a major deterrent to greater exploitation of the work sites.

The productivity of these work sites varies, but useful products are limited to the coconut palm and a few breadfruit trees planted on four or five of the small islets. The coconut palm predominates on most of the small islets. Most of the small islets are not worked as systematically as residence plots, and the coconut trees are overcrowded and choked with much underbrush. Nuts are allowed to sprout and root where they fall. When persons with use rights to one of these plots come to work them, they must cut through the tangled underbrush to collect the fallen nuts. Such hard work is of short-lived utility as the undergrowth grows back all too fast. The problem of rapid growth of choking underbrush is worse on the more southerly atolls that are wetter than Namu.

When a man or woman decides to make copra on a work site, he or she must consider factors such as how long he needs to work in order to make the required amount of money, when a boat may be available, and how much additional help is needed. To clean up the copra as expeditiously as possible, at least two men and two fully active women are needed. The harvester must request help from kinsmen. Thus the work team that goes off to an outer island to make copra consists of the one who has the right to use that plot, the spouse, their children, and certain of their kin. Normally, the group stays six to eight days on one average size parcel, although they may stay as long as six weeks if they have two or more plots close together, that is, within walking distance along the reef. Since these work sites lack proper facilities for fresh water, sleeping, and cooking, the Namu people make their stay as short as is necessary to harvest the copra. The cash returns from the copra sold belong to the couple who exercised their rights; others who helped receive no particular return other than the normal reciprocity in services at the extended kin level.

Income from copra made on work sites is used for purposes other than pure subsistence, namely, as supplementary money for a nuclear family or for a major capital expenditure. Each nuclear family needs some ready cash for church collections, parties for the paramount chief or visitors, rites of passage, and so forth, and copra making is the only source of these funds. When a family needs cash to support a child away at school, to buy an outboard motor, or to pay a Marshallese doctor, then they will ask the 'manager' for permission to work one of their work sites. If a large expense is anticipated, then several plots will have to be worked. The income from this source may thus be considered as different from the strictly subsistence income derived from a residence site. The cash is not surplus. Rather the coconut trees and breadfruit trees, if any, are forms of long-term investments which belong to several kinship groups sharing land rights to that particular plot and which can be drawn upon in times of need. All those who share rights to that plot share the investment and are expected to contribute their labor to keep the plot as clear as possible and to make copra for sale.

Work sites are used then by small groups consisting of members of the personal kindred including affines of the individual who share rights to the location. Over a year, or any given period of time, the work force would be composed of those persons tracing a bilateral relationship back to the ancestor who first received the plot as her heritage.

In summary, land can be put to two kinds of use. Residence sites are under constant occupation while the land beyond the dwelling area is worked for copra at a rate of one or more times a month. Work sites are used only occasionally, at an average rate of two or three times a year according to availability of gas for the boats or need for cash income. The income from copra made on the residence site is used for the everyday needs of all household members. The income from work sites belongs to the individual who initiates the work but with the understanding that the outboard engine, or a student's education, or someone's return to health are all considered as responsibilities of the group that shares rights to that land. The profit accruing to an individual from use of his work sites may thus be seen as profit accruing to the kinship groups whose land has been used after the individual has deducted his pin money.

CONCLUSION

The Namu social system has been examined in terms of the way land rights are allocated and the way in which it allows a number of options. This flexibility permits each individual to have access to scattered but basic food resources. Since land cannot pass outside kinship bonds and resources on this atoll are limited, access to these resources must continue to be spread as evenly as possible throughout the atoll population if the population is to stay viable. Where rights are too unevenly spread, as happens when some sibling sets are disproportionately large, then some will have little or no food, while others have sufficient. Such uneven access to resources is in direct opposition to the ethic that everyone must share however little there is. The structural solution seems to have been to divide up the total number of plots between sisters and their descendants, but there is no regular pattern in the formation of landholding units.

Nevertheless, given the flexible Namu system described above, each person has access to some basic subsistence resources, meager though they may be. The options in different parts of the social system that allow those resources to be maximized are the following: (1) The nuclear family has the freedom to change its place of residence and does so frequently for a variety of reasons. (2) Each individual has some matrilineal, 'other than matrilineal,' and spouse rights to particular parcels of land which he may utilize as the need arises. (3) Where a nuclear family lives and gains a subsistence income is independent of where it makes copra for personal income or capital investment. (4) Tree crops, such as the coconut palm which yields a cash income and the breadfruit tree which yields a basic dietary staple, are in more or less continuous production, yielding a crop that can be utilized at short notice.

When these options are combined, any individual can support himself and his family to some degree. This may be construed as a result of a social system that allows food and cash resources needed by sibling sets of various sizes to be as widely available as feasible.

Therefore, it can be concluded that the multiplicity of safeguards has enabled periodic population imbalances to be self-correcting without necessitating major changes in the overall structure of the system. If it were possible to examine population figures for Namu Atoll at twenty-year intervals since contact in 1880, we might then be able to correlate these with histories of landholding on particular plots and show how the mechanisms analyzed above operated in practice. Unfortunately, we have no accurate record of these events.

NOTES

1. Data were collected on Namu Atoll, Marshall Islands, between February 1968 and February 1969. Fieldwork was funded by a Fellowship and Research Grant from the National Institute of Mental Health, 1–F1–MH–39.045–01 (CUAN) and MH – 11,300–01.
2. Opposing views have been expressed on the nature and relationship of a flexible social system and its resulting effects on land and other resources. Alaric Maude has shown how the access of Tongans to land depends on the degree of independence that exists in the mobility of their nuclear family units (Maude 1965). Barnes in his discussion of the inapplicability of African patterns of social structure to New Guinea Highlands societies has specifically recognized that optation is useful in New Guinea wherever land is scarce (Barnes 1962). Brookfield and Brown in discussing one New Guinea group's control over land have

maintained that if the Chimbu would follow a less rigid structure than that of their present unilineal pattern of inheritance within fixed territories, they would obtain a more equitable allocation of land (Brookfield and Brown 1963:172). Writing of Africa, Goody has used a similar line of argument to describe LoWiili as a patrilineal system which has complementary descent for purposes of land use (Goody 1956:77).

Goodenough's position regarding Malayo-Polynesian organization for access to land remains equivocal. His position in 1955 was that there is a necessary evolutionary link between patrilocality and patrilineality, on the one hand, and between matrilocality and matrilineality on the other. He later modified this position to allow for other combinations, but he still argued for a necessary relationship between descent group structure and residence rule and for the efficacy of the unrestricted descent group in resolving problems of population pressure on land (Goodenough 1963).

The problem of whether principles of membership in a descent group combined with principles of residence are deterministic of a society's flexibility in its access to land is questionable. Both Keesing (1968:84) and Panoff (1970:192) conclude from their respective Melanesian data that residence rights and land use rights operate independently of descent principles. They base their reasoning on the fact that groups composed of persons who are co-residents may differ from groups composed of persons who share land rights. People may manipulate the two variables of residence and land use rights and others to suit their needs as circumstances dictate.

Denying this flexibility, Langness (1964:181), Meggitt (1965:262), and Salisbury (1962) have argued that agnatic descent structure in New Guinea becomes stronger as pressure on land and resources increases.

3. In the past this term has been used for land rights received or inherited from the father (Spoehr 1949:166; Mason 1947; Tobin 1958). However this usage does not fit with my own field data. On Namu the term *ninnin* was used by informants to refer to land one had received from one's father, his father's father or mother, or his mother's father. Thus, I believe the term 'other than matrilineal' rights is a better gloss for the term *ninnin*.

4. Under shifting horticulture, an individual who has land rights to a certain plot may have to wait to plant it until a field crop that belongs to someone else has been harvested. Thus he cannot benefit from exercising his rights to move many times a year because of restricted areas of land that are in continuous production. Use of the products of the coconut palm and breadfruit tree are not so restricted.

5. Namu is the fifth largest producer of copra in the Marshalls according to administrative records on economic development in Majuro. The price of copra in 1968 rose from 4.5 cents to 5 cents per pound. The copra is packed in 100-pound bags, consisting of the meat of approximately 280 nuts. A producer grossed $5 per bag or $100 per ton. Monthly production on Majkin ranged from five bags to twenty-two bags per plot depending on the quality of trees and size of the plot. I calculated that on

Majkin a man working both residence and work sites made $116 per year for his nuclear family.
6. The hospitality of Chief Lejolan Kabua gave me an unusual opportunity to observe these various statuses vis-à-vis one another, especially on occasions of tribute gifts and parties in his honor.
7. Copra taxes on Namu in 1968 were: $.001 (1 mill) per pound of copra to the local council, $.006 (6 mills) per pound of copra to the 'manager' of the plot on which the copra was made, $.003 (3 mills) per pound of copra to the chief of the plot on which the copra was made. This totals $.01. Thus, one cent out of every five cents per pound paid to the producer is taxed.
8. Traditional and modern politics operate side by side on Namu. The picture was confused for me as an outsider because the elected magistrate for the atoll, Lejolan Kabua, is also a chief. Traditionally, a chief made decisions which were passed to his 'managers' and thence to the people. The modern mechanism consists of a magistrate for the atoll, working through an atoll council which has a scribe, and whose membership comprises all of the 'managers' on the atoll. There is also a local community council on each of the three major islets under the leadership of a headman and a policeman. Neither of these are usually 'managers'; both are appointed by the magistrate. Local councils meet once a month and the atoll council meets four times a year. All officials are paid a small salary of $50–100 per annum out of council funds obtained from copra levies.
9. The established religion on Namu is that of the Congregational mission.
10. Land disputes do exist and the court files in Majuro are full of such cases, many of which have been on the books for years. But as long as they do not seriously aggravate either side, they are ignored. Only when major changes threaten a descent group's land do land disputes become a problem.
11. Transportation problems prevented my getting to Mae-Leuen in these same months.

6

LAND TENURE IN THE ELLICE ISLANDS: A CHANGING PROFILE

Ivan Brady

INTRODUCTION

The Ellice Islands are a group of nine small atolls and table reef islands situated just south of the equator and west of the International Date Line in the Gilbert and Ellice Islands Colony.[1] They have been under British administration since the establishment of a protectorate government in 1892. Christian missions have prevailed in the area for more than a century as the result of early proselytization by Samoan pastors of the former London Missionary Society. Both the Ellice church and the colonial government are closely involved with contemporary strategies for living in this region, and their orthodoxies have permeated nearly all aspects of the indigenous society, including land tenure patterns. As economic development plans proceed apace, the growing local interests and participation in market exchange with the wider world are stimulating changes in social and economic organization. The now commonplace diversion of household production efforts beyond immediate consumption needs to include the preparation and sale of copra through cooperative societies has resulted in a partial shift in traditional property concepts and production orientation. Increasing population densities have proved to be incompatible with certain aspects of the traditional land tenure system, inflating an already present overall land hunger.

None of these elements is unique as a source of culture change in Oceania (see Crocombe 1971), but each has had its own particular

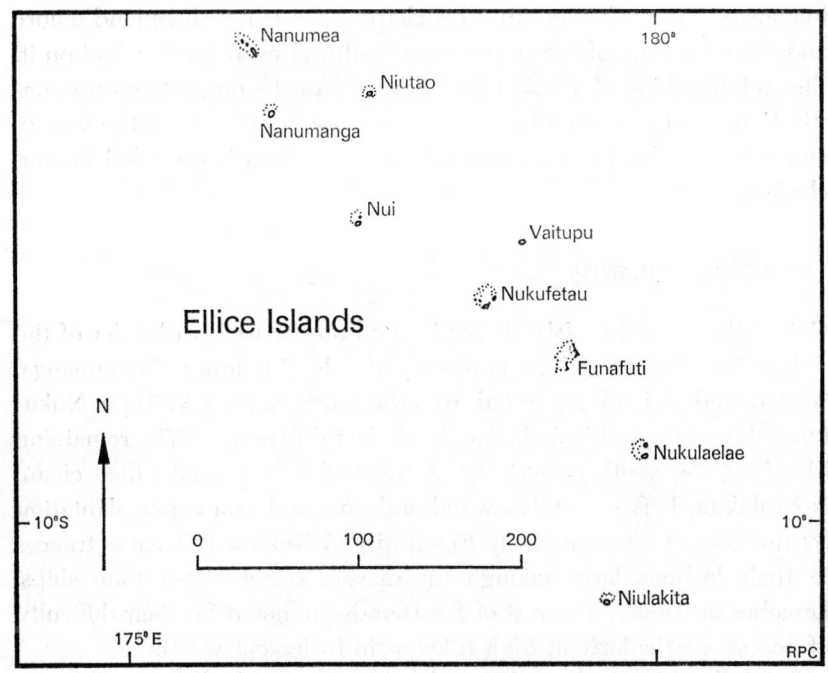

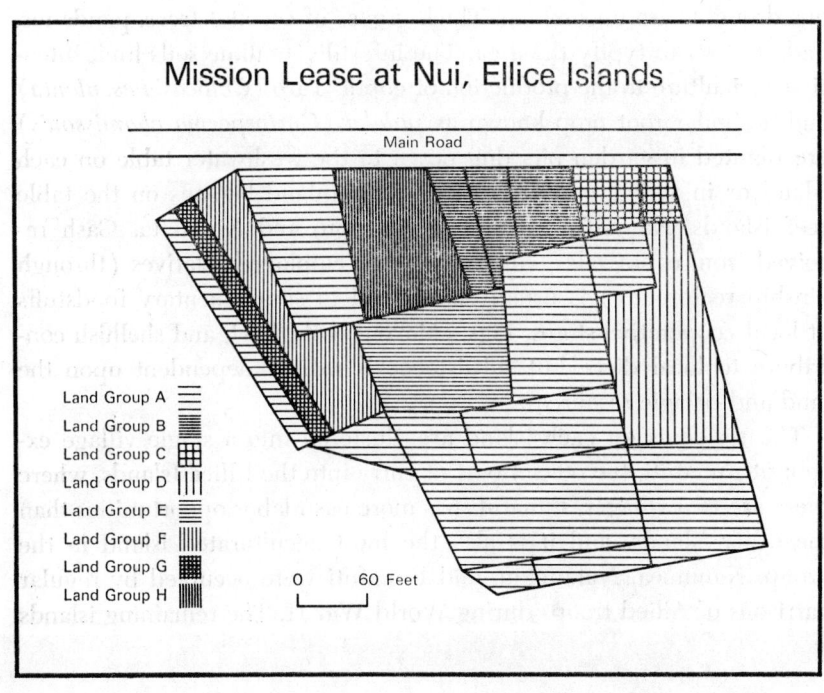

influence in the Ellice group. This chapter describes Ellice land tenure and assesses some of the impact cross-cultural exposure has had on it. The relationships of kinship and land tenure to property-group constitution are demarcated in the process, and an estimate of the variety and extent of land hunger throughout the Ellices is provided in conclusion.

THE ELLICE ISLANDS

Culturally, the Ellice Islands are located on the western border of the Polynesian Triangle. The northern islands, Nanumea, Nanumanga, Niutao, and Nui, are separated from the southern ones, Vaitupu, Nukufetau, Funafuti, and Nukulaelae, by dialect differences.[2] The remaining island, at the southernmost tip of the widely scattered Ellice chain, is Niulakita. It is presently owned and operated as a copra plantation by the Niutao islanders. Only Funafuti and Nukufetau have entrances to their lagoons large enough for marine vessels other than ships' launches or canoes. The rest of the islands are noted for their difficulty of access, particularly at high tides or in inclement weather.

Rainfall averages about 120 inches per year in this region, and serious droughts are uncommon. Thick groves of coconut trees, pandanus, and atoll scrub typify the area. The infertile coralline soils limit intensive agriculture to the production of copra. Taro (*Colocasia esculenta*) and a similar root crop known as *pulaka* (*Cyrtosperma chamissonis*) are planted in garden pits dug down to the freshwater table on each island or in the silty mud bordering the inland lagoons on the table reef islands, Nanumanga, Niutao, Vaitupu, and Niulakita. Cash received from copra sales, employment, or employed relatives (through kinship reciprocity) is usually converted to supplementary foodstuffs at local cooperative stores. Pigs, chickens, wild fowl, and shellfish contribute to local diets, but subsistence is mainly dependent upon the land and pelagic resources.

The residents on each island are clustered into a single village except at Funafuti, the official port of entry into the Ellice Islands, where there are two villages. Funafuti has more cash labor opportunities than the other islands, and it is also the most acculturated island in the group. Nanumea, Nukufetau, and Funafuti were occupied by regular garrisons of Allied troops during World War II. The remaining islands

LAND TENURE IN THE ELLICE ISLANDS 133

were exposed to these alien influences from time to time. The Ellice Islands figured prominently as a staging area for assaults on the Japanese in the Gilberts and elsewhere.

Rough estimates of the total land surface in the Ellice chain suggest that there are about ten square miles of territory, about two square miles of which are taken up by beaches, coral flats, or areas otherwise unsuitable for production. The present population has reached about 6,000 persons, exceeding the figure shown in table 7 for 1968. There are at present about 750 persons per square mile of productive land. Variations in individual island densities are shown in table 8. These densities are not particularly high for rural atoll populations in the Pacific (Hainline 1965; cf. Newton 1967:197), but they are of sufficient magnitude to contribute to overall land hunger, especially when they occur in association with highly fragmented or otherwise maldistributed landholdings.

The early nineteenth-century population was probably stable at about 300 persons per square mile (Newton 1967:202). Blackbirders prowled the Ellice Islands during the latter part of the century with some success, transporting their human cargo to points as distant as Australia and South America (see Murray 1876:375-393). Their effect

TABLE 7 Total Population of Ellice Islands, Selected Years

Island	Early 19th Century[a]	1931[b]	1947[c]	1963[d]	1968[e]
Nanumea	650	770	746	1051	1076
Nanumanga	335	424	524	544	585
Niutao	450	645	644	797	796
Nui	250	410	490	528	569
Vaitupu	400	720	728	823	876
Nukufetau	250	394	524	655	646
Funafuti	280	413	528	687	826
Nukulaelae	300	178	282	317	354
Niulakita	[f]	(40)	(21)	(42)	(54)
TOTAL	2915	3994	4487	5444	5782

[a]Newton 1967. [b]Pusinelli 1948. [c]Pusinelli 1948. [d]McArthur and McCaig 1964. [e]Zwart and Groenewegen 1971. [f]Niulakita was allegedly uninhabited until 1877 or 1878.

TABLE 8 Population Densities of Ellice Islands, Selected Years

Island	Estimated Total Area[a] (sq. mi.)	Density per Square Mile		
		Early 19th Century[b]	1963[c]	1968[d]
Nanumea	1.5	433	700	718
Nanumanga	1.0	335	544	585
Niutao	.9	500	885	885
Nui	1.1	227	480	517
Vaitupu	2.2	182	374	398
Nukufetau	1.2	208	541	537
Funafuti	1.1	255	624	750
Nukulaelae	.9	333	349	394
Niulakita	.2	•	(210)	(270)
TOTAL	10.1	309.2	523.0	561.5

[a]Derived from McArthur and McCaig 1964; Zwart and Groenewegen 1970; Nanumanga: author's own estimate; Nui: Royal Engineers' survey 1962. [b]Adapted from Newton 1967. [c]Adapted from McArthur and McCaig 1964. [d]Adapted from Zwart and Groenewegen 1970. [e]Niulakita was allegedly uninhabited until 1877 or 1878.

on Ellice population stability was negligible in the long run. But the missionary-sponsored abandonment of traditional population control devices (such as warfare, infanticide, and abortion) and the more recent expansion of colonial health and welfare schemes have intensified land hunger problems by stimulating population growth. Only recently have modern birth control methods reached the area. Emigration to Fiji (see White 1965; Bedford 1967) and to urban centers at Tarawa and Funafuti as well as employment on ships and on the phosphate islands of Ocean and Nauru have helped to stabilize or reduce population pressures on individual islands. But these movements have not been sufficient to stem overall population increases, as illustrated by table 7.

LAND ADMINISTRATION: AN HISTORICAL OVERVIEW

Original rights to land in the Ellice group were established through discovery and settlement and were vested in a system of chiefly stewardship. Chiefs held ultimate demand rights on local produce, and they directed specialized production for their own support and for community projects. The highest-ranking chiefs were united on each island as members of the *fono o aliki* 'council of chiefs and elders.' This polity has been replaced by a more modern form of island council government. The members of the island council are not always chiefs today, nor are they recruited explicitly on the basis of their representation of the major descent groups on each island as in former times. Concomitantly, chiefly control over the land and its produce has diminished with the local growth of European democracy and bureaucracy.

The missions have never administered land directly in the Ellice Islands, but in the thirty-year interim between the arrival of the first missionaries and the establishment of the protectorate government some of the Samoan pastors were known to have advised local chiefs in the resolution of land disputes. A few of these pastors also acquired freehold rights to land which have since reverted to the descendants of the original owners (Lake 1948–1949). The ban on customs considered to be repugnant or incompatible with the goals of the church probably contributed to the landownership and registration problems which confronted the early colonial administration. The abolition of ancestor worship and ancestral shrines eliminated some forms of land redistribution which were closely tied to aboriginal religious rites. This also further confused claims made to ancestral land in later years (Lake 1948–1949; see also Gill 1885:25–26).

The political fate of the Gilbert and Ellice islands was a subject of contention as early as 1875 with Germany, France, Great Britain, the United States, and Japan jockeying for position in the Pacific. The Germans secured rights to trade, reside, and otherwise conduct their business at Funafuti in an elaborate treaty signed in 1878, but this proved to be ineffectual in the succeeding course of events (Morrell 1960: 276). Britain declared a protectorate government throughout the Ellice chain in 1892 as a result of a mandate from the crown and with the approval of the inhabitants.

Native courts had been legally established by 1894, and some of the first policies of the protectorate government were aimed directly at ameliorating land disputes. Early land registration efforts proved to be unsatisfactory because conveyance titles were not taken into account, the identification of the person or group from which land had been acquired was omitted, and subsequent transfers of land that had been registered were not accounted for. The relevance of taro and *Cyrtosperma* gardens to total landholdings and the allocation of rights to individual trees separate from rights to the land itself were similarly disregarded or misunderstood (Lake 1948–1949). Some of the early native magistrates complicated matters further—they were later discovered to have increased their own holdings by altering the lands registers and by ruling cleverly in some court cases as interested parties (Lake 1948–1949). (This problem has been minimized today through legislation and revision of the land registration process.)

Nonetheless, the effect of these early administrative policies and practices on Ellice land tenure was negligible until the appointment of the first district magistrate, G. W. B. Smith-Rewse, in 1909. Some of his judgments caused considerable turmoil in land tenure and inheritance patterns throughout the Ellice group. His pronouncements concerning land that had been given to adopted children were followed by abrupt reversals in policy, and in a few instances even the reversals were reversed (Lake 1948–1949). The resultant confusion emerged as a common theme in much of the litigation handled in 1948 and 1949 during the "final lands settlements" (Cartland 1949). Some of the entanglements begun by Smith-Rewse have survived to the present day.

A more formal structure of government began to grow with the annexation of the Ellice Islands to Great Britain in 1915 as part of the newly formed Gilbert and Ellice Islands Colony. Efforts to codify the determination of land titles according to customary law began officially with colony legislation in 1919 (G&EIC Annual Report 1968:81). The first lands commission was created legally in 1918, although it did not begin to function until 1922 under the direction of Arthur Grimble (see chapter 7). Grimble's commission withdrew the official powers of the native magistrates and the island governments to settle land disputes in an effort to curb illegal activities and to halt the rapidly complicating status of local land administration. Local authority in these matters was not returned formally until the Native Lands Ordinance of 1956 amended the 1941 constitution, but informal judgments continued to be made by local leaders in the interim.

Grimble's commission dissolved in 1924 when he was appointed resident commissioner in the colony. Disputes over his commission's interpretations of local custom and some of his judgments in specific cases led to the establishment of a second lands commission in 1934. D. G. Kennedy served as lands officer in the Ellices for this commission until its work was interrupted by the beginning of World War II in 1939

(Cartland 1949). H. E. Maude, native lands commissioner in the Gilberts since 1934, was appointed chief lands commissioner for the whole colony in 1941.

Aided by Maude's expert policies and by funding from Britain, the B. C. Cartland commission convened in 1947. Before its dissolution in 1954, it had achieved a record of accomplishment that far exceeded that of its two predecessors. The lands officer for this commission in the Ellice District, A. G. Lake, completed a legal circuit, hearing land cases and resolving disputes, in 1948 and 1949. The land settlements undertaken by Lake involved more than a thousand cases in addition to finishing up land settlement work begun by Kennedy on about half of the Ellice Islands between 1935 and 1937. Lands courts were instituted on each island, and information was collected for the drafting of the Ellice Islands Lands Code of 1956 (Cartland 1949). As recommended by Maude and implemented by Cartland and Lake, this code was quite closely tailored to local customs. The land registration system devised by the Cartland commission is still in use today, having proved to be at least minimally satisfactory to both the islanders and to the colonial administration.[3]

Early legislation provided that the sale of land to nonnatives was unlawful. These restrictions were relaxed somewhat in 1904 and 1908 through legislation which provided, with minor qualifications, that land could be sold in parcels not exceeding one acre and that leasehold would be granted for a period of not longer than ninety-nine years for parcels not exceeding a total of five acres on each island. The Native Lands Ordinance of 1917 was the first act completely prohibiting land sales to nonindigenous persons in the colony, and it was also the first requiring permission of the crown for leasehold agreements involving nonnative lessors. These provisions were upheld in later legislation, the Native Lands (Leases) Ordinance of 1940. The prohibition on the sale or gift of land to nonindigenous persons continues to the present day; leasehold is subject to slightly more lenient restrictions. Freeholds acquired before this legislation have long since been abandoned or have reverted to the indigenous title holders.

Land administration and adjudication are presently handled by a lands court on each island. The president of this court is appointed by the central government at Tarawa, while the members, apportioned roughly on the basis of one member per hundred persons in the local population, are appointed by the island councils. Lands courts are bound to operate in accordance with existing legislation, but they are given considerable freedom in their interpretation of customary matters which may or may not be spelled out in the regulations. These courts hear and adjudicate land disputes, supervise leases of less than twenty-one years, mark boundaries, mediate and regulate all matters concerning adoption and bastardy, act as a probate court for deceased citizens, and function as a registry for all land proceedings. Litigants have a final appeal privilege from the local courts to the district commissioner, who hears these cases on occasional tours of the Ellice Islands (Hart 1969).

The transformation from chiefly stewardship to lands courts and island councils has taken less than a century to be realized, but, in one sense, the change has not been revolutionary. Government by council has persisted throughout, and this common frame of reference has eased the transition. Yet government has become much more autonomous of other social institutions; leadership selection processes have been lifted out of the kinship matrix and democratized; and legislative penetration of the customary land tenure system has been extensive. Concomitantly, this transformation has had some impact on the functional interrelationships of land tenure, kinship, and the constitution of landholding groups.

LAND TENURE AND KINSHIP

The primary means of access to land in the Ellice Islands is through kin group membership. Customary tenure automatically provides natural children with land use and inheritance rights in their natal groups at birth. The relationships between land tenure and kinship are symbolically isomorphic to the extent that common rights to land imply common kinship and vice versa (see chapter 4). Kinship statuses are defined in large part by the manner in which land and blood are shared with particular persons. Both land and blood symbolize communion with the ancestral past. An extensive analysis of land tenure must therefore be concerned with the structure, organization, and ideology of the local kinship system.

Ellice descent ideology is ambilineal, meaning that it is traced along a continuum from a common ancestor by using links through males or females without set order (Firth 1957:6). This ambilineality is conceptually qualified by a strong patrilateral bias that is manifest in residence, affiliation, inheritance, and succession patterns. The degree or closeness of descent is calculated through generational links to a common ancestor through males only. Agnatic alignments such as these cases are known as *toto maalosi* 'strong blood.' Links to the common ancestor of this agnatic core that include one or more intervening females form a complementary alignment of lesser rank known as *toto vaivai* 'weak blood.' The core and its complement are both subsumed in a single ambilineal descent category that includes living and deceased members by birthright. I call this descent category, corresponding to the Ellice *ngafa*, a maximal ramage.

The widest conceptualization of kinship in the Ellice Islands is the *kaainga* 'bilateral kindred,' which has several more or less inclusive referents including that of "family" in a general sense (cf. Goodenough 1955). One's kindred includes all of the consanguines in the maximal ramages of both parents. Its parameters are the founding or remembered ancestors of the maximal ramages of both parents and all of their known descendants down to and including fourth cousins. Links to more distant members tend to lapse in time, and the bilateral kindred fades out into "nonkin." Occasional groups may be recruited from among the kindred category for special purposes such as participation in weddings and funerals. Overall, the kindred represents people upon whom one can depend for hospitality or assistance when needed. This network of kinsmen, however, is not tied directly to the control and transmission of property. The kindred is a kinship category, not a group, and therefore incapable of fulfilling corporate functions as a complete unit.

The actual groups holding estates of coconut land and taro or *Cyrtosperma* gardens are known as *puikaainga*, the members of which are recruited largely on the basis of common descent in a maximal ramage. The focal point of each land group is a senior *fanaunga* 'sibling set,' all of whom share blood and land by birthright. Children are automatically entitled to share in their natal group's land, so admission to at least one corporate land group is determined and upheld by birthright. Whether primary affiliation at this time is to be with a land group on the mother's or the father's side is determined by parental residence patterns. The usual point of attachment is with the father's side because of the predominance of virilocal residence preference, but residence rules are technically ambilocal. Inheritance within each land group is bilateral, but the proportion given to females when an estate is divided is customarily smaller than that given to males. Children of both sexes are therefore likely to inherit most of their land through their fathers, the eldest male ideally receiving the largest share.[4]

In structure, a landholding group is a reasonable facsimile of the ramage of which it forms a segment. Its primary functions are the maintenance, allocation, and transmission of rights in the estate that its members hold in joint tenure. A change in membership in these groups always necessitates some degree of reallocation of corporate resources to accommodate the inclusion of new members and the displacement of others. The loss of members through death, the incorporation of new members through birth or formal adoption, and the rate of property division have a direct effect on land group constitution. Each group derives its corporate character from its ability to maintain control over its members and its real property holdings over time, including both ancestral land and land acquired from other groups through customary conveyances. Its size and generational depth are therefore predicated directly on fecundity and the rate of property division within it. Depending upon the number of living members and the history of land distribution in each generation, members of the same ramage may have formed several separate land groups. Each of these units is likely to be a lineal or extended family that ranges in size from two to sixty members, with the average nowadays being eight or nine members. Thus a landholding group may be only one of a set of like units, all related to each other by 'ramage category' and bilateral kindred, but each by definition has jurally exclusive control over its own land.

A land group may comprise several households linked together in one or more household clusters, or it may be coextensive with only one household unit. The residential requirement for active members in the land group itself is only that the members must live in close enough proximity to each other to share occasional group activities and to have regular access to the land and gardens they hold in joint tenure. Household residence requirements are more stringent in that all active members must live in close enough proximity to each other to share in the day-to-day responsibilities for production, domestic tasks, and joint consumption of what is pooled on a common hearth. Common residence in a single dwelling unit or aggregation into small household clusters are the normal means for meeting these requirements. Large land group membership promotes the development of household clusters at the expense of more autonomous arrangements so long as the group as a whole continues to share its land on a joint tenure basis.

Each landholding unit is aided in its corporate functions by a *matai* 'manager' who oversees the disposition of the group's strategic resources such as money, land, and canoes. Land estates are registered under the 'manager's' name in the island lands registers, usually prefacing a list of all adult coparceners on the estate. The senior male in the group normally serves as 'manager.' Females may function in this capacity, though they generally do so only in land groups without adult males. Succession to this position may be achieved lineally or laterally, depending upon the composition of the group and in part upon the charisma and abilities of the potential successors. The 'managers' of related land groups are generally real or classificatory siblings who have formed their own groups as the result of previous estate divisions.

ESTATE DIVISION PROCESSES

Barnes defines *segmentation* as "the process by which any social group becomes divided internally and yet retains its own unity and cohesion"; *fission*, on the other hand, is "the process by which a social group is divided into two or more distinct groups, so that the original group disappears as a social entity" (Barnes 1955:20). The problem of determining which is which reduces basically to determining the status of the parent group and noting the presence or absence of unifying bonds once either of these processes has had its play in a particular group.[5]

Internal differentiation in pre-European Ellice ramages was largely segmentary—that is, individual branches within each maximal ramage formed semiexclusive production units that remained tied together through common descent and, more importantly, through joint tenure rights to their ancestral land. Contemporary land groups that remain undivided as joint tenure groups also tend to segment in this manner into subsidiary branches small enough to function effectively as cooperative units. Production units tend to be household clusters rather than individual households under these circumstances.

On the other hand, when division in a land group includes a formal parceling out of the estate among all persons with joint rights to it, the process of division is fission rather than segmentation. Fission dissolves the parent group entirely as a corporate entity, and the emergent groups obtain jurally exclusive rights to their share of the original estate. Fission leads directly to increased plot fragmentation in the land use community, and it undermines the overall solidarity of extended kin networks. Segmentation allows for the internal differentiation of ramage segments without sacrificing much of the integrity of the unifying network, which, as previously mentioned, in the Ellice Islands is based primarily on joint rights to land. Segmentation and fission thus represent differential strategies of resource exploitation.[6]

The transformation from a former predominance of land group division through segmentation to a present predominance of division through fission has been triggered, at least in part, by increased land hunger and the policies of the colonial administration. Legislative sanctions have upheld and increased the autonomy of individual property groups for more than half a century, indirectly fashioning them on a model of European corporate structure. Complicated by increased competition for land, the presence of administrative support for increased autonomy among burgeoning landholding groups has encouraged division through fission rather than segmentation.[7]

It remains to be pointed out that despite the apparent jural autonomy of individual landholding groups, the wide range of cognatic kinship ties in Ellice society makes complete autonomy of produce allocation impossible. Claims of kinsmen on the produce that a land group harvests from its estate crosscut group integrity to some degree. That is particularly true when requests for produce are made by close kinsmen from related land groups through *akai*, a form of solicited gift-giving in which the person approached is formally obligated to honor the request. Nevertheless, many claims on a land group's produce are predicated on the willingness of the target group to honor them, and the disposition of the land itself is a right and a responsibility retained solely by the members of each group in their capacity as a cooperative and corporate unit.

Some other considerations that impinge on the autonomy and integrity of individual land groups are posed by the possibilities for multiple membership in land estates.

PROBLEMS OF OVERLAPPING COMMITMENT

The possibilities for multiple membership in separate land groups are not overwhelming, but they are nonetheless present. Theoretically, the number of groups with which a person can potentially affiliate by birthright in a ramage category is as great as there are separate land groups in each of his parent's ramages. Individuals ideally have a choice of affiliation among related groups through cognatic ties. Continuing division of holdings, in time, reduces the average size of landholding groups; conversely, less division leads to fewer landholding groups which are larger in size than those associated with land that is being continually divided.

It is possible for a primary member of one group to hold rights to land in other groups, so the distribution of landholdings may not be identical for all the members of each estate. Some persons with joint rights to a single estate may also have a few parcels as individual holdings given to them through a completed adoption cycle in another group or through other similar customary conveyances that give the title holder the right to exclude the interests of kinsmen who might otherwise be entitled to a share. A person who is given a parcel of land as a reward, for example, may hold rights to this land to the exclusion of his siblings, despite the fact that this sibling set as a whole may be a primary membership unit in the same estate. Multiple holdings of this kind do not necessarily undermine the corporate nature of individual groups since these groups aggregate on the basis of joint rights to a single estate. But members with holdings beyond this joint share pose a threat of overlapping commitment that can weaken internal group solidarity and may rupture the control that a land group must exercise over its members to maintain its continuity over time.

All land groups are nonexclusive in the sense that establishing primary membership in one group through prolonged association, birthright, or formal adoption does not necessarily require forfeiture of the right to change affiliation to another group if the individual desires to do so and the members of the other group are willing to accept him (see Lambert 1966; Hanson 1971). A formal change in membership may alter immediate access to land and perhaps bind a person to his sponsors through obligations for assistance and allegiance until such time as the obligations are considered to be discharged, but it does not ordinarily alter inheritance privileges in the natal group. The maintenance of multiple rights to land in effect doubles access and inheritance privileges under the present system, posing problems of disaffiliation as well as complicating group allegiance. The biggest problems associated with land transmission lie less with the determination of primary membership in particular groups than with the lack of jural disaffiliation of previous members who are de facto absentees, including those persons who have been formally adopted by other groups.

The potential chaos of multiple membership in the Ellice Islands is mitigated in several ways. One way is that land group membership is inevitably sorted out into primary, secondary, and provisional affiliation priorities. A primary membership is established through active participation in a group in which rights to land have been formally allocated on a basis other than temporary usufruct. Close kinsmen who retain a share in the group's land and who meet the approximate residence requirements outlined above are considered to be primary members. Secondary or inactive members are those persons who have rights to membership in a particular group on the basis of real cognatic affinity and previous residence patterns but who do not presently participate in its activities. These members may be further subclassified. The first priority comprises a core of persons, such as absentee laborers, who have once resided with the group and plan to return to it. As second priority there is a residual category comprising persons who are genealogically qualified for membership in the group but who have never resided with it, such as the children born to previous members after their residential detachment from the group. Provisional members include affines, fostered children, and adopted children, that is, persons who are actively affiliated with a particular group but who rely on principles other than real cognatic affinity for their affiliative bond.

Regardless of the ideal range of ambilateral affiliation, petitions for jural membership by persons other than direct descendants and formal adoptees may be and often are denied today on account of land hunger or sentimental disinclinations in the target group. When recruitment is not automatically determined by birthright, incorporation decisions always rest with the incumbents in the land groups being petitioned. Contemporary land law upholds the right of individual groups to exclude from their estates all previously separated kinsmen (that is, persons whose groups have been formed as the result of previous land divisions within the ramage of the target group) in addition to the right to exclude persons who are not kinsmen at all. Only an estate interest that terminates because of a lack of heirs reverts to the secondary kinsmen of the deceased.[8] This reduces the actual range of multiple membership by reducing its potential.

The combination of increased legal identity as property groups and division through fission has helped to reduce the number of persons other than incoming affines with active rights to land beyond their own primary estate. Persons who do hold active rights of this sort generally offset potential self-interest conflicts by acting as liaison for other members in their primary groups to gain access to the extra territory, either directly for production or indirectly by pooling and sharing the produce harvested from it. Incoming spouses who have been given a portion of their own natal estate as a marriage gift generally pool their holdings with those of the sponsoring spouse and thereby become active members with rights over the use and disposition of the land that subsequently becomes their joint estate (cf. Kennedy 1953:365). This practice also increases the jural distance between the children of the incoming spouse and his or her natal group. The land brought in title by the incoming spouse is intended to be the share transferred through inheritance to subsequent heirs. Normal bilateral inheritance under these circumstances does not extend through the parents equally to their respective natal estates. Concomitantly, ambilateral affiliation privileges are not so easily exercised.

In the event the incoming spouse retains joint rights to his or her natal estate, the sponsoring spouse will usually be allowed access to a portion of it specifically set aside for this purpose. For example, a man whose wife has come to live with him usually will be allowed to work a portion of his wife's natal estate with consent from the 'manager' in her group if the wife's estate is on the same island. It is only through cultivation and maintenance of the marital bond that affines can continue to have access to their spouses' natal estates. These are property relationships that tend to strengthen marital alliances, ambilateral affiliation, and bilateral inheritance for the offspring of parents who maintain joint rights to their natal estates. The maintenance of joint rights by both parents adds to the possible range of active multiple membership for consanguines, but only in groups with which individuals have already established an inheritance claim by birthright. Within the immediate domain of parental estates, an individual will always have established a primary membership keyed to parental residence and tenure patterns. Beyond this immediate domain, the maintenance of an additional active membership is unlikely and infrequent today.

Finally, some of the problems of double inheritance and disaffiliation of previous members who have been incorporated as active members elsewhere are beginning to be reconciled. There are plans on several islands at present to make a change in affiliation more exclusive of natal inheritance privileges than ever before, particularly with regard to adopted children. Legislation is being contemplated that would prescribe the complete assumption of land use and inheritance obligations by adopters, uphold the right of the adoptee's natal group to legally disaffiliate persons who have been formally adopted into another group, and otherwise prohibit double inheritance. Formal incorporation elsewhere would legally cancel the normal bilateral inheritance privileges in the natal group. The option would be to retain natal inheritance privileges so long as affiliations with other groups remain informal. Part of this new plan approximates the indigenous pattern of reallocating inheritance and affiliation rights for children who had been adopted by distant relatives or by nonkinsmen. Kennedy suggests that in former times on Vaitupu once a person was adopted he might even be denied reentry into the meeting house of his natal ramage, being effectively disassociated with it on adoption into another group (Kennedy 1931: 309). Overall, the proposed legislation concerning these matters would expand the range of rights of disaffiliation to include persons adopted by related as well as unrelated groups.

Ambilateral affiliation, adoption, and fosterage were probably sufficient in the past to insure mobility and equity in the distribution of people in relation to domestic production needs and available resources, but the context of these affiliation-recruitment strategies has changed. Formal incorporation in other than the natal group is now a problem that includes groups headed by kinsmen who in all probability would have maintained a joint estate in the past. Fosterage is still an important means for transient or temporary movements among related land groups. But today adoption has become the primary means of changing affiliation within a kinship domain where formal changes in affiliation were once unnecessary. This is a direct result of the decrease in land group size and the increase in jural distance among related groups brought on by the transformation from segmentation to fission. Legislative support of the local plans to implement more exclusive affiliation patterns than are found at present may add further impetus to this transformation and thereby continue to undermine overall ramage solidarity. What effect, if any, this will have on the ideology of descent and group recruitment principles in general is a matter for future empirical determination. But the short-term effects will be to further reduce, or eliminate altogether, many of the problems of multiple membership in contemporary landholding groups.

TENURE TYPES AND DISTRIBUTION

Ellice land tenure pertains either to *fakangamua* 'communal land,' which is shared equally by all bona fide residents of each island, or to *fakangamuli* 'private land,' which is held by separate individuals or land groups within each land use community. The first is the older system, and it represents land held or managed today by the island councils on behalf of local residents; the second represents a subsequent development and is land that is held or managed by managers on behalf of their respective land groups.

It has already been noted that each land group is necessarily an incipient (or an actual) joint estate, depending on whether or not the 'manager' has children, since natural children automatically acquire land use and inheritance rights in their natal estate. In contemporary legal usage this is a form of estate entailment. An individual's freedom to give away any portion of his estate is always constricted by the number of his heirs, if any. The present law pertaining to these matters requires that all children, including formally adopted children, must be allowed to harvest from the landholder's estate and that they are entitled to a share in any subsequent divisions of it except in proved cases of neglect. Thus a married man with children has at least a de facto joint tenure arrangement.

Estates classified as 'private land' can be registered in one of two ways, barring contemporary provisions for leasehold: as *kaitasi* 'joint holdings' or as *vaevae* 'individual holdings.' A joint estate is by definition one in which there is more than one person with active or inactive rights to it. The land of a joint estate is undivided, although this does not imply that it has never been divided. An individual estate is one that has been created through fission in the same generation as the 'manager' in whose name the land is registered. In fact, *vaevae* literally means 'to divide' or 'to separate.' In the strictest sense of the term, an individual estate indicates that a person has rights to it to the exclusion of all other persons except direct descendants.

Individual estates are created through the dissolution of the parent group and a subsequent parcelling out of shares among all persons, usually siblings, with joint rights to the estate. Under this type of tenure, it is also possible for individuals to acquire some land as a gift intended only for them. But, however the land is acquired, reversion from individual to joint tenure is in part a natural consequence of population growth in each estate. Fission is the antithesis of this growth, so the recurrent processes of fission and accretion present a dialectic pattern. A failure to understand this dialectic pattern often leads to ill-founded analogies between individual tenure in places such as the Ellice Islands and individual freehold under Anglo-Saxon law as practiced elsewhere.

The actual number of individual versus joint estates at a given time may give some idea of the balance of fission and accretion processes in a population. A steady rate of fission in joint estates in succeeding generations can easily lead to the impression that individual freehold for the whole population is inevitable. But such data do not necessarily indicate a trend toward the ultimate predominance of one kind of tenure over the other (cf. Bedford 1967:18). The rights that descendants acquire at birth in the Ellice Islands transform individual to joint estates. Overall, the proportion of individual to joint estates results as much from demographic changes as from such other factors as the degree of solidarity and cooperation that obtains within the land groups in each generation.

A comparison of land group census data and entries in the lands registers also shows that de facto and de jure differences between joint tenure and individual tenure are not always reflected accurately in the land registration system (cf. Lundsgaarde 1966; Bedford 1967). Many people with estates registered under individual tenure have subsequently acquired children as heirs and hence have at least de facto joint estates. Thus the actual number of joint estates shown in table 9, a summary of estate registration for all of the Ellice except Nanumea and Niulakita,[9] is higher than indicated because of the number of de facto joint estates which were registered as individual holdings. As registered, however, the data still show a slight preponderance of joint holdings (52.2 percent) over estates listed as individual holdings (47.8 percent).

Table 10 provides an estimate of the percentage of total land area held in each type of tenure. These data suggest that a much greater percentage (71.9 percent) of the land throughout the Ellices is held in joint rather than individual tenure (28.1 percent). Thus, despite a

TABLE 9 Distribution of Tenure Types Among Registered Landholders, Ellice Islands*

Island	Tenure Type				Total Landholders	
	Kaitasi 'joint'	%	Vaevae 'individual'	%	No.	%
Nanumea	—	—	—	—	350	100
Nanumanga	49	28.7	122	71.3	171	100
Niutao	214	50.6	213	49.4	427	100
Nui	103	63.6	59	36.4	162	100
Vaitupu	153	53.5	133	46.5	286	100
Nukufetau	88	45.8	104	54.2	192	100
Funafuti	39	48.1	42	51.9	81	100
Nukulaelae	79	75.2	26	24.8	105	100
TOTAL	725	52.2	699	47.8	1424	100

SOURCE: Adapted from Island Lands Registers (data are for 1969).
*Does not include communal or leasehold land.

TABLE 10 Estimated Percentage of Total Land Area by Tenure Type, Ellice Islands*

Island	Tenure Type				Total plots	
	Kaitasi 'joint'	%	Vaevae 'individual'	%	No.	%
Nanumea	—	—	—	—	1500	100
Nanumanga	552	69.9	248	30.1	800	100
Niutao	1226	67.7	584	32.3	1810	100
Nui	1121	72.3	431	27.7	1552	100
Vaitupu	2714	79.5	699	20.5	3413	100
Nukufetau	1965	62.2	1197	37.8	3162	100
Funafuti	918	67.9	434	32.1	1352	100
Nukulaelae	522	84.0	96	16.0	618	100
TOTAL	9018	71.9	3689	28.1	12,707	100

SOURCE: Adapted from Island Lands Registers (data are for 1969).
*Does not include communal or leasehold land.

steady increase in estate fission rates, and a long-term reduction in the effective size of landholding groups, the balance of land in quantity and type of tenure under which it is registered remains in favor of group rather than individual interests.

COMMUNAL LAND

The concept of communal land in the Ellices is an ancient one that relates back to the time when all the land on each island was under the disposition and management of chiefs. Legendary accounts suggest that joint use of the land and its produce under the management of village chiefs and elders lies at the base of the communal system. The actual nature of this earlier pattern of communal tenure is obfuscated somewhat by antiquity and by the multiple cultural influences in the Ellices since first settlement. But all of the legendary evidence that is available suggests that local chiefs began to allocate land in title to their constituents long before the arrival of the first missionaries (Roberts 1958). Increasing specificity and fission in the allocation of land rights superseded the former system of provisional usufruct under chiefly mandate. This transformation may have been triggered in part by increasing population densities leading perhaps to an overlap in exploited territory and thereby to a more specific definition of territorial and descent group boundaries in terms of ancestral rights and similar forms of temporal priorities (see Sahlins 1958). Present-day accounts still maintain that ultimate title to the land is vested in the populace as a whole by virtue of aboriginal chiefly grants. The dictum that all bona fide residents on each island are entitled to some measure of land as a birthright is probably a remnant of this earlier system.

Most communal land today consists of roads, bush paths, inland lagoons, small plots of land that have gone unexploited because of recent development,[10] and plots of productive land specifically set aside for communal purposes. In general, the produce from communal land is used for local taxes and community festivities. Any remainder is divided equally among the island residents.

Housesites in the village are treated as if they were communal land for purposes of maintaining residential solidarity among the inhabitants on each island. But most village land is actually held in primary or residual title as 'individual' estates. Landholders whose plots are occupied by other persons for use as dwelling sites do not ordinarily receive any compensation for the use of them, but full usufruct and title revert to the registered owner on abandonment of the site. Such sites can be created on mandate from the island council if an individual or group needs one but does not own a suitable plot in or adjacent to the existing village. Another person with local plots may be asked to relinquish without compensation sufficient territory for the housesite if necessary, although it is not unusual for the new tenants to exchange a more distant plot of coconut land for the privilege of occupying the site. Existing produce, such as breadfruit and coconuts, is normally left at the disposal of the residents.

Undeveloped communal land may be improved for use as garden pits by anyone who desires to do so. The developer does not receive title to the land, but he may continue to harvest it on his own, usually without encroachment from others. However, all the produce from communal land, including independently developed sites, technically belongs to the community as a whole (cf. Kennedy 1953:353). The construction of permanent dwelling structures on communal land beyond existing villages is generally forbidden.

Other variations of communal rights to land are limitations on private property. For example, all bona fide residents are guaranteed freedom of access to harvest raw materials from certain kinds of trees and bushes which grow in abundance, regardless of their location. Mangrove trees at Nanumanga are treated in this way. All residents also have rights of access through other people's land to reach their own plots or gardens, although most people use the bush paths. Trespass is defined as "harvesting another person's land without permission." Travelers in the bush are permitted an occasional drinking nut or pandanus fruit from other people's land for nutriment while working, but harvesting for household subsistence without permission is forbidden on any land other than one's own. Ideally, wild birds may be snared anywhere, but the general attitude is that hunting should be restricted to one's own land area. The freedom given to individuals for occasional harvesting varies from island to island. But there is consensus that if a person desires access to someone else's land on a regular basis, he must petition the landowner for permission.

The suspicion that some individuals working alone in the bush were engaged in thievery led to some commotion on Funafuti and Nukufetau in the recent past. Suggestions were made by the island councils that each island should pass a regulation to restrict all individuals from solitary visits to the bush, a prohibition alleged at the time to be an ancient custom on these islands. While there is still some apprehension about thievery from coconut land and garden pits, no regulations have been passed that would preclude solitary harvesting.

The produce from communal land belongs collectively to the citizenry of each island, but jurisdiction over title and usufruct is vested in the island councils. One interesting patch of communal land consisting of about twenty acres of coconut plots at Nanumea is called *manafa tapu* 'forbidden land.' This area is under the management of the Nanumea island council, and money earned from the sale of copra harvested from it is held in trust for the citizenry in the Island (Personal) Fund. The people at Nanumanga say that the land was given to them as a gift from the Nanumeans in pre-European times. The Nanumangan account suggests that the land was a reward for helping the Nanumeans fight off an attack by Gilbertese from Beru. The Nanumeans disagree and say that the story is false, and that the Nanumangans have no legitimate claim to this land.

A slightly different pattern of jurisdiction over communal land occurs at Nui. The island council there has been given title to a large section of coconut land that is worked communally by the island residents specifically to pay annual taxes. The conventional role of island councils as administrators of communal land is simply to act as managers in a role approximating that of a manager in a joint estate. The power pattern at Nui gives the council ultimate rights of disposition and usufruct over this patch of communal land, and the transaction has been entered into the lands registers. This means that the land in question is not held collectively by the citizenry on an equal basis, as on the other islands, and that it cannot be used for purposes other than those explicitly approved by the council. This level of jurisdiction over land used for communal purposes closely approximates the aboriginal system, despite a divergent process of development.

Finally, it should be mentioned that the amount of existing communal land in the Ellice Islands is often overestimated. Only about 2 percent of all the land at Nanumanga, a little more than 3 percent at Nukufetau, and probably not much more than 5 percent on any of the other islands, if that much, is actually communal land.

LEASEHOLD

Three categories of leasehold are presently found in the Ellice Islands. In one form the land is leased, but the lessor retains usufruct rights to the produce and responsibilities for upkeep and taxes. The second form is a full lease in that the tenant assumes all responsibilities for upkeep and taxes and has lease rights on both the land and its produce. In the third form, a combination of the first two, the lessor shares the produce and upkeep responsibilities with the lessee. The government station at Nukufetau is leased under the first category;[11] the government station at Nanumanga, in the second manner; and the Catholic mission at Nanumea, in the third form. The produce from the government station at Nanumanga is reserved for employees who live there and for guests who arrive to stay in the transit quarters. The government station at Nukufetau was formerly leased in the same manner as that of Nanumanga, but usufruct rights on the produce were subsequently returned to the registered owners of the land in exchange for a lower annual premium on the lease. Unlike other lessors, the missions are seldom charged any rent. For this reason, mission leases are better termed usehold or loans although they are technically registered as leases.

Competition between sects and the generation of some rivalry over the proper use of mission-occupied land contributed to a clarification of mission tenure rights after World War II. Some early administrative policies suggested that missions would have a prescriptive right to the land they had occupied for more than twenty-one years. The legality of this policy was challenged by the Cartland commission with the result that missions are entitled to remain on each island so long as they continue to serve the welfare of the people. The right of mission occupancy was thereby returned to the local citizenry, who are the final judges as to whether or not the missons continue to serve their welfare.

Leasehold arrangements that separate rights to land from rights to its produce are a modern form of overlapping stewardship. The earlier forms of differentiating between full and residual rights to land and its produce perplexed the Cartland commission and emerged as a key topic in much of the litigation brought before it. This commission obtained consent from all of the Ellice Islands except Nanumea to abolish these practices. Persons holding rights to trees separate from rights to the land at this time agreed to relinquish the trees to the landholders on receipt of payment (Cartland 1949). No doubt this policy has contributed to the general demise of the system, but it has not eliminated all such arrangements on a customary basis.

A person who has no coconut trees near his garden pits or his cooking house may desire a supply of coconuts to quench his thirst while he works. He may petition a nearby landowner for relief in one of two ways. First, he may ask for long-term usufruct rights to an existing tree near his work area, with the provision that all rights to the tree will revert to the landholder either on request from the donor or death of the user. Second, a man may ask for permission to plant a coconut tree on another person's land for a future supply of drinking nuts. The usual arrangement here is also for rights to the tree to revert to the landholder on request of the donor or death of the user, whichever comes first.

These arrangements are infrequent today because there is a tendency for persons with long-term rights to trees to end up making an illegitimate claim to the land itself. Moreover, except in leasehold agreements, trees cannot be registered separately from the land itself. The present law holds that all produce on each parcel of land belongs in full title to the registered owner(s) of the parcel and that permanent separation in title is prohibited. Without registration and contemporary legal support, a person who enters into a customary agreement to allow usufruct of his trees runs the risk of losing some of his land or at least being brought before the lands court to defend a claim for what was already his.

Leasehold has been encouraged by the administration in recent years as a means for utilizing surplus and neglected land. However, implementation of this policy on the local level has been notably unsuccessful for several reasons, chief among them being that the islanders find the impersonal, commercial relationship imposed by lessor-lessee arrangements unpalatable. Resistance to leasehold in the private domain of each community is all the more interesting since land is often leased willingly and generously to institutional bodies on the government level.

Promoting leasehold in the private sector is in one sense an attempt to reorganize certain customary bonds of the domestic economy. Landholders with surplus or neglected land are constrained from entering into leasehold agreements with kinsmen and neighbors by duties to be generous, the implication being that the prosperous should give rather than sell to the less fortunate. Generalized reciprocity and strong communal bonds promote a noncommercial flow of goods and services within each village in a manner that works to the advantage of the disadvantaged (see Sahlins 1965; Brady 1970). Most of this material flow is conducted on an egalitarian basis since only token differences exist today between chiefs and commoners. Commercial transactions are generally inappropriate in this domain, and the prevailing egalitarianism fosters resistance to more impersonal arrangements that threaten the customary status quo. Conservatism, under the present circumstances of increasing land hunger and kinship conflicts over commerce, also promotes suspicion of the administration view that leasing unused or neglected land to others nearby will provide for better land utilization, increase production, and thereby put more commercial and noncommercial goods into circulation.

On the other hand, a commercial relationship already exists between each community and its modern leadership, so leasehold in this domain presumes no striking reorganization of domestic relationships, at least not beyond those that have already occurred in the last century. The island governments, the Colony Wholesale Society, and the local cooperatives function as points of liaison between the Ellice domestic economy and wider markets. Commerce, including leasehold, is appropriate within this wider sphere. In fact, leasehold with agents from beyond the domestic economy is valued as an additional source of income and is even sought after with enthusiasm on some of the islands. This does not alter the resistance to leasehold involving fellow islanders.

Land sales between villagers have met with similar opposition, only in this instance the opposition covers all land sales regardless of the identity of the principals. Nui, Nukufetau, Nanumea, and Funafuti islanders explicitly opposed the sale of land on their islands when the present lands code was being drafted and requested that it be prohibited in the code. However, since then at least one cash sale of coconut land at Funafuti and a few sales of garden pits at Nui have been recorded in the lands registers. An exchange of plots is preferred as a more customary means of offsetting maldistribution and land neglect, but even here the constraints of customary equivalency are operative.[12] The sale of land is generally opposed on any account. The following examination of the variety of land titles in the Ellice Islands reveals some of the customary modes of land conveyance that are preferred to buying and selling.

LAND TITLE DISTRIBUTION

It was noted above that the persons registered as land group managers do not necessarily have sole jurisdiction over their holdings. The closest approximation of full title rights, such as those in English freehold tenure, occurs in cases where the manager has no children and holds his land under individual tenure. But corporate holdings under joint tenure, whether registered as such or not, predominate on each island, so the freedom of individuals to give away any portion of their estate often rests on consensus among all of the remaining persons who have a share in it. Moreover, the lands court may prohibit or revoke a transfer of land in title to individuals outside the donor's group if, in the court's opinion, the transfer would in any way deprive the natural heirs of land resources deemed necessary for their support. These restrictions, and an increasing perception of land hunger, help to keep transfers of land beyond individual group boundaries to a minimum, as the following data reveal.

Most land in the Ellice Islands is transferred directly to lineal descendants through bilateral inheritance on the strength of consanguineal ties. There are other customary means of acquiring land, however, and these means vary somewhat from island to island. Table 11 gives the distribution of registered land titles in 1969 for all of the Ellice group except Nanumea. Land "titles" in this instance are descriptive labels entered in the lands registers that refer to the means by which particular landholdings were acquired. For ease of presentation, the various titles referred to in table 11 are coded with the use of roman numerals.

Title I refers to *ngafa* 'consanguinity,' which is the term entered in the lands registers to show that a particular person or group has acquired land through bilateral inheritance from blood kin. Title II refers to *mavaenga* 'will,' which is used to indicate that rights to the land registered were acquired formally through provisions made in a will. This formal transfer of property through testament is singled out by informants as the primary difference between titles I and II. Other than this, nearly all of the title II cases are identical with those of title I in that they involve property transmission from one or more persons to their immediate descendants; only a small fraction of the conveyances under either title involve the giving of land to persons other than immediate next-of-kin.

Title III, *tamapuke* 'adopted child,' refers to land given by adopters to their adoptees as part of the adoption agreement. Land transfers of this nature are mandatory in all formal adoption arrangements, unless the adoptee is proved in court to be guilty of neglecting or abandoning the adopters. Title IV, *tamafuataka* 'bastard,' is entered in the lands registers to indicate that the owner has right to the land by virtue of his or her being an illegitimate child. Ellice custom and current land legislation stipulate that the genitor of an illegitimate child must provide some land for it. If the child is not taken in as a joint member of his genitor's estate, the genitor must transfer at least one plot of coconut land and one garden pit to the child as compensation. Such transfers are normally registered under title IV only at Funafuti, Nanumanga, and Vaitupu (see table 11). The other islands prefer to avoid some of the stigma attached to bastardy by registering these transactions under title III. Since this can only be done as the result of a formal adoption, the possible embarrassment attached to title IV often encourages adoption transactions in the event of bastardy. In any case, the formal transfer of land to illegitimate children legitimizes and validates their status as members of the local community in particular kinship positions.

Nearly 95 percent of all landholdings on the seven islands surveyed are held in titles of types I through IV, and I assume that a comparable distribution occurs at Nanumea. About 84 percent of the landholdings represented in table 11 were acquired through direct inheritance from lineal ancestors, illustrating some of the effects of fission on kin group separation and, concomitantly, the strong conservatism of contemporary landholders in giving land to persons beyond their own landholding groups.

The remaining eight types of titles shown in table 11 pertain to only 5 percent of all holdings. These less frequent modes of land conveyance range from a formal exchange of plots (title V) to land transferred as a result of a lands court decision as compensation for grievances against particular individuals or groups (VI). Other modes include gifts for kindness (VII), land given as a share in an estate for special assistance such as saving someone's life in the event of a natural catastrophe (VIII), and gifts that initiate as generalized reciprocity from a sibling

TABLE 11 Registered Land Titles in the Ellice Islands by Type of Title (Indicated by Roman Numerals)*

Island	I No.	I %	II No.	II %	III No.	III %	IV No.	IV %	V No.	V %	VI No.	VI %
Nanumanga	151	88.3	15	8.7	2	1.2	1	.6	1	.6	1	.6
Niutao	277	64.9	101	23.7	27	6.3	0	0	16	3.7	2	.5
Nui	119	73.4	5	3.1	17	10.5	0	0	0	0	16	9.9
Vaitupu	207	72.4	8	2.8	9	3.1	51	17.8	2	.7	3	1.0
Nukufetau	154	80.2	16	8.3	13	6.8	0	0	1	.5	0	0
Funafuti	65	80.2	2	2.4	4	4.9	9	11.1	0	0	0	0
Nukulaelae	80	76.2	2	1.9	10	9.5	0	0	3	2.9	0	0
TOTAL	1053	73.9	149	10.5	82	5.8	61	4.3	23	1.6	22	1.5
(Cumulative)		73.9		84.4		90.2		94.5		96.1		97.6

SOURCE: Adapted from the Island Lands Registers, data as of 1969.

*I. *Ngafa* 'consanguinity': inheritance from a consanguine. II. *Tongi* (*Mavaenga*) 'will': transfer of land by testament. III. *Tamapuke* 'adopted child': land given to adoptees. IV. *Tamafuataka* 'bastard': land gift to illegitimate children. V. *Fesuiaki* 'exchange': formal exchange of land plots. VI. *Ikunga o te Fono Manafa* 'lands court decision': a transfer of land as compensation, in consequence of a lands court decision.

TABLE 11 Registered Land Titles in the Ellice Islands by Type of Title* (cont.)

Island	VII		VIII		IX		X		XI		XII		Total
	No.	%	No.	%	No.	%	No.	%	No.	%	No.	%	
Nanumanga	0	0	0	0	0	0	0	0	0	0	0	0	171
Niutao	0	0	1	.2	0	0	2	.5	0	0	1	.2	427
Nui	2	1.2	0	0	0	0	1	.6	2	1.2	0	0	162
Vaitupu	5	1.7	0	0	0	0	0	0	1	.2	0	0	286
Nukufetau	0	0	6	3.1	2	1.0	0	0	0	0	0	0	192
Funafuti	0	0	1	1.4	0	0	0	0	0	0	0	0	81
Nukulaelae	7	6.7	0	0	2	1.9	1	1.0	0	0	0	0	105
TOTAL	14	1.0	8	.6	4	.3	4	.3	3	.2	1	0	1424
(Cumulative)		98.6		99.2		99.5		99.8		100		100	

*VII. *Meaalofa* 'gift': any land given freely as a gesture of 'kindness'. VIII. *Tofi* 'share': land given for special assistance in general. IX. *Fauaunga loto malie* 'senior sibling set is agreeable': gift of land initiated by owners as generalized reciprocity. X. *Tino tausi masaki* 'person who cares for the sick': land gift for nursing the sick or aged. XI. *Taungasoa* 'friend': land gift to a friend as a result of strong affective ties. XII. *Avanga* 'spouse': generally land given to a wife by a husband who dies without children.

unit in a joint estate (IX). A person who cares for the sick or aged may receive land specifically for assistance rendered in this capacity (X). Gifts of land to friends as a result of strong affective ties (XI), or to a spouse, generally to a wife in the event her husband dies without immediate descendants (XII), are also very explicit and infrequent modes of land conveyance. Many of these categories are not mutually exclusive (especially VII–XII). The factors that determine which entry is to be made in the lands registers are often predicated on the composition of the lands court in terms of customary experience on different islands, and on the level of specificity required by the principals in each transfer. Some of the ambiguity derives directly from efforts by the island executive officers, who are responsible for recording land conveyances in the lands registers, to provide short glosses for complex customary principles.

The number of customary means for acquiring land from nonkinsmen was, by all accounts, much greater in the past, and it may be expected that they were also more frequent. Half of the methods for transferring land listed by Kennedy (1953) as having been in use on Vaitupu in former times are now obsolete. For example, in the days when infanticide was practiced, a childless couple could get a chief's consent to adopt someone else's third child in order to save it from being killed by smothering. Technically, the child became an adopted child, but children adopted in this manner were differentiated from other categories of adopted children. This custom disappeared, of course, with the legal prohibition of infanticide. Several other methods of acquiring land through adoption have disappeared as a result of colonial and missionary interference (cf. Kennedy 1953:355ff.).

The custom of transferring land to betrothed persons or their families was once commonplace but has since disappeared. Conveyances of this sort usually involved a transfer of land from a male child's parents to a female child's parents when marriages were prearranged and the children betrothed at an early age. If the marriage failed to materialize in later years, all land conveyed through these means reverted to the donors (Kennedy 1953:356). If an early betrothal failed to result in marriage on account of the premature death of the betrothed male, his land group might transfer some land to a child of the girl's family as a token of default. Similarly, adult males who made their own arrangements for marriage occasionally transferred a few plots of land to an intended bride or her family as an inducement for them to consent to the marriage.

Kennedy also reports that a woman's family might have been given a gift of her husband's land for help given toward the accumulation of the bridewealth necessary for the marriage of a son or daughter. Both matrilateral and patrilateral kinsmen combine their efforts to produce the necessary goods and foodstuffs for each side. A large contribution from matrilateral kinsmen occasionally triggered a reciprocal gift of land from the patrilateral kinsmen of the bride or groom. Land is no longer given for these reasons, but all contributors to bridewealth or dowry stockpiles are given some of what is received from the opposite side.

Another mode of land conveyance that Kennedy mentioned (1953: 355) for Vaitupu and which is known to have been used also on Nukufetau and Funafuti involved a child believed to have been saved from death or serious illness by the religious intercession of priests or seers. The religious specialist was fed by the sick child's family during the treatment. On the patient's recovery, the healer is reported to have given a gift of his own land to the child as a permanent gift, that is, with no contingencies for reversion to the donor. Through some complicated interplay between divine assistance, the spirit medium's success, and the patient's recovery, the healer became obligated to reciprocate with a gift of land. The precise motivation for this behavior is beyond accurate recall today because the practice has been obsolete for more than a century. Divine intercession on behalf of a sick person is nowadays rewarded through a gift other than land to the local pastor by the family of the person saved.

Contrary to the above case, surgeons were formerly given land for their services in healing the sick (Kennedy 1953:356), as were other kinds of specialists such as midwives and canoe craftsmen. Fishing experts were once given land in exchange for their services and the teaching of technical knowledge. The heirs of sailing experts who had been lost at sea were formerly obligated on some of the islands to give land as compensation to the families of crew members who had perished with the experts.[13] Land was also once given as a gift to traders or beachcombers who came to reside on the various islands in the group, in addition to being acquired through warfare and conquest. These modes of land conveyance are obsolete today, although, as noted above, it is still possible, with lands court approval, to make gifts of land to persons who physically assist the aged or sick.

Finally, Kennedy (1953:357) notes that, in former times, land might be transferred to the wife of a childless couple on death of the husband, as a reward for her behavior and to insure her well-being after the husband's death. The most common way to do this was to have the husband make an outright gift of land to the wife in the presence of witnesses. Kennedy reports this specifically as a Nanumea custom. But it was also present on Nukufetau, and at least one case registered under the title of "spouse" at Niutao (see table 11) fits this description. An alternative with the same end is to have the husband adopt a child as his legitimate heir. The wife's interest in her husband's estate then continues so long as she remains the child's guardian. This practice is not unusual today, although it technically becomes a by-product of an adoption transaction.

LAND AND GARDEN BOUNDARIES

Section 7 of the Native Lands Ordinance of 1922 stated that landowners were duty bound to mark out and define their boundaries by planting trees or placing rocks in identifiable alignments or otherwise marking their boundaries in a manner satisfactory to the lands commission. The maximum fine for persons not complying with this measure was one pound sterling plus court and land measurement costs, if any. Most boundary markers today consist of slashmarks made in trees, strategically placed cloth remnants, bottles, rocks, cans, or such impermanent items as palm fronds upended in the ground. Alignments of trees and garden plants tend to be ambiguous. The most permanent boundaries are set off by large trees or natural landmarks such as coral outcroppings and shorelines, although these change in time through accretion and erosion. The cost of accurately surveying all land and garden plots on each island, particularly on those islands with excessive fragmentation of holdings, has undermined the practicality of official installation of more permanent boundary markers made of cement or metal.

Disputes over land boundaries are a common source of litigation in the lands courts.[14] The ambiguity of many boundaries puts the courts at a definite disadvantage in resolving these disagreements. Local informants argue that some persons may engineer litigation over land boundaries in anticipation of the court's being unable to arrive at an accurate resolution of the dispute and concluding the case by dividing the disputed territory equally between the litigants. A boundary hedger who presses a claim with this result may then end up with more land than was actually his in the beginning, and he may have it legally registered in his name to protect him from further recourse by his neighbors.[15]

A typical kind of boundary hedging between persons with adjacent and irregularly shaped plots is illustrated in figure 7. Landholder X's

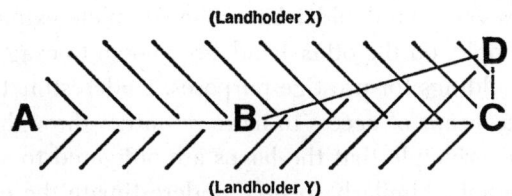

Figure 7. A hypothetical example of boundary hedging.

boundary is really A–B–D. If landholder Y only infrequently visits or neglects the B–C–D area, X may claim his boundary at points A–B–C–D, especially if the trees from B to C happen to be in some regular alignment.

Land boundary lines tend to run perpendicular to the coastline, with the longest tracts thus formed being subdivided by lines running parallel to the shore.[16] Plot divisions tend to be much more irregular in shape on the wide islets, on the table reef islands, and near the villages than they are on the narrow stretches of atoll land.

The map on page 131 illustrates a typical kind of irregularity in plot size and shape found in village areas. Although this particular map happens to be of an area leased by a single body, a former mission, the overall configuration derives its patchwork character from land group fission and house-site accommodations over several generations. Parcels near the village also tend to have better-defined boundaries than do more distant plots because of previous disputes. In general, land increases in value with its ease of access from habitation sites, and boundary disputes seem to increase accordingly.

Standard units of plot sizes were established in the Ellice Islands for the first time in 1957 and 1958 for tax purposes.[17] The measurements were carried out by pacing, and each landholder had the responsibility of reporting his holdings to the island council. This information was recorded and correlated with named sections that had been roughly mapped and indexed by the previous lands commission. Each plot was rated as good, fair, or bad according to its estimated productive value. Taxes are now assessed on land size and quality from these original estimates, usually at a few cents an acre. Complaints have been filed in recent years on several islands concerning inequities in this system, both in the method of measuring area and in the method of taxation.

Not everyone can give an accurate accounting of the size of his land plots, nor does every landholder know the complete extent of his holdings. Many people, on the other hand, are known to exaggerate the extent of their holdings for prestige purposes. Underestimation is usually employed as a means of access to more resources through kinship reciprocity on the principle that the haves are obligated to share produce with the have-nots. Similarly, people underestimate the extent of their solvency in order to minimize taxes, although the leeway for exaggeration or underestimation here is narrowly defined. Regular interaction and close-knit communication in each village promote a general knowledge of approximate landholdings, and boundary disputes help to define for everyone the total holdings of the contestants.

Some plots in the lands registers are recorded simply as *ngalo* 'lost.' The most commonly 'lost' or forgotten plots are those located some distance away from the villages. 'Lost' plots tend to be more common on the atolls than on the reef islands since many of the more distant islets on the atolls are worked with much less regularity than are even equally distant plots on the reef islands. Canoe jaunts to islets on some of the atolls may entail a six- or seven-mile journey away from the village area, whereas none of the plots on the reef islands are separated by more than a mile or so, and they can be reached by foot or bicycles. Difficulty of access also inhibits productivity and leads to the neglect of many plots.

NEGLECTED LAND AND ABSENTEE OWNERSHIP

Problems of neglected land and absentee ownership vary considerably from island to island. Table 12 illustrates the disparity in the number of absentees registered as landholders at Nanumanga and Nukufetau in 1969 according to the type of tenure under which their land was

TABLE 12   Absentee Landholders at Nukufetau and Nanumanga*

Island	'Joint' Tenure				'Individual' Tenure			
	Male	Female	Total	Acreage	Male	Female	Total	Acreage
Nanumanga	3	0	3	11.6	2	0	2	1.4
Nukufetau	34	6	40	188.6	14	6	20	28.0
TOTAL	37	6	43	200.2	16	6	22	29.4

SOURCE: Adapted from Island Lands Registers (data are for 1969).
*These absentees are scattered over the Gilbert and Ellice islands, Ocean Island, Nauru, Christmas Island, the Tokelaus, and Samoa. Niutao absentees in 1968 included 11 males and 1 female holding about 8 acres; Vaitupu had 25 absentees in 1967 holding approximately 58 acres, excluding gardens.

registered. Absenteeism under joint tenure generally poses no real problems of upkeep and use while one of the landholders is away from the island—other members of the estate will usually remain behind and continue to work the land.

Absenteeism under individual tenure, however, usually necessitates the appointment of a caretaker. In return for usufruct privileges, caretakers are charged with the upkeep of the land in the owner's absence. Despite the fact that kinsmen or close friends are the most likely appointees for caretaking, their lack of title to the land provides no incentive for improvements. A frequent complaint from the caretakers themselves is that they "do not have enough time" for upkeep as prescribed by the island regulations. The inheritance of land from islands other than the inheritor's home island often creates a need for appointing a caretaker, but this is not always done. When an absentee landholder has neither a caretaker nor a joint estate with active members, the land is either neglected entirely, or nearby landholders harvest it without permission. Both contingencies can lead to problems.

The Neglected Lands Ordinance of 1959 provides that the central colony government at Tarawa may purchase neglected land at a price determined by its relative overall quality or by its estimated annual copra value. Landholders who fail to prove that their land is not neglected within six months of notification of the government's intention to buy the neglected parcels forfeit the right to retain them. This ordinance also includes provisions for formally inspecting land that was once determined to be neglected, but was later improved by the owners, for a period of five years after first notification.

Not many of the local owners fully understand this legislation, and some have the impression that the government may arbitrarily take their land if it chooses to do so, whether the land is actually neglected or not. Nevertheless, the presence of this legislation has had a coercive effect on several landholders to improve the quality of land which otherwise might have been neglected. Lack of enforcement of the ordinance, however, has reduced its impact, and there have been disagreements on each island as to what actually constitutes "neglected land." There is not much land on any of the islands that would clearly qualify as neglected on the basis of its never having been cleaned of debris or harvested. It is the occasional cleaning and harvesting that lead to difficulties. Local regulations generally prescribe weekly upkeep. This often poses serious difficulties for landholders with widely scattered and highly fragmented holdings.

Other attempts by the government to offset absentee ownership and neglected land problems have included a policy of encouraging persons from overcrowded islands to emigrate to those islands where they have sufficient land for their support. The islanders have also been encouraged to exchange plots with absentee owners from different islands and to lease unused or neglected land to families with insufficient holdings. No significant implementation of these schemes has been realized to date. A lack of customary equity in exchanges of plots that differ widely in quality and size, a general resistance to leasehold in the domestic sphere of each island's economy, and a general inability to match up land-hungry families with more distant holdings have mitigated these plans.

LAND HUNGER

Where tenure rights are based on kinship and subsistence depends mainly on the land, survival depends on sufficient land and a means of access to it. Highly fragmented and otherwise maldistributed holdings may impede productivity in various ways and thereby contribute to land hunger.

"Land hunger" refers here to a perceived or actual scarcity of land resources. In general, an actual condition of maldistribution may be said to exist when land resources are allocated in a manner that makes it difficult or impossible for an individual to harvest minimal subsistence requirements,[18] or when the population of a land use community is distributed in a manner that leads to the overwork of small holdings and the ineffective use of larger holdings.

The first kind of maldistribution is most commonly associated with high fragmentation, that is, when a multiplicity of separate parcels is bound up in a single estate, none of which alone is sufficient for the support of the landholder. This can be offset by consolidating holdings through exchange, reducing fission rates in landholding groups, and reducing the flow of land parcels to nonkinsmen. The second kind of maldistribution is most commonly produced by differential property division and birth rates in the land use community. It can be offset by relocating disadvantaged landowners to areas more favorable for their subsistence, by increasing the yield from present holdings, or by acquiring neglected land for reallocation to groups with insufficient holdings. All of these have been tried by the administration in the Ellices.

Discounting differences in cash subsidies through employment, subsistence income through kinship reciprocity, dependence upon marine resources, and individual consumption rates, my own estimates combined with some from the administration (Cartland 1949, 1952) suggest that about one acre of productive land is a minimal per capita requirement for subsistence in the Ellice Islands. This means that thirty to thirty-six coconut trees and about a thousand square feet of garden pits are needed to sustain each person in meeting minimal dietary requirements.[19] Extensive data for more accurate estimates of per capita consumption in terms of the number and weight of coconuts used for all purposes (which include human consumption, pig food, and copra production) are not available at present. My survey of households at Nanumanga in 1969 revealed a crude daily consumption rate for each household that ranged from ten to thirty-five nuts for all purposes. Comparable figures for households at Nukufetau ranged from six to twenty nuts per day, and the sample taken at Funafuti revealed a range of zero to fourteen nuts per day. The lower range from Funafuti is due to a high rate of local employment. Cash income allows for the purchase of supplementary foodstuffs from the local cooperative retail outlets and thereby reduces dependence upon the land.

Accepting that one acre of productive land is a reasonable estimate of per capita subsistence requirements, the optimum population density would be something less than about 640 persons per square mile. If the land unsuitable for production is subtracted from the total land area, the present overall density averages about 750 persons per square mile of productive land. Only Nanumea, Niutao, and Funafuti exceed 640 persons per square mile (see table 8). But other factors such as highly fragmented holdings and an inequitable distribution of landholders over the available resources contribute to the actual land hunger index. Population density by itself is an insufficient indicator of overall land hunger.

Table 13 is a ranked index of fragmentation of landholdings for all of the Ellice group. It is based on the number of plots per capita, which is a function of both previous magnitudes of fragmentation and population densities; the mean size of plots in acres, on the assumption that a smaller mean plot size indicates greater land fragmentation than does a larger mean; and the number of registered owners per thousand in the local population, on the assumption that a higher number of registered owners per thousand in population indicates greater fragmentation than does a lower number. The relative rank on these subindices was averaged to produce an overall fragmentation rank for each island relative to the others (column four). Nukufetau and Niutao show the greatest fragmentation on this index, while Nanumanga and Nukulaelae are tied at equal ranks for the least fragmentation.

Table 14 relates to the maldistribution of land resources. It is based on the amount of good-to-fair-quality productive land among the total number of registered landholders on each island except Nukulaelae, where data were not available.[20] Table 15 is an expression of table 14 in percentages. These data clearly indicate male biases for inheritance and control over land. Females in each case tend to hold smaller parcels than males, and the number of male titleholders significantly exceeds that for females on all islands but one. Nui has an equal number of male and female title holders in this distribution. A careful check of previous landholdings by sex of the registered owners on Nui reveals that registered male landholders ordinarily outnumber registered female landholders here as elsewhere in the Ellice Islands. The equal distribution recorded for Nui in table 14 is due as much to chance as it is to the possibility of a lesser patrilateral bias in land distribution as compared to the other islands.

Since males are much more likely than females to become household heads and land group managers, an unusually large percentage of males with one acre or less of good-to-fair-quality land can be used as

TABLE 13 Ranked Index of Land Fragmentation in the Ellice Islands

Island	Number of plots per capita	Rank (1 = highest)	Mean size plots in acres	Rank (1 = lowest)	Number registered owners per 1000 in population	Rank (1 = highest)	Overall Rank (1 = most fragmented)
Nukufetau	4.9	1	.24	1	260	4	1
Niutao	2.3	4	.25	2	514	1	2
Vaitupu	4.1	2	.42	4	336	2	3
Nui	2.7	3	.43	5	232	6	4
Nanumea	1.39	7	.64	6	324	3	5
Funafuti	1.6	6	.41	3	98	8	6
Nukulaelae	1.7	5	.76	8	173	7	7*
Nanumanga	1.37	8	.70	7	259	5	8
Mean	2.5		.46		275		

SOURCE: Computed from data in Island Lands Registers; population figures from Zwart and Groenewegen 1970.
*Tied with Nanumanga in overall rating for least degree of fragmentation. Ranking resolved with other data such as number of plots per *Matai*: Nanumanga = 4.7; Nukulaelae = 5.6. Otherwise an equal rank in this column of 7.5 may be assigned to each.

TABLE 14 Approximate Quantities (in Acres) of Good-to-Fair Land Held, by Sex, in the Ellice Islands

Island	0-1.0 acres			1.1-2.0 acres			2.1-3.0 acres			3.1-5.0 acres			5.1 acres +			Total		
	Male	Female	Total	Male	Female	Total	Male	Female	Total	Male	Female	Total	Male	Female	Total	M	F	Total
Nanumea	110	82	192	29	26	55	29	12	41	24	11	35	23	4	27	215	135	350
(Cumulative)	(110)	(82)	(192)	(139)	(108)	(247)	(168)	(120)	(288)	(192)	(131)	(323)	(215)	(135)	(350)			
Nanumanga	37	39	76	14	8	22	8	7	15	18	5	23	29	6	35	106	65	171
(Cumulative)	(37)	(39)	(76)	(51)	(47)	(98)	(59)	(54)	(113)	(77)	(59)	(136)	(106)	(65)	(171)			
Niutao	190	155	345	37	15	52	15	3	18	9	3	12	0	0	0	251	176	427
(Cumulative)	(190)	(155)	(345)	(227)	(170)	(397)	(242)	(173)	(415)	(251)	(176)	(427)	(251)	(176)	(427)			
Nui	23	15	38	9	17	26	4	9	13	12	9	21	33	31	64	81	81	162
(Cumulative)	(23)	(15)	(38)	(32)	(32)	(64)	(36)	(41)	(77)	(48)	(50)	(98)	(81)	(81)	(162)			
Vaitupu	81	69	150	51	13	64	23	7	30	22	4	26	15	1	16	192	94	286
(Cumulative)	(81)	(69)	(150)	(132)	(82)	(214)	(155)	(89)	(244)	(177)	(93)	(270)	(192)	(94)	(286)			
Nukufetau	49	33	82	23	15	38	19	6	25	19	6	25	19	3	22	129	63	192
(Cumulative)	(49)	(33)	(82)	(72)	(48)	(120)	(91)	(54)	(145)	(110)	(60)	(170)	(129)	(63)	(192)			
Funafuti	16	18	34	17	6	23	4	1	5	10	1	11	6	2	8	53	28	81
(Cumulative)	(16)	(18)	(34)	(33)	(24)	(57)	(37)	(25)	(62)	(47)	(26)	(73)	(53)	(28)	(81)			
TOTAL	506	411	917	180	200	280	102	45	147	114	39	153	125	47	172	1027	742	1669
(Cumulative)	(506)	(411)	(917)	(686)	(611)	(1197)	(788)	(656)	(1344)	(902)	(695)	(1497)	(1027)	(742)	(1669)			

Source: Adapted from Island Lands Registers (data are for 1969).

a crude indicator of seriously maldistributed holdings. The sample is large enough to assume that differences in dependence upon these holdings will average out in the long run. On this index, Niutao has by far the greatest maldistribution in the group—75.5 percent of all registered males have one acre or less and more than half of these have less than one-half acre. Nui has the least maldistribution—28.4 percent of all registered males have one acre of land or less. Correspondingly, no individual at Niutao controls more than five acres of good-to-fair-quality land, while nearly 40 percent of the registered owners at Nui have holdings that exceed five acres of comparable quality.

Lacking data on the distribution of all kinds of resources per capita on each island for an index of absolute land hunger, a crude estimate was devised using other indices. The results have been incorporated in table 16. Column I, adapted from table 13, includes a population density measure per total land area on each island which is expressed in the amount of good-to-fair-quality land per capita. Column II is an index of maldistribution of landholdings on each island; it is a combined rating based on the degree of fragmentation and skewing in the distribution of average size parcels among the members of each land use community adapted from tables 13 and 14. Column III represents an average rank for each island based on the sum of the rank order values in columns I and II. Admittedly crude, it gives, nonetheless, an overall and relative estimate of land hunger in the Ellice Islands. Nukulaelae shows the least and Niutao the most overall land hunger on this index, and this is consistent with all other estimates.

All things considered, it is evident that land hunger may be more apparent than real in some cases. It has not yet reached a level at which most residents are faced with imminent starvation on account of insufficient or maldistributed resources. The diversion of household produce as generalized reciprocity to the have-nots, cash income for supplementary foodstuffs, optional affiliation, marital alliance patterns, and dependence upon marine resources tend to offset some of the problems of land hunger to varying degrees. Yet a local perception of land hunger does prevail to the extent that it often directly influences behavior in inheritance, affiliation, and marital alliance strategies. Definite calculations are made in an effort to maximize alliances with persons or groups who hold superior resources. Land-hungry groups often attempt to link up with land-wealthy groups through marriage, adoption, and even friendship. Land-hungry groups can neither afford to incorporate

TABLE 15 Percentages of Good-to-Fair Land Held, by Sex, in the Ellice Islands

Island	0–1.0 acres			1.1–2.0 acres			2.1–3.0 acres		
	Male	Female	Total	Male	Female	Total	Male	Female	Total
Nanumea	51.3	61.0	54.9	13.5	19.5	15.7	13.5	9.1	11.7
(Cumulative)	(51.3)	(61.0)	(54.9)	(64.8)	(80.5)	(70.6)	(78.3)	(89.6)	(82.3)
Nanumanga	34.9	60.0	44.4	13.2	12.3	12.9	7.6	10.8	8.7
(Cumulative)	(34.9)	(60.0)	(44.4)	(48.1)	(72.3)	(57.3)	(55.7)	(83.1)	(66.0)
Niutao	75.7	88.0	80.8	14.7	8.5	12.2	6.0	1.7	4.2
(Cumulative)	(75.7)	(88.0)	(80.8)	(90.4)	(88.6)	(93.0)	(96.4)	(98.3)	(97.2)
Nui	28.4	18.5	23.5	11.1	20.1	16.0	4.9	11.1	8.0
(Cumulative)	(28.4)	(18.5)	(23.5)	(39.5)	(38.6)	(39.5)	(44.4)	(49.7)	(47.5)
Vaitupu	42.2	73.4	52.4	26.6	13.0	22.4	12.0	7.4	10.5
(Cumulative)	(42.2)	(73.4)	(52.4)	(68.0)	(87.2)	(74.8)	(80.0)	(94.6)	(85.3)
Nukufetau	38.0	51.4	42.7	17.9	23.8	19.8	14.7	9.5	13.0
(Cumulative)	(38.0)	(51.4)	(42.7)	(55.9)	(76.2)	(62.5)	(70.6)	(85.7)	(75.5)
Funafuti	30.2	64.3	41.9	32.1	21.4	28.4	7.5	3.6	6.2
(Cumulative)	(30.2)	(64.3)	(41.9)	(62.3)	(85.7)	(70.3)	(69.8)	(89.3)	(76.5)
TOTAL	49.3	55.4	54.9	17.5	26.9	16.8	9.9	6.1	8.9
(Cumulative)	(49.3)	(55.4)	(54.9)	(66.8)	(82.3)	(71.7)	(76.7)	(88.4)	(80.6)

SOURCE: Adapted from Island Lands Registers (data are for 1969).

TABLE 15 Percentages of Good-to-Fair Land Held, by Sex, in the Ellice Islands (*cont.*)

Island	3.1–5.0 acres			5.1 acres +			Total		
	Male	Female	Total	Male	Female	Total	Male	Female	Total
Nanumea	11.2	7.8	10.0	10.5	2.6	7.7	100	100	100
(Cumulative)	(89.5)	(97.4)	(92.3)	(100)	(100)	(100)			
Nanumanga	17.0	7.7	13.5	27.3	9.2	20.5	100	100	100
(Cumulative)	(72.7)	(90.8)	(79.5)	(100)	(100)	(100)			
Niutao	3.6	1.7	2.8	0.0	0.0	0.0	100	100	100
(Cumulative)	(100)	(100)	(100)	(100)	(100)	(100)			
Nui	14.8	11.1	13.0	40.8	39.2	39.5	100	100	100
(Cumulative)	(59.2)	(60.8)	(60.5)	(100)	(100)	(100)			
Vaitupu	11.5	4.3	9.1	7.7	1.1	5.6	100	100	100
(Cumulative)	(92.3)	(98.9)	(94.4)	(100)	(100)	(100)			
Nukufetau	14.7	9.5	13.0	14.7	4.8	11.5	100	100	100
(Cumulative)	(85.3)	(95.2)	(88.5)	(100)	(100)	(100)			
Funafuti	18.9	3.6	13.6	11.3	7.1	9.9	100	100	100
(Cumulative)	(88.7)	(92.9)	(90.1)	(100)	(100)	(100)			
TOTAL	11.1	5.3	9.1	12.2	6.3	10.3			
(Cumulative)	(87.8)	(93.7)	(89.7)	(100)	(100)	(100)			

TABLE 16 Estimated Rank Order of Land Hunger in the Ellice Islands

Island	Per Capita Holdings		Estimated Maldistribution[b] (1 = lowest)	Overall Land Hunger (1 = lowest)
	Acres[a]	Rank (1 = highest)		
Nukulaelae	1.446	2	1[c]	1
Vaitupu	1.478	1	4	2
Nui	1.202	3	3	3
Nanumanga	1.309	5	2	4
Nukufetau	1.059	4	7	5
Nanumea	0.607	6	6	6
Funafuti	0.455	8	5	7
Niutao	0.538	7	8	8

[a]Adapted from Island Lands Registers and Zwart and Groenewegen 1970. [b]Adapted from tables 13 and 14. [c]Rank inferred from Bedford 1967:xvi.

new members through birth or adoption, nor can they tolerate an outflow of their real property through customary conveyances to members of other groups. They tend to maximize the dispersal of their members through employment elsewhere and adoption by other groups as mechanisms for both decreasing dependence on their existing resources and increasing supplementary income through kinship reciprocity.

The establishment of an external copra market has inflated the value of coconut land and partially redirected production schedules. Land is no longer valued only as a direct source of subsistence or for its communion with the ancestral past. It now has a cash income value that provides for additional subsistence and the acquisition of many manifestations of Western lifestyles that have come to be desired, such as outboard motors, motorcycles, metal kitchenware, household radios, and sewing machines. Strategies for access to land take these factors into account, and the notion of relative land hunger is affected accordingly.

The growing perception of land hunger has had an adverse effect on the actual level of land hunger by increasing competition for land and thereby inflating group fission and plot fragmentation rates. Concomitantly, many traditional modes of reallocating land and redistributing the population within land use communities have become increasingly difficult to implement. Outside contact has complicated these patterns by contributing to population growth and by stimulating market participation while production remains largely on a traditional basis.

SUMMARY AND CONCLUSIONS

The two most dominant forces of culture change in the Ellice Islands have been the Samoan pastors, as agents for the London Missionary Society, and the colonial administration. Their cumulative influence over the last century has stimulated a number of changes in traditional land tenure patterns, although kin group membership is still the primary means of access to land. The abandonment of ancestor worship and conversion to Christianity undermined chiefly powers and eliminated many forms of land reallocation which were bound up with pre-European religious rites. The former system of chiefly stewardship over the land has been replaced by a more Western form of administration. The transformation from a council of chiefs and elders to the island council polity was not dramatic in a structural sense, but it has led to a much more evolved form of leadership that is predicated neither on kinship nor on chiefly rights of succession. Lands courts have been established on each island as part of this political transformation, and they have been charged with the responsibility for administering all land matters. The members of these courts are not always chiefs, nor are they recruited solely on the basis of representing each of the major ramages on their islands as in the previous polity. Land management that closely approximates the aboriginal system is confined today to relations between the senior members of 'land groups' and the coparceners on their estates.

Despite the relative success of the administration's efforts to codify customary land tenure, land legislation has upheld and increased the jural autonomy of landholding groups on a model of European corporate integrity. The effect has been to encourage fission in these groups, and an unintended by-product is that overall ramage solidarity has been undermined in the process. Landholding groups have grown smaller in active membership, genealogical depth has become shallower, and estates have become much more fragmented than in earlier times as the result of a transformation from division through segmentation to a preponderance of division through fission. Aboriginal ramage segments holding joint rights to an ancestral estate once encompassed major sectors on each island. An average landholding group today includes only eight or nine active members, all of whom are likely to live in a single household. These groups tend to aggregate into household clusters in the absence of regular fission. Persistence as a viable economic and political unit is predicated directly on residence patterns and the maintenance of joint rights to land.

The abolition of overt infanticide, abortion, and warfare as population control devices has contributed to the present magnitudes of land hunger on each island, as have certain aspects of economic development under colonial guidance. Traditional property concepts and production schedules have been altered to accommodate increased participation in the copra market. Land has developed a cash value that is determined by the market price its produce will bring. Cash income takes some of the burden off the use of land for direct subsistence, but competition for land has increased with growth in the local population and with expansion of the range of commercial rewards for copra production. Strategies for access to land take these factors into account, and the perception of relative land hunger is affected accordingly.

Despite some disparity in the levels of perceived and actual land hunger, it is evident that land hunger problems have fostered conservatism in the alienation of land to nonkinsmen, pushed several modes of land conveyance into obsolescence, constricted the adaptive mobility of individuals among related landholding groups, inflated estate fragmentation and group fission rates, and increased land litigation over estate boundaries and inheritance rights. Unlimited population growth has proved to be incompatible with the traditional rule that provides land for all bona fide members of each community by birthright, particularly in conjunction with the predominance of group division through fission rather than segmentation. These and other land tenure problems associated with population pressure have pointed to a need for new or modified forms of land allocation that will offset rather than promulgate perceived and actual land hunger.

The colonial orthodoxy has failed, at least partially, to provide viable substitutes for the abolished or otherwise modified traditional means of maintaining homeostasis between local populations and their natural resources. But it is of some interest to note that considerable leeway remains for the resolution of some of these problems at the local level. Administrative designs have given the lands courts considerable freedom in their interpretation of customary matters, and there is now an active legislative process for the islanders to implement changes in their own life strategies on a formal basis. This capability combined with a realization of the commercial fishing industry (whose feasibility is presently being explored under government sponsorship), the institution of a successful birth control program, and the development of greater possibilities for migration and employment elsewhere hold some promise of alleviating for future generations some of the land tenure and land hunger problems of the present.

NOTES

1. Data for this chapter were gathered while I was conducting doctoral dissertation research in the Ellice Islands in 1968 and 1969 with support provided by a U.S. Public Health Service (NIMH) Research Grant (MH 11629) and Fellowship (MH 40529) and by the Department of Anthropology, University of Oregon. Additional information was obtained in 1971 on a Summer Research Grant from the National Science Foundation (GS 29695). This assistance is gratefully acknowledged. I also wish to thank Henry Lundsgaarde, Ron Crocombe, Barrie Macdonald, Harry Maude, Bernd Lambert, Beth Dillingham, and Vern Carroll for their valuable criticisms of earlier drafts of this chapter.
2. The people at Nui speak a Gilbertese patois as the result of conquest and settlement by warriors from the islands of Tabiteuea and probably Beru. Among other diagnostic linguistic features, the remaining northern islands have an [h] in their phonemic inventory that is absent in the southern islands.
3. Cartland's commission overlooked the registration of landholders who were not resident at the time of establishment of the new lands registers. This oversight has since been corrected by district officers.
4. The customary patrilateral bias for land inheritance can be disregarded with lands court approval. Landholders at Vaitupu are ostensibly free to allocate their land in whatever proportions they choose, barring complete disinheritance of any natural heirs.
5. Some difficulty with the segmentation-fission dichotomy emerges because of the conventional use of the English term *segment*. Segments can be viewed as the empirical results of the operation of both segmentation and fission processes.
6. Sahlins has asserted the same principle in his 1958 thesis concerning differential adaptation to high-island versus low-island environments in Polynesia.
7. Note also that the Ellice Islands Lands Code (Section 4, iii) provides that a manager may stipulate that his estate may not be divided for at least one generation after his death. This applies to Nanumea, Nui, Vaitupu, Funafuti, and Nukulaelae. This provides a possible check on group fission because of the functional interrelation between landholdings and

land group constitution. But, with lands court approval, consensus among the living coparceners may override the conditions of a will at Nukufetau, Nanumanga, and Niutao.

8. Inheritance under these circumstances is rare, but when it does occur, the number of claimants by virtue of the cognatic next-of-kin principle may be so large that it leads to an impractical division of the deceased's estate. A compromise allocation is usually devised to reduce unnecessary land fragmentation.
9. Data on this topic from Nanumea were not available because shipping irregularities in the colony prevented a visit of sufficient duration to gather the necessary information. Niulakita is deliberately excluded here because its status as a copra plantation owned by the Niutao islanders precludes comparison with the remaining eight islands.
10. Islets on the atolls or stretches of coastline are examples. The earth fills built by the U.S. Army at Nanumea during World War II are now treated as communal land.
11. Government stations generally include hospitals, offices, and schools.
12. Land has been exchanged a few times for canoe sails at Nanumea, Niutao, and Nanumanga. Gardens have been exchanged for *puka* trees (*Pisonia grandis*), which are used for canoe hulls, at Nui. But all such transactions are now generally discouraged by the community at large.
13. Similarly, land is no longer forfeited as retribution for offenses against the chiefs as in former times. Until a decade ago, however, recalcitrant persons in each village could be admonished through the island council by having their share of commercial produce withdrawn until amends were made.
14. Although some of these disputes may lead to heated arguments, they rarely deteriorate into actual violence.
15. Just how frequent boundary hedging is in the Ellice Islands is difficult to say because of its illegal nature, but I suspect that it is not as common as many persons on each island believe.
16. Property divisions in former times often extended into the immediate ocean or lagoon so as to incorporate fishing territories. Boundaries demarcating these marine territories were fixed with reference to points ashore.
17. A "size 1 land" measures 10 x 20 yards throughout the Ellice group, except on Vaitupu where it is 20 x 20 and on Nukulaelae where it is 40 x 40.
18. Owing to parcels that are too small, too distant, or too irregular in shape to be worked productively.
19. Protein in local diets is derived from fish, shellfish, pork, poultry, eggs, coconut meat, *Cyrtosperma*, and taro; carbohydrates from unpolished rice, wild sugar cane (on islands where this grows), and fruits; some minerals and vitamins are obtained from the carbohydrate-producing items listed and from fish, birds, coconut toddy, fresh coconuts, bread, pork, and taro; fat sources include coconuts, fish, liver, butter, and lard drippings. Rice and flour from the local stores provide adequate dietary substitutes for garden produce. Toddy palms are less important for dietary reasons when sugar is available from other resources.
20. Bedford 1967 includes some comparable data for this island.

THE EVOLUTION OF TENURE PRINCIPLES ON TAMANA ISLAND, GILBERT ISLANDS

Henry P. Lundsgaarde

INTRODUCTION

From the moment in 1892, or shortly thereafter, when British government officials compiled the first land registers in the Gilbert Islands "both native and European officials commenced giving numbers of land decisions, altering the registers to such an extent that by 1918 they were considered to be virtually useless. In the case of the native officials this was only to be expected, for however trustworthy a Gilbertese may be on ordinary matters, when it comes to land he throws all vestiges of honesty away. . . . The European officials no doubt did their best, but their decisions were based on no study or knowledge of native custom, they were coloured by purely European ideas of ethics and law, and the decisions of one District Officer often completely contradicted those made by his predecessors" (Maude 1937).

Maude's observations express the frustration felt by any government officer charged with the duty to adjudicate a Gilbertese land dispute in which tenure rights often are asserted by means of oratorial skill, personal prestige, or blunt political pressure. His comments also caution against seeing the present-day land tenure system as undisturbed by outside influences. The presence of British government administrators for nearly four generations, together with other factors, has in fact served to modify aboriginal tenure practices in numerous ways. It must suffice, in the interest of brevity, to acknowledge the historical and innovative effects of the British presence and to proceed from the as-

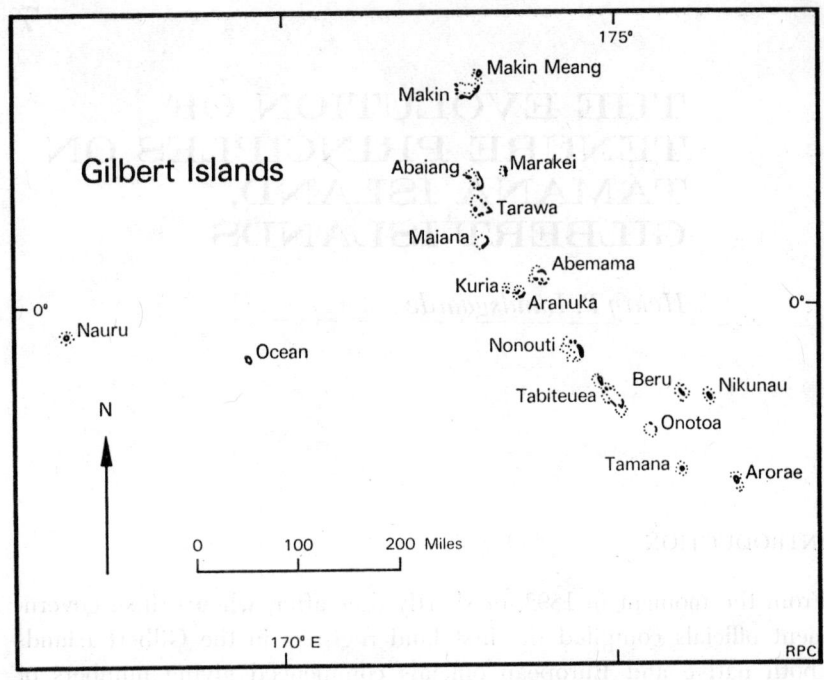

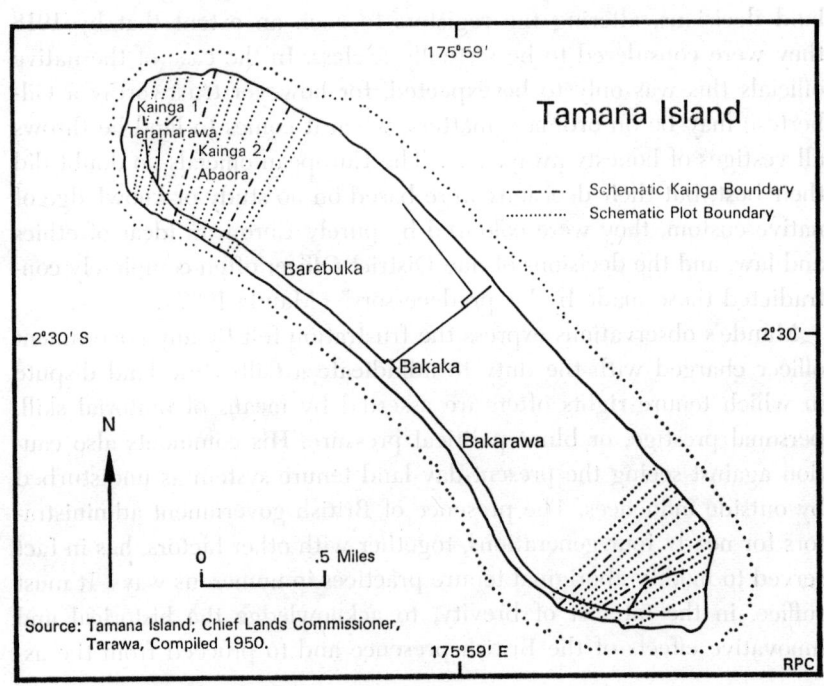

sumption that Gilbertese land tenure practices reflect multiple cultural adaptations to colonial rule.[1]

How we then conceptualize a complex land tenure system, with roots in native custom and colonial law, and how we start the analysis will, of course, color any subsequent generalizations about the system as a whole. Although one approach is not necessarily better than another, it is useful to contrast two prevailing but polar perspectives of Gilbertese land tenure. First, the official or administrative perspective generally seeks simplification by way of property registration, codification of formal procedures to be followed in adjudication, and by maintaining legal supervision of land transactions. Second, by contrast, the anthropological and analytical perspective seeks understanding from a study of the total social network in which real property forms one focus of interpersonal relations. It is thus quite clear, for example, why a European colonial administrator may come to view social custom as a source of ambiguity and trouble and why an anthropologist will at times find the governmental emphasis on legislative codification and court procedure an expedient whitewash shielding a lack of knowledge of the indigenous culture.

Within the brief time span between 1892 and the present, there have, in fact, been colonial administrators who have proceeded in their work with Gilbertese land tenure from both of these perspectives. Some colonial administrators have in the past interpreted their work as a means to superimpose a layer of Western civilization on a native society by introducing writing, systematic record keeping, and—at the pinnacle—legislation for the guidance of public affairs. Others, in addition to following these nominal civilizing efforts, took it upon themselves to understand the native culture from the viewpoint of the individual, the village community, or an island social organization. Despite the merits of this more empirical and inductive approach—associated with the names of B. C. Cartland, R. Cowell, A. F. Grimble, H. E. Maude, and M. M. Townsend—it has been broadly denounced by many, including the present administration, as romantic, unrealistic, and unprogressive. Or, it has been chastised as a continuation of Grimble's "museum policy."

Although it may be said of the late Sir Arthur Grimble that he democratized the feudalistic land tenure system of the northern Gilberts to a point of administrative confusion, it is misguided effort to equate his administrative errors with a false or unrealistic perspective. Grimble worked from the assumption that no outsider either could or should dissertate authoritatively on Gilbertese land tenure without also being aware of and knowing the historical, political, social, or cultural context in which the system is embedded (see Grimble 1929).

H. E. Maude, who worked as lands commissioner in the southern Gilbert Islands in the 1930s, went beyond Grimble and achieved more than his predecessors in the process. In fact, Maude went so far that he never adjudicated a single land dispute without the aid of an interpreter, despite his own fluency and superior knowledge of the Gilbertese language. Maude demonstrated, in his dual role as scholar and administrator, the necessity of placing specific land tenure problems within the broader context of Gilbertese culture. This perspective, which by no means seeks to ignore the catalytic effects of administrative innovations on the present system, seeks to understand and explain how people actually behave with respect to the use and control of real property.

Land tenure in the southern Gilbert Islands, as of the mid-1960s, could be broadly characterized, therefore, as a composite system of legal and customary principles rooted in aboriginal Gilbertese custom as well as in English administrative customs (Lundsgaarde 1968a:117–130). This amalgamation of tenure principles which originate and evolve from the duality of the colonial social structure both simplifies and complicates descriptive analysis of local land tenure practices. Ethnographic description, for example, is much simplified by the availability of lands registers, written regulations and ordinances, and recorded minutes of court actions involving land litigation and settlement. If, however, we rely too heavily on these ready-made tools of investigation, the superficiality of our understanding will be all too readily apparent. Gilbertese land tenure touches on every single social institution imaginable. Kinship, marriage, adoption, status seniority, and group affiliation are but a few of the more conspicuous elements of Gilbertese social organization that, in one way or another, involve what Epstein has aptly termed a "simultaneity of interests" in the ownership, use, and conveyance of real property (1969:117).

I will focus primarily on data from Tamana Island. The field data on Gilbertese land tenure from this island provide a fixed point of reference from which to compare interisland variations. The Tamana Island land tenure system is one which, unless otherwise indicated, is characteristic of the more general tenure patterns on Nonouti, Tabiteuea, Beru, Onotoa, Nikunau, and Arorae islands. As with all of these islands, land tenure on Tamana is part of a broader system of kinship and contractual relations symbolized by various rights in real property.

In addition to the ethnographic data collected on Tamana Island during fieldwork from September 1964 to January 1965, I have relied upon my own field data collected on Nonouti and Tabiteuea islands and have excerpted other data from government documents on file at the Gilbert and Ellice Islands Colony archives at Betio, Tarawa Island. For a comparison of these data with tenure practices in the northern Gilberts the reader should consult Crocombe (1968:27–37) and Lambert (1971:146–171).

TAMANA ISLAND

On most maps, the 2½ by ¾ mile dimensions of Tamana Island are rarely dignified by a single ink blot from the cartographer's pen. Yet this island located at 02°30'09" south latitude and 175°58'48" east longitude is home to 1,241 Gilbertese. It has the highest population density (about 0.82 persons per acre) of any of the sixteen islands in the Gilbert archipelago. Because of the human crowding that naturally results from such a high density ratio, one might expect to find a comparatively higher number of disputes involving land ownership and use than might be the case under less crowded circumstances. However, this does not appear to be the case at the present time (cf. Lundsgaarde 1968b:86–93).

Three hamlets—Barebuka, Bakaka, and Bakarawa—form one continuous north-south village settlement on the lee and western side of the island. The official 1963 census showed a total of 248 separate households with an average of 4.91 persons per household (McArthur and McCaig 1964:88, 261–262). Tamanans, who relish their reputation among fellow Gilbertese as being kind and happy, have not had to cope with the disconcerting Protestant and Catholic factionalisms that prevail on all of the other islands except Arorae. The 99 percent conversion of Tamanans, together with their close neighbors on Arorae Island, to the Protestant faith has, since the latter part of the nineteenth century, set these islanders apart from their fellow Gilbertese. They seem to enjoy their local reputation of being more cooperative and community minded than most other Gilbertese. Whether the powerful influence of the Protestant church plus the size and isolation of the island community may have fostered these attributes as a combination of faith and necessity is left as an open question.

All Tamanans subsist on a primary diet of coconut, taro (*Cyrtosperma chamissonis*), pandanus, papaya, and a variety of different fish. These foods are supplemented by such imported luxuries as rice, sugar, flour, and tea. Domesticated pigs and chickens are foods reserved for special social events. Unlike the atoll-type islands—Nonouti, Tabiteuea, Berue, and Onotoa—Tamana has no lagoon area, no natural fishponds, and no extensive reef platform on which to build coral-stone fish traps. The relative ease with which Tamanans can exploit deep-sea fishing resources, however, provides them with a constant and plentiful source of animal protein (see Catala 1957). Land boundaries, unlike those on the atolls and other reef islands like Nikunau Island, do not include areas on the narrow reef platform surrounding the island.

The entire island is divided into 116 named tracts known as *kainga*. Each *kainga*, 'estate,' is subdivided along an east-west boundary line into any number of smaller land parcels (see map p. 180). Each of these parcels is registered in an official lands register that is kept up to date by a Gilbertese scribe. The scribe notes all land transactions in this register.

The scribe also issues, records, and validates all wills pertaining to real property, and he reconciles entries in the lands register with any actions brought before the native lands court. The entry for each parcel of land lists information on all of the following categories.

The first entry lists the name of the hamlet and 'estate' section on which the parcel of land is located. Most parcels form a narrow strip that spans the entire island in an approximate east-west direction. Any smaller parcel that departs from this pattern may carry an additional entry.

Land areas, with the notable exception of lands leased to government or mission agencies, are not surveyed, and boundaries, which are a continuous source of litigation, are haphazardly demarcated. Boundary markers may consist of a notch or two in a coconut tree, an overturned piece of coral rock, or a simple gravemarker. Upon close examination of any contested boundary line the principal parties to a dispute will commonly try to establish the true line with evidence that at times baffles both casual spectators and government officials alike. For example, a party may testify, "I know that the boundary line runs right here, because my father used to take me here as a child and he told me that this was the true boundary line." In defense of these practices, it may be said that the Gilbertese probably conceptualize land dimensions more like topologists than like geometricians. As a direct outcome of registration, individual parcels are now numbered in consecutive order within the boundaries of individual 'estates.' For example, the northernmost parcel of 'estate' No. 1 is recorded in the lands register as parcel number one, the following parcel as number two, etc. The number of individual parcels within any given 'estate' may vary from one to as many as fifty-five.

A typical entry in the lands register that describes a land parcel registered to a woman by the name of Nei Eriera Materei reads, "Nei Eriera Materei, 80w, 5N, M, mt." This decodes as "Tekarara 'estate' in Bakarawa hamlet (80), parcel number twelve (w), approximately five acres in size (5), of medium productive quality (N), received by the present owner from her male ascendant (M), and held in concurrent or joint ownership title with her sisters (mt)." All other real properties registered to Nei Eriera Materei or any other title holder could be looked up and documented in this way.[2] This system of land registration, allowing for minor local variations, is repeated on all the other islands in the archipelago. The brevity and informality accorded uncomplicated title recording procedures are illustrated in the following cases.

Case 1 (Tamana Lands Court 20/1964). A, a woman, appeals to the lands court to approve and record title to some of her lands in the name of B, her daughter. B consents to the wishes of her mother and agrees to accept single title to her mother's land parcels. The lands court "agrees to the formal transfer and registration of lands conveyed as a gift, and therefore records B as the new owner of the parcels Tawana, Tumairang, and Temankateainga."

Case 2 (Tamana Lands Court 21/1964). A, a man, appeals to the court to register title to land parcels given to him by B. B, who has formally adopted A's mother as his 'grandchild,' has given his consent to the transfer. The lands court rules that "since B has given his consent to the action, A will be registered as the owner of the lands Teinati and Tekauake."

Case 3 (Tamana Lands Court 22/1964). A, the Tamana Island magistrate, appeals to the jurors on behalf of the London Missionary Society to settle a disputed claim between the church and B, a person who claims to own a small taro pit located within the physical boundaries of the lands leased to the church. The jurors rule in favor of B's claim: "The right to the taro pit rests with B since the London Missionary Society was never given title to the taro pit."

Land parcel size is indicated by noting its approximate acreage. However, since no numerical standards are employed to measure actual parcel dimensions there is no accurate way of knowing the exact size of a land parcel. The Gilbertese speak freely of the land parcels as being of one, two, or three acres and their annual land tax assessments are based on these approximate entities. Land parcel quality is a more accurate reflection of reality. The Gilbertese follow a tripartite classification that discriminates between land parcels on the basis of relative productivity—good or excellent, medium or average, and poor or unproductive (cf. Mason 1960:1–17; Catala 1957).

The entry under what is simply the name of the title holder shows the name, sex, and type of title held by the registered person.

Case 4 (Tamana Lands Court 22/1957). A, a woman, appears before the lands court to transfer the title of her deceased mother's lands to her own name. Her father and brother are still living although neither appeared before the court. A's brother was temporarily away from the island while employed on Ocean Island. "The members of the lands court agree that A should receive title to the lands belonging to her deceased mother. She will be registered as the owner of parcel No. 1 on Taramarawa 'estate,' parcel No. 24 on Matarei 'estate,' and taro pits previously recorded in section No. 30 as pits number 3133–3137. If there is any capital share from A's mother, it should be shared equally with her brother upon his return from Ocean Island."

Exclusive or single title is indicated by the presence of one name only.

What we might term concurrent or joint title is indicated by adding one or more of the following statements to the name of the senior person among any number of joint title holders. For example, an entry which lists the title as "Ten Bauro Eribati *ma tarina*" indicates that Ten Bauro holds title to a parcel of land 'together with all of his brothers.' Similarly, "Ten Bauro Eribati *ma manena*" means that Ten Bauro holds title to a parcel of land 'together with all of his sisters.' The combination *ma tarina/ma manena* 'together with siblings of same/opposite sex' is also possible.

Case 5 (Tamana Lands Court 29/1957). A appeals to the court on behalf of himself and his sister, B, for conveyance of full title to the lands formerly held by their deceased father. The lands court "agrees that the lands of A's father should be registered in A's name on behalf of his sister. (All individual land parcels, taro pits, and soaking ponds are thereupon itemized and entered in the register under A's name 'together with his sister.') The capital share of the deceased should also be given to A. If there is any other money left by A's father, it should be shared equally between A and B."

A less common type of entry lists the name of a person together with his children. In very exceptional cases in which two title holders are not related to each other, the names of both persons are listed together. Two joint title holders theoretically hold equal rights to their common property. However, the name of the person who is listed in the lands register is most often a senior kinsman or the person who customarily enjoys a higher status than his junior kinsmen and who has the final authority to speak on behalf of his juniors in any dispute arising between his kinsmen and other islanders. A person cannot, however, in any way transfer any part of the jointly held land to any other person without first obtaining the consent of his juniors or co-owners.

Case 6 (Tamana Lands Court 25/1951). A, a sister of absentee respondent B, appeals to the court for recognition of her right to derive a living from lands jointly registered to both of them. Although A has not been denied access to these lands outright, she claims that her brother left his lands in care of C, a third party. In addition to this, however, her brother specifically asked A to care for an old woman during his absence. A, who admits to being on unfriendly terms with her brother, requests that title to two land parcels from the jointly held estate be conveyed to her. The lands court refused to partition the estate in B's absence but upheld A's right "to derive her livelihood from all the land parcels currently registered in her brother's name."

Case 7 (Tamana Lands Court 26/1957). A and B, who are brothers, appear before the court together with C, B's daughter. A has initiated an appeal for redistribution of their jointly held estate, because he claims that B is enjoying the benefits of a larger share of their common estate. Since all parties with a vested interest agree to redistribution and reregistration, the court "will comply with the wishes of the three persons who have appeared before the court. The lands will be redistributed and the former registration will be cancelled from the lands register." The two brothers are registered for approximately equal shares and C is given separate title to one land parcel.

Although colony law explicitly prohibits the sale or alienation of native lands to non-Gilbertese, it is common practice for government and mission agencies to enter long-term leasing contracts with Gilbertese landowners. In the following case we can observe how such a lease is created. The lease is granted on the principle that all persons with a vested interest in the leased properties must be unanimous in their consent.

Case 8 (Tamana Lands Court 9/1959). All parties with a vested interest in the parcels on Taiku 'estate' have been brought before the court to voice their consent to a long-term lease of these lands to the colony government. After all parties have expressed their consent, the magistrate enters the terms of the lease in the court record. The owners have given their consent to lease their lands on Taiku 'estate' for twenty-one years and have consented that their estate may be used for the construction and operation of the government primary school. The court further notes that "the conditions of leasing have been carefully explained to all the landowners."

Conveyance. Each title contains a separate clause that shows how the present title holder(s) acquired title to the property. The most common entries in this category, which reflect the streamlining and simplification resulting from the work of the most recent colony-wide lands commission in the early 1950s, include title transfers by way of direct inheritance from either a male ascendant or a female ascendant. Since both men and women can hold exclusive title to real property they are also capable of conveying title to any or all of their children. These methods of conveyance, together with other and less frequent ways of transferring title to real property, will be discussed separately and in more detail below.

CONVEYANCING

In 1964, there were a total of 639 persons on Tamana Island who held some kind of legal title to one or more of the 2,243 parcels of land. Each registered titleholder held an average of 3.5 parcels. A more detailed picture of the land distribution patterns on Tamana Island is presented in tables 17 and 18.

The data in tables 17 and 18 indicate that men have a slightly better chance than women to become, or be registered as, land title holders. If an estate is held by two or more persons, it is the male, if of age,

TABLE 17 Number of Land Parcels on Tamana by Sex and by Title of Ownership

	Male		Female		Total	
Title	No.	%	No.	%	No.	%
Exclusive	930	41.5	872	38.9	1802	80.3
Concurrent	354	15.8	87	3.9	441	19.7
Total	1284	57.3	959	42.8	2243	100

SOURCE: Tamana Island government records (data are for 1964).

TABLE 18 Number of Land Parcels on Tamana by Sex and by Productive Quality

	Male		Female		Total	
Quality	No.	%	No.	%	No.	%
Good	477	21.3	357	15.9	834	37.2
Medium	391	17.4	335	14.9	726	32.4
Poor	416	18.5	267	11.9	683	30.5
Total	1284	57.2	959	42.8	2243	100

SOURCE: Tamana Island government records (data are for 1964).

who is the most likely person to be registered as the custodian for the jointly held estate. This fact merely agrees with the slight status bias favoring men that governs Gilbertese social relations. But it is important to notice that women are capable of holding any form of title to real property and that their somewhat lower social status ranking does not affect the number and quality of land parcels that they receive or transfer from others. These statistics are supported by the statutory provision that allows women to acquire, possess, and transfer title to lands on an equal basis with men. This fact is important because men traditionally enjoy a higher social rank than women and because men dominate most transactions connected with land utilization and changes in ownership. The data in table 19 clearly reflect this male bias, but they do not invalidate the generalization that men and women, with respect to real property, exercise potentially the same kinds of rights and privileges.

The numerical data on land tenure patterns are corroborated by various lands court decisions recorded in the 1950s. All of the following cases serve to exemplify the application of one or more tenure principles to the formal adjudication, mediation, or arbitration of a concrete case involving the conveyance of land rights.

TABLE 19 Land Transfer Patterns on Tamana

Beneficiary	Benefactor				Gifts	
	Male		Female			
	No.	%	No.	%	No.	%
Male	771	58.9	381	55.9	132	52.4
Female	538	41.1	301	44.1	120	47.6
Total	1309		682		252	

SOURCE: Tamana Island government records (data are for 1964).

The most common mode of land conveyance is by direct inheritance. Rights by inheritance are conveyed either as *te mwi ni mane* 'from a male ascendant' or as *te mwi n aine* 'from a female ascendant.' Application of the inheritance principle may be complicated by any number of factors. Of these factors, the number, relative age, and sex of the legal heirs bring forth questions of equity. This is particularly true if the estate is small or of variable productive quality and if the legal heirs contest an even distribution of land parcels among all heirs on grounds of superior claim right. We have already seen how the principle of mutual consent is applied in cases involving joint land use and separation of title by estate partitioning (see cases 6, 7, and 8). In the following two cases we learn how additional consideration of male status superiority and consanguinity, as opposed to female status and adoption of collateral or affinal persons, can create an uneven distribution of the shares conveyed to male and female heirs.

Case 9 (Tamana Lands Court 19/1957). A, the widow of B, appears before the lands court to request that the estate of her deceased husband be distributed to B's sons only. A and B had three sons and three daughters. The court acknowledges A's privilege to propose the reconveyance of her deceased husband's estate, but they reject in principle A's wish to exclude B's daughters from the inheritance. "The members of the lands court agree that B's estate should be conveyed to his heirs. It is decided that title to B's entire estate should be conveyed to B's eldest son, as principal title holder, together with his younger siblings as residual title holders." The lands court, while it denies A's petition to convey separate title to her three sons and exclude her daughters, resolves the immediate issue of direct inheritance by accommodating the social principle of male status superiority with the legal device of joint ownership.

A similar case illustrates how additional facts, such as the availability of a written will and an adopted child, can complicate a conveyance by inheritance.

Case 10 (Tamana Lands Court 14/1957). A, a deceased woman, had testamented most of her land parcels to her adopted son. Smaller allotments of land parcels and taro pits had been willed to her four nephews and nieces. The will is contested by one of A's nephews on grounds that the estate of a childless person by law should revert to his nearest consanguineal relatives. It is the desire of this nephew to reduce the share willed to A's adopted son by one-fourth or, in essence, to restrict the inheritance share of the adopted child to one parcel of land. The case is further complicated by the additional knowledge that A herself was adopted and thus received part of her estate as 'the land of an adopted child.' The lands court decides, "Four of the heirs have not opposed the lands willed to A's adopted child. Only the land parcels conveyed to A by her adoptors should revert to their kinsmen. The remaining estate will be divided equally between A's own adopted child and her four consanguineal kinsmen mentioned in the will." While the lands court allowed heirs to contest the equitable distribution of inheritance shares, it also upheld the principle that a person adopted as a child has equal inheritance rights with natural children or consanguineal kinsmen. It is implied that the share conveyed to A's adopted child will revert to A's nephews and nieces only if the adopted person dies without natural issue.

The final case of inheritance involves a number of conflicting claims involving a written will, adoption, bastardy, a gift of land for nursing, and the rights of an absentee heir.

Case 11 (Tamana Lands Court 56/1951). Two women, A and B,

appear before the Tamana Lands Court to settle a disputed claim to the ownership of X, a land parcel. A, the appellant, is acting on new information concerning the former ownership of X. Because of this information, she feels that she has a superior claim to the parcel by virtue of lineal descent from the original owner. Land parcel X is claimed on behalf of C, its present owner, by B, his half-sister who is acting as his representative. As can be seen in figure 8, A's grandmother and B's

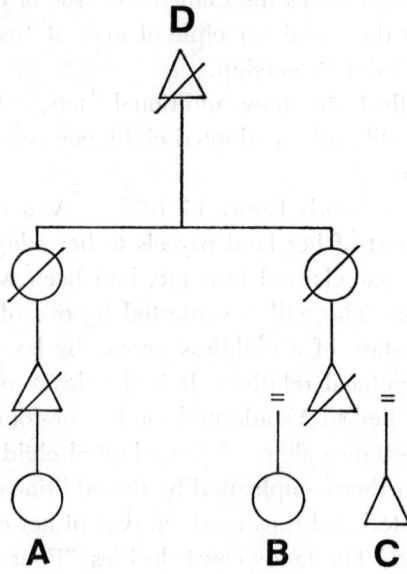

Figure 8. Case II genealogy.

grandmother were sisters and joint owners of the estate which the two sisters had received from D, their father. It is alleged that these sisters divided their father's estate by transferring title to all their jointly owned lands to A's grandmother. This was allegedly done because she had given D title to X during the other sister's absence from the island. Further complications arose when the daughter of A's grandmother's adopted sister willed a parcel of land to D after she had been nursed by D's father. The Tamana Lands Court rejected A's claim and upheld C's title to land parcel X.

It is not clear why the lands court chose to uphold C's claim to X, because mutual consent among all interested parties was not obtained prior to the official conveyance. Despite this, B's son received X, which technically should have reverted to A's grandmother, and he in turn conveyed X to his bastard son. It may be assumed that the lands court denied A's claim to X because her claim only concerned one parcel of land and because that parcel had been formally conveyed to D as 'the land of a bastard child.' Although this mode of conveyance is relatively infrequent, it may nevertheless precede a claim by direct inheritance (see table 19 under "Gifts").

I will now give examples of other modes of conveyance to illustrate how the tenure system allows individual land owners some slight latitude in land transference outside direct inheritance relationships. All of the following modes of conveyance can for all practical purposes be said to have the effect of statutory principle, because many traditional land transfer patterns have been codified in the Provisional Tamana Island Lands Code.[3] Such codification, as said above, does not necessarily determine the outcome of a particular case. The following case illustrates how the Tamana Lands Court in fact chose to ignore the statutory requirement that all bastard children receive title to one share of land from their progenitor's estate.

Case 12 (Tamana Lands Court 28/1957). A, the mother of a child born out of wedlock, appears before the court "to inform the court that the father of my child is B." The magistrate, speaking on behalf of the jurors, almost purposefully abandons judicial principle for common sense when he advises A that "the lands court readily recognizes the fact that B is the father of your child for the reason that B's parents, on the birth of the child, came to assist you to take care of him. Since the child is already well cared for, there is no further need to make arrangements for the child from the father's side."

On a later occasion, involving another case of bastardy, the lands court chose to follow the letter of the statute.

Case 13 (Tamana Lands Court 85/1958). A, the mother of a child born out of wedlock, appeals to the court for the support of her child. "The father of my child is B." B, the respondent, replies, "The child is not mine. It is true that I have had a private affair with the woman, but I am not the man who has fathered her child." The magistrate does not waste much more time on the case, but concludes that "the lands court confirms that the father of A's child is B as he himself has testified that he has had a private affair with A. The child will be registered as the legal owner of a land parcel located on the southern half of [the father's] 'estate.'"

A bastard child is by colony law entitled to receive title to one parcel of land from the estate of his most probable father. A title conveyed in this manner is recorded as 'the land of a bastard child.' Such a conveyance is subject to very few limitations or restrictions because mutual consent among the donor's consanguineal relatives or any other persons with residual interest in his estate is not required before the transaction can be completed. If, on the other hand, a man feels that he is only a probable and not the only possible father of the child, as in case 13, he may contest the title transfer and delay any final court decision about title transfer for some time. In cases where there is a reasonable uncertainty about the genitor's true identity, the lands court will usually defer action on the case for some years. The court simply waits until the child has grown sufficiently so that the court can choose a father for the child by comparing its features with those men who have admitted to having sexual relations with the child's mother. It is in this way that the duty to convey land title falls on the most probable father.

A land title conveyed under these circumstances may revert to the donor or his heirs if the illegitimate child dies without issue. This restriction appears to be the only limitation attached to the conveyance of title to a bastard child. It is otherwise legal for the new title holder to reconvey title to land received in this manner to his own adopted child or to give it as a gift to any other person without seeking the consent of the original title holder.

The reversionary limitation that attaches to many title transfers is most clearly expressed in instances of death without issue. If a title holder dies without issue, including adopted children, his entire estate reverts to his nearest consanguineal kinsmen. This general rule, which can easily generate various claims and counterclaims if the deceased person's estate is large or particularly valuable, is clearly expressed in a boundary case from Tamana. This case shows how joint title holders can protect their future estate interests against counterclaims by others.

Case 14 (Tamana Lands Court 1T/1958). A and B, two brothers, appeal to the lands court for title to part of the estate now held by C, their deceased mother's sister. C has never borne any children and is now too old to have any. Title to the jointly claimed lands is registered in C's name "together with A and B." C does not oppose the partitioning of the jointly held estate but requests that only her share of the estate be separated and that the remainder be left in joint tenancy with

A and B. For some unknown reason, the court agrees to partition the estate by giving C single title to one-fourth of the original estate while A and B are allowed joint tenancy to the other three-fourths. What has happened in this case is probably that A and B simply wish to secure their interest in the lands jointly held with their mother's sister. Although C would not be able to dispose of any part of the estate without first obtaining the explicit consent of A and B, it is much safer for the two brothers to take this official step prior to C's death. This eliminates any possibility of claims on their share by others unknown, who after C's death might claim ownership rights in the estate on grounds that they had either nursed C during her final debility or sickness or that C had made them a gift in return for some other favor.

A gift of land donated to a person in return for an act of kindness is known as *te aba n akoi* 'the land of kindness.' If such a transfer is contested by surviving heirs, the donor must be able to satisfy the lands court that the gift will not in any way jeopardize the welfare of the heirs. Such a claim would not be difficult to contest by the deceased person's natural or adopted heirs because, to be legal, the title transfer should have taken place when the donor was still alive and at a time when he could have obtained the consent of his future heirs. To my knowledge there are no cases which illustrate any claims against heirs for a land conveyed in this manner. There is more difficulty, however, with claims arising from the conveyance of land as *te aba ni kuakua* 'the land of nursing.' Such a conveyance is usually interpreted as a means to reduce the inheritance share of a person's heirs because they have somehow failed to take proper care of an ill or dying parent.

Generally speaking, any landowner has the right to donate one parcel of land to any person who has nursed or aided him during a period of illness or debility. A person's children would normally be expected to take care of their parent during such times of hardship. The child who assumes most of this responsibility may be given a parcel of land in recognition of his extra services. However, any stranger or nonrelative, who in the absence of a debilitated person's own children volunteers his services, may also be entitled to receive title to one parcel of land. If a nurse who is not related to the person whom he has nursed claims a share of a deceased person's estate, he must be prepared to prove neglect on the part of the children or relatives of the deceased.

Case 15 (Tamana Lands Court 20/1951). A, a woman, appeals to the lands court for a share of the estate owned by B, a deceased woman. A claims to have nursed B during the illness which resulted in B's death. A further claims that B's relatives failed to take care of their disabled and sick relative and that A was the only person who looked after B during the latter's illness. The lands court deferred any decision on A's claim until such a time that B's relatives could be summoned to court. It is not known from the records if A ever prosecuted her claim again or if the lands court made any attempt to summon B's surviving relatives to give testimony before the court.

Although this case is undecided, it illustrates a principal element of Gilbertese land litigation: any person who initiates a title claim to a parcel of land must act on his own initiative, and he often must demonstrate the legitimacy of that claim against great odds. Conveyance of land title as an act of reciprocity or as a gift is best facilitated when the donor is alive and can obtain the explicit approval of his heirs and kinsmen. Conveyances of this type most commonly involve marriage, adoption, exchange, or direct payment for a valued service. For example, at marriage a girl's father may give his daughter exclusive title to one parcel of land. In exceptional cases, a bride may receive a parcel of land from both of her parents. Such a gift does not exclude the girl from her normal inheritance privileges but merely provides her with one extra share as a form of dowry. A girl cannot claim to receive this share unless it is freely given to her, and it is said that parents seldom if ever give gifts of land to a daughter who remarries after divorce or widowhood.

In cases of adoption, which are quite frequent in Gilbertese society, the adopter fulfills his part of the adoption arrangement by formally transferring title to one or more parcels of land to his adopted child (see Lambert 1970:261–292; Silverman 1970:209–235).

A person can be adopted as either a 'child' or 'grandchild.' If he is adopted as a 'child,' he acquires the status of a natural heir. If adopted as a 'grandchild,' he becomes the recipient of one parcel of land from the adopter's estate. In both types of adoption the adopter must obtain the consent of his siblings, future heirs, or joint title holders before he can formalize the adoption. If an adopted child dies without issue, the land received in adoption will revert back to the nearest consanguineal relatives of the adopter. This implies that title to a parcel of land conveyed to an adopted child can only vest when the adoptee has offspring of his own. Since it is very rare to find land conveyances to adopted children who are not already in some way related to their adopter(s), it may be concluded that conveyance by adoption is an intrafamilistic device for reallocating land rights among those who already have a simultaneity of interests in a common family estate (Lundsgaarde 1970a:236–260).

Extrafamilistic conveyances, as we have seen, are extremely rare. In exceptional cases two title holders may decide to make an even exchange of two land parcels. Such an exchange is subject to the usual limitations imposed by the rule of consent. There is a noticeable reluctance on part of Gilbertese landowners to avail themselves of this option. In a very exceptional case a person may acquire title to a land parcel by outright purchase. Acquisition of title by purchase is a very recent practice, and it is presently limited to purchases of land parcels in the less densely populated islands in the archipelago.

In addition to the land conveyances involving reciprocity for an act of kindness or service as a nurse, the Tamanans infrequently will convey title as 'the land of suckling' to a person who has served in the capacity of wet nurse to the title holder's child.

All of these modes of conveyance were said to be in practice on Tamana Island in 1965. When queried about other conveyancing practices, informants denied that there were any. Yet it is evident from comparative data from other islands in the southern Gilberts that many more such principles have been employed in the more recent past (cf. Townsend n.d.). A reduction in the number of conveyance principles have followed hand in hand with the introduction of land registration records and a governmental policy of encouraging codification of individual island land tenure customs. The disproportionate number of titles conveyed by direct inheritance as opposed to other modes of conveyance may also be correlated with the exponential growth of the Gilbertese population in the twentieth century. It is more than likely that further study will reveal a direct and inverse relationship between the variety and number of noninheritance conveyancing principles and land scarcity. Whereas land ownership in the past was conceptualized in terms of wealth, prestige, and political capital, today it has come to signify the difference between life and death.

INTERESTS IN LAND AS PROPERTY

It is readily evident that the Gilbertese people have a variety of interests in land as an economic resource. It is much less obvious how such fundamental economic interests possibly correlate or conflict with a multitude of social, legal, and political interests that concern land as property. Yet it is these interests which ultimately determine how individuals and groups actually benefit from land as an economic resource. I shall attempt to outline some of the ways in which the Gilbertese conceptualize land as property by distinguishing among interests in land that vest in individuals, groups of persons, or in more loosely defined corporate entities. It must be emphasized that the expression *interests in land* refers to a variety of customary and legal rights which allow persons to control real property and that I use the word *vest* to denote a fixed right of enjoyment.

I have distinguished between individual and joint title. The illustrative court cases have exemplified the principal role of mutual consent in all land transactions involving the conveyance of title from one person to another. Analysis of these various modes of conveyancing and the restrictions placed on each of these can be most helpful in furthering our understanding of the rights and duties that define different kinds and degrees of land ownership.

We have already observed, for example, how both men and women as individuals can hold separate title to parcels of land. The right of individual ownership is affected neither by a person's sex, his age, nor his marital status. But we have also observed how a title holder must obtain the consent of others before he can undertake a title transfer. This alone serves to illustrate the significance of the reversionary interest that resides with the landowner's consanguineal kinsmen. This kind of limitation of a person's ownership rights also suggests that his estate interests only vest for the duration of his own lifetime.

Compared to English and American common law traditions, a Gilbertese landowner does not have what we would define as fee simple interest in his estate. One might then ask what ownership attributes remain if a title holder lacks the basic power to dispose of his lands as he wishes. Although there is no simple answer to this question, it is clear that exclusive or single title confers a great deal of social authority, power, and prestige upon the individual title holder. An exclusive title holder has the authority to decide how his landholdings shall be used and by whom, and he can evict those who illegally trespass upon his property. Most importantly, he can generally control the activities of his future benefactors by controlling the redistribution of individual land and taro plots by allocating smaller or larger or productive or unproductive parcels as he sees fit. An exclusive title holder can also command services and labor from those who reside on or derive a living from his estate. He can, in other words, discriminate in the allocation of substantial rewards to his heirs and relatives without necessarily disinheriting or otherwise ignoring the privileges of his kinsmen.

When two or more persons are registered as joint owners they exercise much the same rights as a single title holder. The basic difference between the two forms of estate interest is that there is an even greater limitation on their powers to redistribute land parcels to descendants and others. We might say that a joint title holder is bound by a duty to his title co-holder not to disturb the title until such a time that they can agree to partition the estate. It is important to note that joint tenants always are related to each other as either consanguineal or adoptive kinsmen. Two unrelated persons such as a husband and wife are never registered or treated as joint title holders of the same estate. In some cases, however, a widow may be formally appointed by the lands court or informally by her deceased husband's heirs as caretaker of her husband's undivided estate. This situation normally arises only if there are young children who are not yet capable of succeeding to the legal responsibilities of estate ownership.

Before analyzing any rights and interests that may come about as a result of caretaking, it is necessary to look briefly at the category of persons that must be consulted before a title holder takes any action with respect to the redistribution of his estate. These persons comprise a corporate entity that cannot be said to have any vested interest in a particular estate. Such persons simply have a series of privileges which complement the duties of a title holder.

I am now talking about that category of persons who must give their consent to a title holder's actions concerning his estate. We have already observed in the previous cases how various land transactions were finalized or postponed on the basis of the presence or absence of parties who were required to consent to a particular transaction. The privilege to give or withhold such consent from a title holder's proposed land transaction resides, in order of importance, with his siblings if the estate is undivided, natural or adopted children, collateral ascendants and descendants, and tertiary relatives who can demonstrate consanguineal ties to the title holder. It is now clear why this aggregate of persons is labeled a category rather than described as members of a group.

The Gilbertese concept of *utu*, defined broadly as 'family' and 'persons defined as consanguineal kinsmen,' is the most inclusive label which can be used to describe this unspecified category of persons (see Lundsgaarde and Silverman 1972:95–110, for a detailed discussion of Gilbertese kin groups and categories). A person who can claim to be of the same *utu* as a title holder has a residual right in the title holder's estate. Since, legally, his interests in that estate do not necessarily vest in the estate, he can only exercise his rights when the title holder or his legal heirs propose a change or redistribution of the properties included in that estate. Therefore, the rights of consanguineal kinsmen might be described as residual, conditional, or provisional. The precise description of these rights, which vary considerably under different family circumstances, is less important than awareness of this link between property rights and kinship affiliation.

As is evident from other chapters, the interplay between property rights and kinship affiliation is beset with analytical complexities. It is, for example, very difficult to separate the rights and duties of kinship from the obligations of 'estate' ownership. To illustrate the social basis and interrelatedness of these different variables, I will examine a court case from Nonouti Island which calls attention to the interplay between estate interests and kinship obligations.

Case 16 (Nonouti Lands Court 39/1961). A, a young man, has initiated formal legal action against B, his father, on grounds that his father has prevented him from deriving a living from the family estate. A testifies, "Both my father and my stepmother have been most unjust toward me, and I no longer reside with them. I have come before the lands court to appeal for separate title to one parcel of land on my father's 'estate' and for one of his taro pits so that I may make a living for myself. My father has warned me not to trespass on his lands. I am his only child."

The father replies to his son's charges by saying, "I have not quarreled with my son, and I have asked him to build his house next to ours, but he has refused to do so. When my son went abroad to work for the British Phosphate Commission, he never sent anything [i.e., money or goods] back to us. Despite that, I have already registered one taro pit in my son's name. I only own one parcel of land which I hold in joint ownership with my brothers and sisters. Since we have not yet divided our common estate among ourselves, I do not have any lands registered under my own name."

One of the lands court jurors then testifies on behalf of A's action by stating, "I can verify that A has always helped his father by providing him with coconut toddy and other necessities. When A returned from his job on Ocean Island, he once again assisted his father who refused his help."

The Nonouti Island magistrate, speaking for the lands court, curtly states the court's decision: "As B himself has stated . . . he does not object to his son's desire to derive a living from his estate, and B is free to work his taro pit as he pleases. If a second appeal is made to this court, it will be necessary to establish whether or not a wrong has been committed, and if so, it may be necessary to divide the disputed estate."

It could be argued that the magistrate's decision totally ignores A's legal rights to claim a share of his father's estate on the grounds that B has prevented his son from obtaining a livelihood from his estate (paragraph 1, section i, of the Native Lands Ordinance, 1956). On the other hand, it is very clear from this and similar cases that the lands court often seeks to mediate and arbitrate rather than adjudicate disputes between close relatives (see Lundsgaarde 1970b:242–264). To force the issue any further, the son would have to do one or more things to return the case to the lands court. He would have to demonstrate that his father had in fact physically prevented him from obtaining a satisfactory livelihood from the 'estate' and he would have to rally the support of his father's co-owners to his cause. Without any support from his senior kinsmen, it would be exceedingly difficult for A to benefit from a court settlement, because the issue then would probably appear as a contest of authority between junior and senior kinsmen. In such a contest, the junior member would have much to lose and little, if anything, to gain by his protest. We might also say that A's action has led us directly to the question of ownership versus possession.

Would it be correct to say, for example, that the lands court in fact denied A's legal claim to ownership when it was established that he already had possession? I think so, because ownership in the minds of most Gilbertese is associated with social status and kinship seniority. I would prefer, therefore, to treat ownership of real property together with kinship authority as one category and to conceptualize possession as a lesser type of right or privilege enjoyed by dutiful heirs. To discover who owns what property and why, we must begin to ask who is related to whom and how. One cannot sensibly comprehend the ideological basis for Gilbertese land tenure practices without linking together Gilbertese conceptions of family and proprietorship.

While any type of ownership title confers a series of rights, privileges, immunities, and powers upon an owner, it is important to re-emphasize that each title holder is bound to his kinsmen, co-owners, or even affinal relatives by a variety of both legal and moral duties.

To study ownership and possession in the context of Gilbertese land tenure is not an easy matter. We are dealing with a mixture of Gilbertese and British legal traditions which at best allow us to apply such concepts as official title, legal capacity, and legal power to describe a wide assortment of positive legal attributes invested in one or more landowners. In the most simple form, we could therefore define a landowner as a person who is registered with the local island government as the title holder of a particular parcel of land and is generally entitled by law to decide how and by whom his property is to be used or redistributed within the broad limitations set forth in the Native Lands Ordinance (see Lundsgaarde 1966:Appendix D–2).

Such Gilbertese administrative officials as magistrates, jurors, and scribes who sit on the island lands court should ideally decide property disputes in accordance with the statutory provisions spelled out in the Native Lands Ordinance or the local island's lands code. This would mean, for example, that the lands court would accept registration (i.e., title) as equivalent to absolute ownership. The lands court does in fact decide individual land claims either by classifying each new case in accordance with the statutory regulation which more or less fits the circumstances of the case or by ignoring the code in favor of any other authority that may help resolve a dispute. This other authority is best defined as Gilbertese tradition. In this context Gilbertese tradition would be defined as the rights and duties embedded in a matrix of cultural values, morals, beliefs, and attitudes concerning interpersonal relationships and rules of social conduct.

I am now prepared to argue that any investigation of Gilbertese ownership, possession, or use of real property will lead to a consideration of the subtle social distinctions between the categories of kinsman, spouse, relative, and stranger. I will attempt to illustrate how the relative position of a Gilbertese within his consanguineal 'family' and his affiliation with other similar 'families' through marriage or adoption exactly determine his capacities for controlling real property.

A Gilbertese becomes a blood relative by being accepted as the legitimate offspring of a married couple. An affinal relative is not conceptualized or regarded as a relative by the Gilbertese. As seen above, a bastard child may in fact be disclaimed by its known and natural father. In such a case, the father will transfer title of one of his lands to that child as prescribed by statute and thus exclude that child from membership in his 'family.'

A child, a youth, or a young adult, even if married and a parent himself, is under the direct authority of his parents and his senior kinsmen. The authority of senior kinsmen, which is considerable by our standards, is sustained by their legal powers to control the 'family estate.' The rights and privileges of land ownership and possession traditionally reside with senior kinsmen. Since both men and women can independently hold title to lands, a legitimate child will in fact belong to two different 'families.' He will simultaneously be a member of his father's and his mother's consanguineal 'family' units.

If only one senior person within the same 'family' and residential unit holds title to land, he is spoken of as the landowner. A landowner is free to use his lands as he pleases provided, of course, that his actions do not violate the nominal regulations prescribed by the Native Lands Ordinance, 1956 (G.E.I.C. 1963). Paragraph 1, section i, of this ordinance defines the authority of a real property owner as follows: "An owner controls the use of his property except that if it is proved to the satisfaction of the Lands Court that an owner is preventing his issue from obtaining a livelihood from his land, the Lands Court may order that some of his property be set aside for the maintenance of his issue. The Lands Court may also direct that the owner shall not make use of such property himself. The ownership of property set aside in this way is not transferred" (G.E.I.C. 1963:8).

It must be emphasized that this paragraph defines what I term *exclusive ownership* or *single title*. As long as a person is alive his title to real property is immune from the claims of others. Included with the title, however, is the important provision that others may use and possess part of that estate if they are closely related to the title holder. This means that close kinsmen can claim tenure privileges to part of an estate owned by a blood relative. They make such a claim operative either by obtaining the explicit consent of the property owner himself or, if the relationship between the two persons is not an amicable one, by bringing the matter before the island lands court.

The power or control exercised by a title holder is not lessened by the rights of others to seek redress before the lands court. In fact, a landowner can sustain his authority over his junior kinsmen in a number of different ways. For example, he may legally refuse to part with any of his land parcels when he is too old to work his 'estate' himself, or he may threaten to transfer title to nonrelatives. In these and similar ways a title holder can influence the behavior of others. Land allows a person to create loyalty, if not devotion, and respect in his subordinates and successors.

Examination of lands court cases reveals that Gilbertese landowners often do use their position to reward dutiful and obedient children or, as may be the occasional case, to make the future prospects for disobedient children as grim as possible. Real property in the past as well as in the present may be said to be a significant regulatory device for managing family relationships.

A contractual relationship comes into existence when two qualified persons enter a more or less formal agreement to honor an obligation. In the Gilbertese case, one can speak of contractual relations in marriage, some types of adoption, and a residual category of formalized friendship arrangements. I will briefly describe adoption and friendship as forms of a contractual agreement and then turn to a more detailed analysis of the marriage contract.

An adoption creates a series of new relationships between the adopter and his kinsmen—siblings, parents, and natural children—and between the adopter and the natural parents of the adoptee. Adoption most commonly takes place within the 'family,' that is, the preferred adoptee is already related to the adopter. Adoption of this type, which may be either of a 'child' or a 'grandchild,' is used to redistribute lands within the 'family' in such a way that those with less property will obtain a more adequate share of the ancestral estate. An adoption contract between two relatives may be interpreted as a way to extend inheritance privileges to collateral relatives. The total effect on the overall system of tenure is that individual land parcels remain with a particular family unit for a long period of time. In consequence, the landholdings of persons belonging to the same family are contiguous, or at least part of the same 'estate.'

The performance of a personal service, such as taking care of an estate for an absentee owner or helping another in times of illness or debility, can also give rise to a contractual relationship. We can recognize here the basic elements of a contract, that is, the public recognition of a relationship involving legal rights and duties, the distinction between casual and binding agreements, and recourse to formal procedures for invoking a breach of promise or forcing a settlement. For example, a debilitated person who allows another person to assist him with household chores, to procure food, or to provide medical assistance is bound by a moral duty to reward his caretaker with a formal gift of land.

Here it is again significant to note the restriction on such transfers specified by paragraph 5, section ii, of the Native Lands Ordinance, 1956: "If the member's [sic] of the owner's family refuse to nurse him, then a stranger [i.e., a nonrelative] may be regarded [sic] for nursing him. An owner may not choose a nurse from outside his family unless he has successfully prosecuted them in the Native Court under Island Regulation No. 62" (G.E.I.C. 1963:9). In any case involving a contractual relationship, it must be assumed that one of the principals is a property title holder and the rights of a title holder to dispose of his property are conditioned by his relationships to his kinsmen. These assumptions may be clarified by considering Gilbertese marriage as a primary relationship between two family units as symbolized by the ceremonial union of two junior family members. For example, the marriage on Tamana Island described below shows how a modern Gilbertese marriage ceremony is the result and cause of a series of family negotiations and transactions in real property.

Marriage has become a religious ritual which symbolizes the acceptance of Christian ideology. This ideology does not conceptualize marriage as part of a complex network of property relations. Yet it is perfectly clear that traditional property relations have continued even with the acceptance of a new religious and moral ideology.

During the course of fieldwork, I had numerous opportunities to attend and observe a variety of modern Gilbertese marriage ceremonies. One of these may serve to illustrate the multiple dimensions of the marriage contract. The bride belonged to the 'family' that had come to regard me as theirs, because I lived on their 'estate' and did most of the detailed genealogical and case study work with members of their 'family.' The groom was a young man from Bakaka hamlet. The religious ceremony took place in the London Missionary Society church.

Few people were in attendance at the church ceremony and that was perhaps just as well. The groom was drunk. He had been drinking great quantities of the local brew—fermented coconut toddy. Drinking any alcoholic beverage, particularly on predominantly Protestant Tamana Island, is regarded as unacceptable, if not altogether sinful, behavior. He had been granted specific permission to imbibe, however, by his elders on the grounds that he should be allowed to calm his nerves before the event that would elevate a careless bachelor to a responsible householder and a future parent. Although the young man dropped the wedding ring on the floor of the church, the missionary in charge of the ceremony, as well as the other Gilbertese missionaries and church deacons who were present, did not seem to mind.

Following the ceremony, the bride and groom led the church attendants to an adjoining building in which more than one hundred relatives of the couple were seated in preparation for 'the feast with the missionary.' But just as the young couple sat down and eased themselves toward the eating mats, the alcohol got the better of the groom, and he turned to his bride and vomited on her dress. Two of his senior kinsmen helped the young man to his feet and quietly led him home to his father's house. The bride briefly stepped outside to shake the vomit from her dress. She returned to the room and the feast proceeded as if nothing had happened. The small church choir entertained the participants during the meal. When the eating mats had been cleared the people, as is the custom, stretched out on the floor to digest, rest, and enjoy the conversation.

Solemn speeches were offered by the missionary and representative elders from both families. The missionary was presented with handsome gifts of new and colorful lavalava cloth. The bride left with a group of her husband's kinsmen. She was destined to spend three nights at her father-in-law's house.

In pre-Christian times the bride would be required to give public evidence of her purity. Following the couple's first sexual intercourse the bride would give her mother the sleeping mat on which the marriage had been consummated. The blood on this mat, accepted as prima facie evidence of the girl's virginity, was proudly exhibited by her mother. The wedding guests would share the parents' pride by smearing their faces with the bride's blood. A bride was accepted on the principle of *caveat venditor* or, if unable to satisfy her husband of her virginity, she could be rejected and the marriage annulled. This principle, the test of virginity, is said to be followed by a few moderns although some husbands claim that they do not care one way or another about their wife's premarital habits.[4]

After three days, I was invited to join a group representing the bride's family charged with the responsibility for "fetching the bride and groom." We arrived at the groom's place of residence and were formally seated directly across from an equal number of men representing the groom's family. We shared a special meal prepared from the finest local foods. During the meal the men from both sides engaged in what appeared to be a formalized exchange of derogatory comments about the other side's family. They said, for example, "This is the toughest chicken that I have ever tasted," and "I regret that our children will not see food like this at your house." Immediately following the meal, several girls appeared and began to peel off our clothes. Each person had anticipated that this would happen, so everyone was decked out in several layers of new lavalava cloth and a brand new singlet. The meaning of this was simple—we were symbolically exchanging valuables to signify the union of two separate families.

The bride and groom, who were passive participants in all of this, now rose and came with us. They were destined to spend three days at the bride's household before they would finally establish their new home on the 'estate' belonging to the groom's father.

Although it is unwise to test a reader's patience too long by lingering on anecdotal descriptions of fieldwork experiences, I do believe, however, that the synoptic description of this wedding touches on many fundamental principles of Gilbertese land tenure. I will now expand the discussion of this particular case to illustrate the wide ramifications of the Gilbertese marriage contract.

The church ceremony represents a public means of expressing faith in the basic truths of Christianity. Marriage is a spiritual union of a man and a woman, not merely a permissible sexual arrangement between adults, and it is a relationship which presupposes the creation of a Christian family. The Gilbertese accept these basic views, believe them to be correct, and as with most other religious faiths, it is believed that the formulation and execution of these principles in actual practice sets man apart from other animals.

These idealized precepts of marriage as a holy union contrast rather sharply with the pragmatism of Gilbertese life. For example, the marriage described above, like most other Gilbertese marriages, was carefully arranged by the parents. Parents of marriageable young people attempt to choose a spouse for their son or daughter on the basis of the ability of the future spouse to work hard at the tasks required of adult persons of their sex and on account of the real property which will become available to the couple for their immediate use and the property which in due time will pass into their possession and eventual ownership.

It should also be noted that the sequence of feasts held to celebrate the marriage, including the ceremonial exchange of clothing by two groups of family representatives, suggests that Gilbertese marriage involves more than the change of social status for two persons. In fact, the festivities at the groom's house were mixed with more serious business. During the three day stay at the groom's house, the groom's father announced to his kinsmen which land parcels he intended to give to his son at an unspecified future time. Both the bride and groom were also told exactly which parcels of the family estate they would be allowed to use, that is, treat as theirs. Similarly, when the groom was brought to the bride's place of residence, he was shown which lands they could use. The bride's father also announced that he wanted to give his daughter a gift in the form of 'the land of a woman.'

The most intriguing part of all this is the fact that the groom's father publicly promised future title to the estate for which he was now giving the couple full possession. The bride's father, on the other hand, took immediate steps to transfer a land parcel to his daughter. His gift of land would not, however, subtract from the expected inheritance share going to the daughter at the time of her father's death or final estate settlement. I interpret the action of the bride's father as equivalent to giving someone a bonus for having conformed to the wishes of a benefactor because this gift of land was entirely voluntary. There is no way in which a girl can legally claim or demand such a parcel of land from either of her parents who in turn are not bound by any duty except perhaps a moral one to give such a gift to a daughter upon her first marriage.

If, on the other hand, a girl should be rejected by her husband or if the girl has a bad reputation, that is, making her an unlikely marriage prospect, she may be given the smallest possible share that parents can give to a child. Because of this, a girl who engages in premarital sexual relations cannot hope to marry as prosperous a man as might otherwise have been the case.

Parents of a girl, therefore, negotiate the marriage contract with the parents of a boy with at least two things in mind: the girl's reputation in the community and their own willingness to compensate for previous indiscretions with future title rights to real property. The Tamanans now disclaim that they pay any serious attention to whether a girl is a virgin before her first marriage.

There are other more elaborate and traditional forms of property transactions that originate with a single marriage contract. If, for example, a young bride wants to cater to her husband's father's brother by serving him special foods at community or family feasts, by annointing him with coconut oil during dances, or by granting him sexual favors, she would become eligible to receive a parcel of land as 'a land of love,' 'a land of kindness,' or as 'a land of an in-law.' These gifts of land from a man to his brother's son's wife could vary in both size and quality. The particular mode of conveyance also tells us something about the nature of the relationship between the two persons—only a 'land of an in-law' gift would imply that they were sexual partners.

It should also be noted that the approved sexual relationship between in-laws, in addition to formalizing a relationship between a man and his brother's son's wife, could exist between a man and his wife's mother or sister (Maude 1963). Although the custom is no longer practiced on Tamana Island, its faint survival on other islands attests to the numerous possibilities for land exchanges resulting from a single marriage. Land transactions between in-laws not only symbolized the unity of two larger family units, but proved to be an effective device for consolidating land holdings. We can be quite certain that a desire for highly prized parcels of land, in the past as well as in the present, competes favorably with any romantic, religious, or sexual motives affecting the creation and continuity of a Gilbertese marriage. A couple can reap substantial inheritance benefits for their children by remaining married, and it is still risky business to ignore the wishes of parents.

The facts of life in the Gilberts are obvious to most islanders—a person with few parcels of land at his disposal is destitute, and a person with no land whatever lives a marginal social existence. The status of a Gilbertese is in more than one sense equivalent to his 'estate.'

On the one hand, a person is guaranteed by birth certain land use privileges together with the prospect of future land ownership by virtue of his membership in a category of consanguineally related kinsmen. Ownership and possession of land and other forms of real property allow a person to provide for his children and aging parents; it lends stability and security during old age and debility; and it guarantees a significant political voice in the community. The powers of a title holder are only limited by his kinship role and by law. Traditional morality demands that kinsmen reciprocate and cooperate in the management of 'family' resources. Present-day Gilbertese land laws require a title holder to obtain the consent of his kinsmen before he initiates any property transaction that might involve any lessening of his kinsmen's residual tenure rights.

On the other hand, a spouse, adopted child, or friend of a land title holder, may also come to enjoy both use and ownership rights otherwise reserved for consanguineal kinsmen. Title rights in real property remain totally unaffected by a person's marital status, because any married person can convey title to his estate without obtaining the prior consent of his spouse or fictive kin. A comparatively complex system of reciprocal rights and duties together with the occasional use of various 'gift' conveyances safeguard the individual's ability to survive and protect him against any fortuitous inequities in the enjoyment of real property.

CONCLUSION

The systematic codification of Gilbertese land tenure principles and the enforcement of property laws by native courts and colonial administrators have virtually eliminated the unhappy prospect of anyone's becoming landless and economically destitute. The relative prosperity of Gilbertese tenants is today threatened by the increasing reduction in both size and quality of land parcels that an individual owner can hope to use and control. Continuation of the land tenure system described in this chapter must sooner or later create a critical shortage of available land parcels. The numerical growth of the Gilbertese population as a whole promises to precipitate the ongoing processes of estate fragmentation.

All of the cases examined in this chapter illustrate the seriousness with which the Gilbertese regard land ownership and use. The quantitative data on succession suggest a growing preference for direct parent-child title transference together with a corresponding decline in the number of land gifts to nonrelatives. These realities point to a dilemma for the Gilbertese. If the people, in an attempt to adapt to economic changes and a strictly monetary economy, lessen their traditional emphasis on family and kinship bonds, they will simultaneously disturb the tenure principles created and perpetuated by a reliance on these bonds. Although I hesitate to characterize the Gilbert Islands as a so-called developing nation, there can be no doubt that even the most remote island setting will feel the impact of modernization. Wage-earning opportunities outside the colony have created a false sense of progress in the minds of some who now feel that land ownership is only a traditional mode of survival. The future chances for deriving a living from wage income alone must realistically be viewed as a possibility reserved for a very small minority of islanders (cf. Couper 1967:68–86).

Similarly, the Gilbertese cannot look to emigration as a way to lessen the numerical pressure on their resources because other Pacific island communities now face much the same problems of land scarcity. The tenacity of traditional modes of coping with existence if exposed to novel circumstance and foreign setting is amply illustrated by data from the relocated Gilbertese communities in the British Solomon Islands Protectorate and the Banaban Gilbertese on Rambi Island in the Fiji Islands (see Maude 1968:315–342; Knudson 1964; Silverman 1971).

NOTES

1. It is a pleasure to acknowledge the many constructive criticisms and suggestions of an earlier draft of this chapter that were made by all the volume contributors together with Harry E. Maude and Martin G. Silverman.
2. In addition to the registration of individual land parcels, it is standard practice to treat each of the following as a real property subject to the same limitations of ownership that pertain to land:

   (a) *Te rua:* A taro or *babai* pit. *Te babai (Cyrtosperma chamissonis)*, taro, is the only crop systematically cultivated by the Gilbertese. Taro plants are grown in large pits excavated deeply enough to allow for a constant supply of water (cf. Catala 1957:67–75). A large taro pit may be subdivided into smaller sections owned by different persons. Ownership of a taro pit or any part thereof is recorded in the same manner as lands.

   (b) *Te niba:* A small excavated pit capable of holding one taro plant only. On Tamana Island there are very few large taro pits. Taro cultivation is thus predominately confined to *niba* pits.

   (c) *Te nei:* A small brackish pond filled with stagnant subsurface water. It is used exclusively by women who use it to soak both pandanus and coir sennit materials employed in the manufacture of mats, thatch, and rope. Ponds owned by two or more women are marked by boundaries. Ownership is transferred to female relatives only. On the southern atolls, *nei* also denotes a large fishpond used, paraphrasing Catala (1957: 136), to "park" small fish of the species *Chanos chanos*.

3. The following is a free translation of the Provisional Lands Code for Tamana Island. It was adopted by the Tamana Island Council on June 16, 1950. The code is used as a general guideline for local government officers charged with both judicial and administrative duties. It should be viewed as a shorthand expression of local land tenure customs rather than as a legal document imbued with full statutory powers. The original Gilbertese language version of the lands code is on file with the Tamana Island government.

1. *Registration.* Ownership of lands, taro pits, *niba*, and soaking ponds shall be established by entry in the lands register. Only the native magistrate, Chief Kaubure, and lands scribe may make entries in the lands register. They shall only enter judgements given by the lands court, and they must give the number of the relevant case in the minutes book and sign and date all entries. Pits, ponds, and *niba* which are not registered may be used by the owner of the land on which they are situated.
2. *Partition of Estates.* A father or a mother may give a land *inter vivos* to his or her child if the lands court approves the conveyance. The lands court shall inquire into the opinion of the other children of the prospective donor before deciding whether the conveyance shall be approved. If the court considers that the remaining land of the parent is insufficient for the other children, it shall not approve the conveyance.
3. Parents may bequeath their lands jointly and an offspring may dispute the partition on the grounds that he or she has received land from only one of his or her parents. If each offspring has received sufficient land for his or her support, the lands court shall confirm the partition.
4. A parent may partition his lands to his offspring by will in the manner he wishes, but he must provide each of them with sufficient land for his support. An offspring may not be disinherited even if guilty of neglecting his parent.
5. Normally the share of a son shall exceed the share of a daughter, but if giving a son a larger share would entail leaving a daughter without sufficient land for her support, their shares may be made equal. The dowry granted to a daughter on her marriage may only be taken back by the parent if the daughter is guilty of neglecting the parent or if insufficient land is left for the support of the parent's remaining children.
6. *Wills.* The will of a landowner shall be confirmed by the lands court if it conforms with the provisions of this code. A written will may not be superseded by verbal bequests but may only be amended in writing. Verbal bequests will not be upheld by the lands court if they are disputed, and the court shall in such cases effect a partition without paying regard to the disputed will.
7. *Death without Issue.* The court shall divide the lands of a deceased landowner without issue among his next of kin in such a manner as to avoid excessive subdivision, and it shall take into account the needs of the heirs. The shares of males and females shall not normally differ. When

two brothers or sisters or a brother and sister are joint owners of land received from a parent and one of them dies without issue, the other shall obtain sole possession of the land to the exclusion of the remaining brothers and sisters.
8. *Multiple Marriages.* When a landowner has had offspring by more than one spouse, such offspring shall have equal claims to his lands on his demise.
9. *Adoption.* A 'land of the adopted' may only be given if the adoption has previously been approved by the lands court. An adoption shall be approved by the land court if it is confirmed that the natural children of the adopter or his next of kin if he has no natural children will be left with sufficient land for their support after the gift of a 'land of the adopted.' If, however, the natural children are guilty of neglecting their parent or live elsewhere and cannot look after him, the adoption may be approved regardless of their claims. An adoption may be annulled by the lands court on the request of the adopter if it is confirmed that the adopted child has not fulfilled his obligations. If an adoption has not been annulled prior to the death of the adopter, the adopted child may be granted a 'land of the adopted' by the lands court notwithstanding the failure of the adopter to make such a bequest.
10. Only a brother or sister of the natural parent may adopt a child as his or her son or daughter. In such adoptions the child may inherit land from the adoptive parent and his or her spouse and may be disinherited by the natural parent. In all other adoptions the child shall inherit land from his or her natural parents. An only child may not be adopted as a son or daughter but only as a grandson or granddaughter.
11. An adopted grandson or granddaughter may not be given more than one land plot, one pit, one pond, and five *niba* by the adopter. The adoption of a stranger is not prohibited. If the adopted person dies without issue, the 'gifts of the adopted' shall revert to the donor or his heirs. If the adopted person dies leaving issue, the 'gifts of the adopted' shall pass to such issue, and the reversionary interest of the donor is lost.
12. *Mutual Adoptions.* When two persons adopt each other's children and only one of such persons makes a 'gift of the adopted,' he or his heirs may demand the return of such a gift.
13. *Land of a Bastard.* A land given by a father to his illegitimate offspring shall revert to his estate if (1) the recipient dies without issue and has not bequeathed the land as a 'land for nursing' or a 'land of the adopted'; and (2) provided that the original donor or his legitimate children have nursed the deceased during his last days.
14. A 'gift for nursing' may be given only by a will which is confirmed by the lands court. It may be given to a stranger only if all the members of the donor's family refuse to undertake to do the final nursing before the donor's death. A 'gift for nursing' shall not exceed one land plot, one pit, one pond, and five *niba*. Reversion shall be as for a 'gift of the adopted.'
15. *Land Gifts and Sales.* Land may only be given or sold if the consent of the next of kin and of the lands court is granted. The next of kin are the children of the landowner or, if he is childless, his brothers and sisters or, if he has no brothers or sisters, his aunts and uncles or their children on the side of the parent from whom the land was received.

16. *Exchanges.* Landowners may exchange lands if the lands court gives its consent. Such consent shall not be given if the lands differ considerably in value. It is immaterial whether the lands are both on Tamana or whether one is on another atoll. Pits may be similarly exchanged. The reversionary rights attached to a land given in exchange shall be transferred to the land received in the exchange.
17. An absentee landowner shall be free to chose whomsoever he desires to use his land, and his next of kin may not dispute his choice.
18. *Improvements.* When a person wishes to dig a pit, pond, or a *niba* on the land of another person, he must first obtain the consent of the landowner and the lands court. After the pit, pond, or *niba* is constructed, he shall report the fact to the lands court, and when the construction has been confirmed by inspection, it shall be registered in the lands register by the lands court.

4. The following notes have been excerpted from an unpublished document containing the resolutions adopted by the London Missionary Society (L.M.S.) Conference held on Abaiang Island on 10–13 December, 1957:

(1) *Pagan Marriage:* The marriage of a man and a woman who have already lived together before they married, is considered a pagan marriage, and Christians are, therefore, forbidden to attend the wedding feast when such people are married. And about the new way of marriage, as ministers have now been allowed to perform marriages, Christians are forbidden to attend a wedding feast in honour of a marriage performed by the Magistrate. Christians may have, and join, the wedding feast of a true marriage performed by a Minister.
(2) The feast at midnight after the couple have been together for the first time. Christians are forbidden to have a feast at midnight in honour of the first being together of the couple; for it is disgraceful to know it. Christians are forbidden to have a feast in honour of it because it is a pagan custom.

The following paragraph, excerpted from the same document quoted above, is but one example of the doctrinal thinking that sustains religious factionalisms: "(8) Religion and government. L.M.S. adherents on all islands should unanimously aim at selecting Christians to fill government posts as far as possible so that the government is not in the hands of pagans or Roman Catholics."

8

LAND TENURE IN A TEST TUBE: THE CASE OF PALMERSTON ATOLL

Ron Crocombe

INTRODUCTION

Palmerston Atoll provides a rare example of a land tenure system which has been developed in isolation by persons with minimal knowledge of other tenure precedents. Whereas less than a hundred years ago all rights were claimed by just one man (though his claim was in dispute) distinct rights have since emerged at ten separate levels.[1]

An effective claim to Palmerston was made by William Marsters on the grounds of long undisturbed possession and the investment of labor and capital. Today, rights are based primarily on inheritance from Marsters, through one or another of the three lineages which derived from his three wives to form the basic social division on the atoll today.[2] Other rights in the atoll are the sovereign rights shared by the governments of New Zealand and the Cook Islands.

The growth of the system is clear. For many years the atoll was worked as a single unit under Marsters's autocratic control. As resources were limited and their exploitation offered economic, social, or psychological advantages to persons with superior rights to them, disputes arose when his sons came of age. Marsters found it necessary to share some of his rights with them and made laws for this purpose. After his death, disputes not provided for in Marsters's laws seem to have been dealt with on an ad hoc basis until their continuing occurrence led the heads of the three lineages to lay down additional laws. With the increasing complexity of relations between men and land and

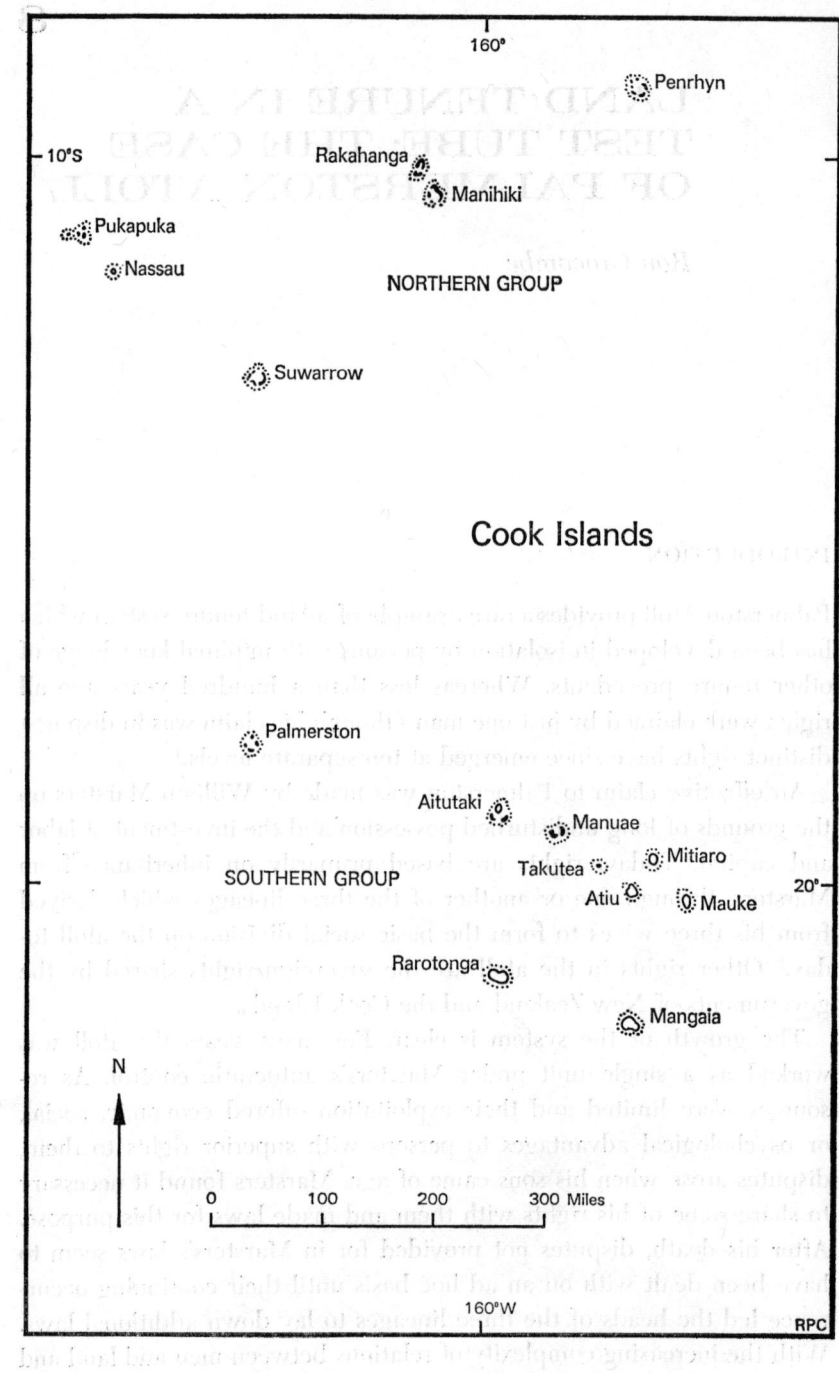

the increase in the atoll's population, an increasingly complex system of land tenure evolved and continues to evolve. It is interesting that such a tiny population (ninety-five at the time of this study) living in such extreme isolation built a relatively complex system of tenure. The system which functions today is the product of the atoll's human history, which has been greatly conditioned by the physical and cultural context.

Palmerston is a very isolated, small atoll of the northern Cook Islands.[3] The reef, which measures about 7 miles from north to south and about 5 miles from east to west, covers about 3,600 acres, and the lagoon, completely enclosed by reef, about 5,000 acres. Several shallow natural depressions in the reef provide narrow, and at times dangerous, passages into the lagoon for small boats. The total land area is only 357 acres spread over six main islets and a number of smaller islets and sandbanks. The islets are composed of coral rubble and sand and are of very limited fertility except where humus has developed a thin topsoil in the interior areas. Although rainfall averages 83 inches per year, water supply is limited by lack of storage, as the natural freshwater lens is quite small. Hurricanes have struck with destructive force about once each decade. Serious hurricanes destroy the main land-derived foods but do not greatly affect those from lagoon, reef, or sea.

By comparison with larger atolls, Palmerston's population density is not high.[4] The atoll was not inhabited at the time of European contact although there is evidence of former habitation by Polynesians (Gill 1885:37). For Polynesian people with a preindustrial technology it was probably not permanently habitable because it is subject to drought, hurricane, and tsunami.[5] The introduction of improved water and food storage facilities, radio, and relief supplies has made it permanently habitable, but not for many people. The islanders do not remain on Palmerston and become so numerous that survival is threatened. Most of them emigrate, and those who remain do so because of assumed material, social, or psychological disadvantages elsewhere.[6]

Throughout the history of the atoll various human inhabitants, as well as some nonresidents, have tended to claim certain rights for themselves, at the expense of the rights of others, beyond those that are likely to give them extra material advantage. That is, they have manifested what is probably a universal human tendency to expand their physical area of influence. However, they have been willing to concede

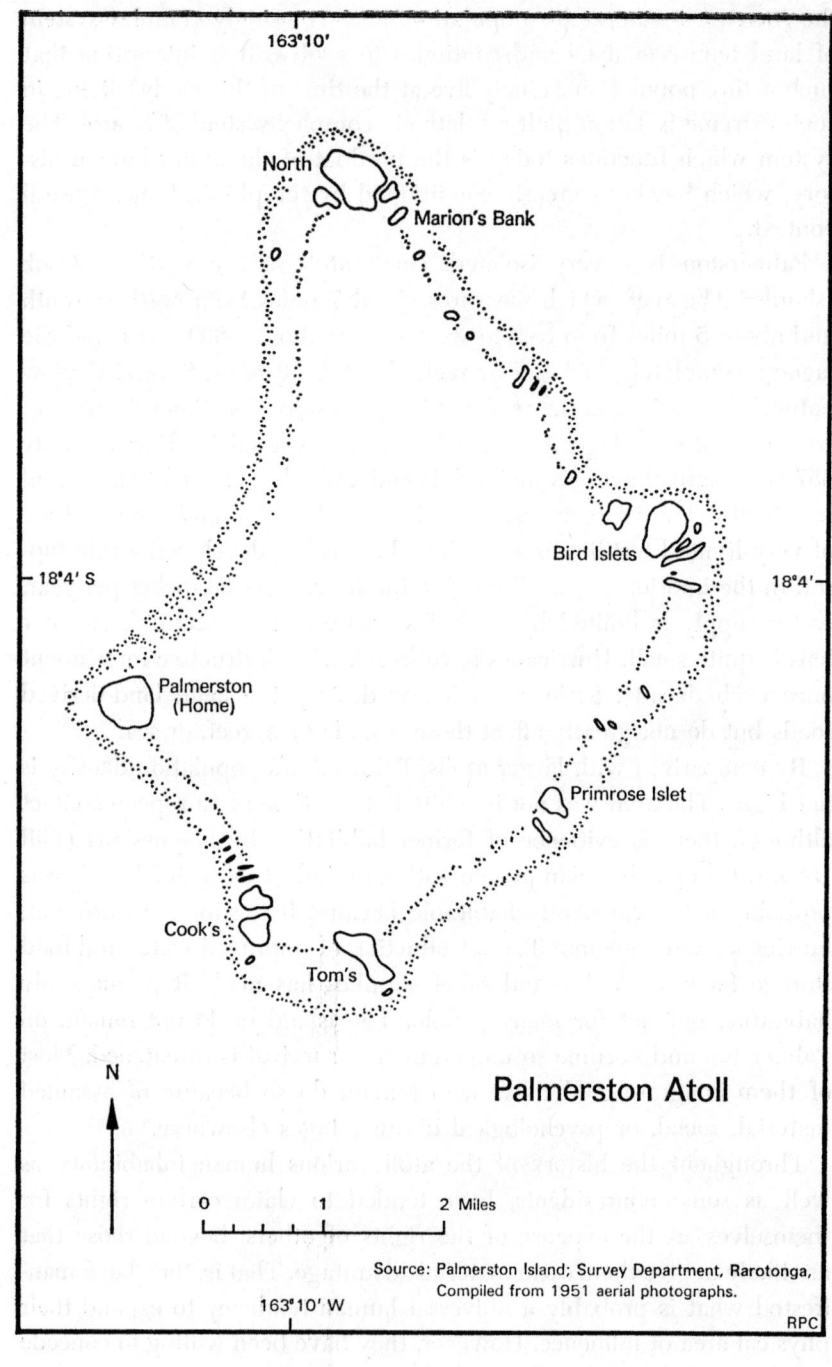

THE CASE OF PALMERSTON ATOLL

spatial rights to others in return for control over them, superior status to them, or some other advantage from them.

This is exemplified in the strongly possessive attitudes toward some sandbanks that are only used for a few unimportant products that could just as easily be found elsewhere.

No surveying equipment has been used on Palmerston. It has never been worthwhile for any external agency to send such equipment in, and the islanders today want to keep it out.[7] There are no written records or registers of land rights and the existing system apparently functions adequately without them.

Land boundaries are most commonly marked by puka trees or by double rows of coconuts. One party owns each row, and the boundary is an unmarked line between them. With the exception of the settlement area, where rows of stones or lilies mark the boundaries, boundaries between the three lineages are straight lines running from the beach on the ocean side to the beach on the lagoon side. Boundaries within lineages are marked by artificial soil ridges in the case of garden pits,[8] and by stones, trees, and footpaths in the case of arrowroot plots and house sites. Individually held trees are notched or otherwise marked, but as marks are neither adequately standardized nor sufficiently clear, some confusion and petty dispute result.

Probably in part because of the technical difficulties of demarcation, the beaches, reefs, and lagoon have never been subdivided in any way and are not claimed by any particular segment of the population.

The main agricultural implements are bush knives for copra cutting and shovels for garden culture. Axes are used for tree felling and carpentry tools for construction. Simple fishing gear is the other main technological aid to production.

Contact with the outside world is limited to radio and to the visit of a trading schooner about once or twice a year. Cruising yachts call rarely, and once every few years a vessel of the New Zealand navy pays a brief visit during training exercises.

Resources suitable for human exploitation include fish, shellfish, crustaceans, seaweeds, turtles, coral, and other products of the reef, lagoon, and ocean. The land grows a number of plants, mostly introduced by humans. Some seabirds nest on the atoll or rest there during migration; bosun birds settle from about July to December. Crabs are found, and turtles come to certain islets to lay their eggs. Pigs, fowls, and dogs are domesticated.

Most foods and raw materials are obtained or produced by the household which uses them. The exploitation of surplus beyond subsistence is limited by the environment, by the small quantities that are or could be produced, and by the long distance to markets. Few products are economic to transport, let alone process, preserve, and package, under such circumstances.

In the 1950s goods and services were mostly financed through the sale of copra.[9] Salaries and allowances from government employment brought in more cash than copra, but it was very unevenly distributed as the only salaried posts were those of resident agent, radio operator, teachers, medical assistant, and meteorological observer. Most of these posts were held by Palmerston people.[10] Much smaller quantities came as gifts from absent relatives, friends, and wellwishers and, after hurricanes, from relief organizations. The government and the Cook Islands Christian Church sent some supplies for the school, medical dispensary, church, and so forth. There is a very limited and spasmodic sale of dried fish, bêche-de-mer, live turtles, and turtle shells, as well as of a few artifacts of wood, coconut fibres, pandanus, and shell. These items are sold to passing ships or sent to relatives in Rarotonga, Aitkutaki, or Manihiki for sale, barter, or gift exchange. Total cash income averaged perhaps NZ$35 to NZ$40 per capita per year.

In the days before radar and electronic stormwarning devices, the greatest source of many foreign products was shipwrecks, vessels carrying timber from the west coast of America to Australia being the most common victims. The church and almost all houses on the atoll today are built from materials retrieved from wrecked vessels.

Apart from their own personal codes, values, and expectations, the first persons on Palmerston were in a socio-cultural vacuum. The atoll belonged to no one and fell within no legal jurisdiction. Relations with others who landed were strictly ad hoc, as illustrated by the killing and spearing of beachcombing seamen there by one another in 1811 (Rhodes 1937:176). British naval vessels had power to deal with disputes involving British subjects on unclaimed islands of the Pacific such as Palmerston, but their calls were decades apart. The declaration of the British protectorate in 1888, annexation by New Zealand in 1901, and the establishment of the internally autonomous government of the Cook Islands in 1965 placed the atoll in an increasingly complex framework of law and culture.

The social pattern during most of the nineteenth century was under the authoritarian control of Marsters himself.[11] Following his death in 1899, however, a much more complex pattern developed. Insofar as this related to land tenure, it is outlined in the following sections.

The total population as of 20 November 1959 was ninety-five, of whom twenty-seven belonged by descent or marriage to the "first family," that is, the lineage which traces descent from the first of Marsters's three wives; thirty-eight to the "second family"; and nineteen to the "third family." The other eleven (two schoolteachers and one medical assistant and their families) were strangers,[12] but each was associated with one of the three lineages for many purposes. Fifty-six of the ninety-five were primary school children or infants, and only fifteen were males over fifteen years of age. This indicates a high degree of out-migration by adult males.

THE ACQUISITION OF RIGHTS

In the early nineteenth century various Europeans visited and lived on Palmerston for short periods (Burland 1966; Maude and Crocombe 1962:36) and in the 1850s an Englishman named Jeffrey Strickland lived there and claimed ownership by sole occupation. He is said to have handed over his rights and titles[13] in the atoll to Captain Bowles of the *Merchant of Tahiti* in return for a passage to Tahiti, and the Tahiti merchant John Brander claims to have bought the rights from Captain Bowles. William Marsters arrived on the island on the schooner *Aorai* on 8 July 1863, probably as an overseer of a few Tahitian laborers to exploit existing produce and to plant more coconuts on behalf of Brander,[14] whose ships collected produce there until his business got into difficulties.

The rights of Brander, and later his heirs, and Marsters were in dispute for many years, but Marsters remained in possession. The British crown exercised nominal jurisdiction over the atoll and claimed limited land rights to the extent that it granted leases and licenses to uninhabited and unclaimed islands in the western Pacific.[15] On 6 January 1888 Marsters applied to the high commissioner for the western Pacific in Fiji for a lease over the atoll and was issued a temporary lease on 24 July 1888.[16] Brander's heirs continued to claim the atoll, but on 23 May 1891 the high commissioner granted Marsters a license to occupy

Palmerston for twenty-one years.[17] Marsters claimed exclusive rights to the atoll on the grounds of long exclusive possession and on the claim that he had planted 200,000 coconut palms at his own expense.

After the 1891 license expired, it was replaced in 1913 by a lease from the Cook Islands administration which expired on 1 January 1933. For nine years thereafter the occupants had no legal title, but their occupation was so well established and their land of so little value that their rights were never challenged. However, a Rarotonga company claimed to have a bill of sale over the atoll and used this as a threat to make the islanders sell their produce to the company. A new twenty-one-year lease was drawn up in 1941,[18] and in 1954 an act of the New Zealand Parliament[19] vested the atoll permanently in the "Native inhabitants of the Island of Palmerston and their descendants" who were described as "the descendants of the said William Marsters." Whether by intention or not, this wording restricted the rights to those descendants, about 12 percent of the total, who were then resident, i.e., "Native inhabitants," of the atoll and to *their* descendants, whether resident or not. An undemarcated area of ten acres was reserved for government use. In April 1965 when the Cook Islands became an internally self-governing territory of New Zealand, new rights of control were created at that level. They have not, to my knowledge, been exercised.

Although Marsters won exclusive title vis-à-vis nonresident claimants (apart from the British crown, which he welcomed to guarantee his rights), his rights were being challenged from within. He had three wives on Palmerston, all Polynesians from Penrhyn atoll some six hundred miles to the northeast. He had children by all three, and descent from one or another wife—through the male line in cases where both parents are his descendants—provides the basis for the division of land and society on Palmerston today.[20]

Marsters lived by supplying passing ships with fresh foods, firewood, salt pork, dried fish, and coconut oil, either for shipboard use or for resale. During the early years of his residence he employed islanders from Atiu and Penrhyn, but later used his own growing family as labor. John (or Juan) Fernandez, who was probably of Portuguese-Indian ancestry, lived on Palmerston for most of the period that Marsters did. He is spoken of as foreman, but actually Marsters himself controlled the atoll and all its commercial transactions along patriarchal lines, allotting work to each man each day. The men rostered to gather fish or other food had to supply the whole population, for all lived in one settlement and ate together. Each of Marsters's wives had a separate sleeping house, but all used the one eating house.

By the 1880s the provedore and salt-pork trades had died out, and copra became the main source of cash income. By this time Marsters's sons were maturing and demanding a share of the income, so he gave each son half of the value of the copra the son made, but of that half he had to give one-third to his mother. Coconut trees were still planted by the whole group under the patriarch's control, and copra was still made as and where he ordered. After a time, the sons formed themselves into three groups for copra making, each grouping comprising the resident issue of one wife plus adoptees. The custom of giving a one-third share to the mother was continued by most children until all three wives of William Marsters were dead.

When close to death, Marsters realized that the economic system could continue only if there was effective leadership. The absence of any other person with his unique status precluded a continued authoritarian structure, and the tensions between his three families made it unlikely that any high degree of joint action would be maintained. He accordingly decided that, after his death, the system of division of income from joint production should be replaced by a division of the land itself, and that his authoritarian powers should be replaced by more comprehensive laws.

Having gone to sea at an early age from his home city of Birmingham, Marsters is unlikely to have known much about English land tenure. His three wives, having left Penrhyn very young, probably knew little of its tenure system. Moreover, for the first twenty or so years it is unlikely that any thought was given to internal rights, for Marsters ruled the island on authoritarian lines. Thus when he was faced with the necessity to make a tenure rule, he had no clear precedents to draw from. In any case, there would be limits to which external precedents would fit the local situation. As shown in the following sections, external precedents are, even today, of quite limited relevance for Palmerston.

DISTRIBUTION OF LAND RIGHTS BY AREA

Until 1898 all land, trees, crops, pigs, and poultry were regarded as being owned by William Marsters.[21] At that time, it was alleged that the first lineage (i.e., the resident descendants of the first wife) had stated that the second and third lineages would be banished when the old man died. This led the latter two lineages to request him to make clear provision for them. Accordingly, in 1898 he went round Home Islet[22] and, by pace and compass, divided it into three portions of approximately equal area. He showed the lineages how the division should be done and left them to divide the other islets. They did this soon after his death.

On Home Islet he gave the eldest resident son from his first wife the choice of the three portions into which the islet was divided. The son chose the central portion for the first lineage.[23] On the next islet the senior member of the second lineage was given first choice. First choice on the next islet was given to the leader of the third lineage and so on.

Primrose Islet was divided in half for two unmarried daughters, and Primrose Bank was given to the third unmarried daughter. Of these three unmarried daughters, one belonged to each of the three lineages, and in practice these areas have always been worked as the lands of the respective lineages. The only other exception to the division on a lineage basis was Mary Ann's Bank, which was allotted personally to Marsters's second wife, Mary Ann. Some say it should be Marion's Bank, named after Marsters's eldest daughter by his second wife. In 1959 it was worked by the leading nuclear family of the second lineage, though some claimed it should have been used by all the second lineage.

Before his death Marsters declared the reef and lagoon to be the common property of all—no individual rights could be acquired in either.

On the death of William Marsters in 1899, the lands were worked as three separate units, though some years earlier the three lineages had begun to operate as distinct units for the making of copra and in dividing income.

The livestock were divided among the three lineages, but because of the absence of fences it was difficult to keep the three lots distinct. In William Marsters's time no pigs were penned, for he believed that they improved the soil by aerating it while rooting. Shortly after his death, however, a law adopted by the lineage heads in council made it compulsory for all pigs to be penned on the land of the owning family. This law still applies today.

William Marsters had nominated his eldest resident son to succeed him as head of the atoll but gave him no rights over the lands of the other lineages. As he was absent from the atoll for many years, there was considerable dispute as to whether any individual was head of the island or whether the heads of the three lineages exercised independent authority. This was not finally resolved until 1921 when the resident commissioner of the Cook Islands reaffirmed, administratively rather than legally, the head of the first lineage as head of the atoll. This principle has been followed since.

Hurricanes and wave action have altered the size and shape of some islets, but the law is that the original boundaries must remain. When additional land is built up it belongs to the lineage to whose land it has been added. In a sense then, boundaries extend into the lagoon, but do not take effect unless the lagoon floor is raised above water level. The following case shows, however, that rights based on this premise are subordinated when someone has a clear claim to the land (usually sand!) concerned.

In a unique case on Tom's Islet a small area of land was washed by a storm to a new position in front of the land of another lineage. Even in the new position, however, it remains the property of the former lineage. It was explained that this was not new land but old land removed.

Most of William Marsters's descendants now live away from the atoll. Several children of the three wives went to Penrhyn atoll where they were accorded rights in the lands of their mothers' families. These rights are retained by their descendants in Penrhyn to the present day. All other rights off the atoll have been acquired by marriage, inheritance to the next generation, permission, purchase, or lease.[24] Marriage has been the most common avenue of access to land in other islands of the Cook group, especially Aitutaki, Manihiki, and Rarotonga.

No rights in this category belong to the clan as a whole or to all members of it—only to individuals or small descent groups.

DISTRIBUTION OF LAND RIGHTS BY RESOURCES AND FUNCTIONS

Rights can be delimited by area, but various rights in the same area are differentiated by the resources exploited or the purpose served.

The largest land area is devoted to coconuts. Copra is the sole cash crop and coconuts are an important food. William Marsters ruled that coconut palms were to be owned in common by the lineage on whose land they grew. From that time copra was cut by each lineage as a whole, and the income shared equally by its men. In some cases, however, equal shares were given to each nuclear family, or other ad hoc arrangements were made. This system of dividing copra income was long a matter of contention—it was alleged that some lineage heads took excessive personal shares or showed favoritism in distribution. The governor-general of New Zealand, during a visit in 1926, therefore ruled that within each lineage shares must be exactly equal for each person, irrespective of age, sex, or status.[25] This ruling has not always been followed.

In 1922, due to disagreement over the distribution of money, the lands of the second lineage were divided into six portions—one for each of the four sons and two daughters of William Marsters by his second wife. Neither of the daughters lived on the atoll, both having married on Aitutaki. By emigration, adoption, and selective inheritance these six portions had come by 1959 to be held by the three resident sections of the second lineage. Three portions were held by the largest section of the lineage, comprising four resident nuclear families; two by the smallest; and only one by the second largest. One of the two nuclear families of this latter section took its copra shares from the less populous first lineage, with which it was linked by adoption. The two smaller sections of the second lineage decided to work their lands, for copra making only, as a single unit. The history of the six original portions is still remembered, however, and periodic readjustments are likely to continue as matters of verbal negotiation rather than definitive settlement.

During 1945 and 1946 all three lineages pooled their copra and all resident descendants took equal shares of income. Thereafter the second lineage withdrew. The first and third lineages continued to work together and pooled not only the copra, but also the coconut lands, as the third lineage then contained only one working man and one nuclear family. When other members of the third lineage returned to Palmerston, it resumed its former status as a fully separate lineage.

Until 1957 the second and third lineages allocated the money to the heads of the working families. At that time it was alleged that the headmen of the lineages were taking more than their share. As a result of this serious dispute, the resident commissioner of the Cook Islands insisted that these two lineages allocate the money as the first lineage

THE CASE OF PALMERSTON ATOLL

had done since the governor-general's visit of 1926—equal per capita shares of the income irrespective of age or sex. This practice has been followed since.[26]

During my stay the rule being observed was that members of the second lineage were to get an equal income. The largest section of the lineage cut all the copra from its three portions of land. The rest of that lineage cut copra on their portions only until they reached a quantity per capita equal to that of the largest section. This did not use all their nuts, but as income was to be equal for all, additional cutting would have lead to uneven incomes. The larger section asked if they could cut half the surplus copra on the other portions. This was refused on the grounds that when the advantage had been with that section several years before, they had refused to share the surplus. In these circumstances use of land by lineage sections has led to reduced output and income, as well as to increased dispute. Members of the lineage maintained that the rule of equal division within each lineage was required by the government in Rarotonga. There was no legal basis for this view, though it accorded with the governor-general's 1926 ruling.

Coconuts belonging to the lineage are frequently placed under a *rahui* 'customary prohibition' which precludes their use other than for copra making.[27] For domestic purposes, however, lineage heads sometimes allow a ration of nuts, usually two or three per person once every two to seven days.

New Zealand's Protestant ethic influenced land utilization too—the 1941 lease required the lessees to keep the islets fully planted with coconuts and "use all diligence in the making of copra . . . so that the output and sale thereof will be as great as possible."

The most important vegetable on the atoll today is the tuber *Cyrtosperma chamissonis* which must be grown in swampy conditions. The first tubers are said to have been brought from Penrhyn and Manihiki in the 1890s and planted in a small natural swamp, but they were soon destroyed by pigs. Early this century, after the penning of pigs became compulsory, the tuber was replanted. To extend the plantings, artificial swamps called pits were made by digging the sand to the water lens. This was a major undertaking as some pits had to be dug ten feet deep before being filled with leaves, rotting wood, and soil to form humus. Some digging was done by individuals but most by companies of men, usually within a lineage, which dug ten feet square for each member in turn. The garden area was then regarded as the sole property of the individual, though in practice there are limits on disposition and on the period one can be absent without losing rights. The garden pit and plots within it are distinguishable from the garden itself, and rights to each may be held by different parties.[28]

The main area of garden pits is on Home Islet, with those of the first and second lineages lying on their respective sides of the major boundary between them. The first lineage had no pits on other islets, but members of the second lineage had smaller pits on North Islet and Tom's Islet. The third lineage had its main pits on Tom's Islet and smaller pits on North Islet and Home Islet.

Other vegetable crops grown in these pits include taro, sweet potato, and bananas.

The greater amount of labor, necessitating more frequent and prolonged visits, seems responsible for the fact that there is stronger personal identification with garden land, and more assertion of rights to it, than with any other land except house sites.

Arrowroot has grown in small quantities for many years, possibly since precontact times.[29] As it continues to be edible even if left unharvested, it is an excellent emergency food. After the 1926 hurricane the people realized the need for more arrowroot and each person planted some. The individual did not have to ask the head of the lineage where to plant, though in most cases it was done by arrangement with him. A person can clear a patch of unallotted lineage land and plant arrowroot on it for himself, and that land is spoken of as his for such time as he uses it for arrowroot. Arrowroot takes three to five years to come into bearing. It is usual not to harvest the whole crop, but just to lift the number of tubers required at any one time and to replant in their place immediately. As a result, many of the owners have been in possession for many years. Arrowroot land is considered to be owned by the person who planted the arrowroot or by anyone to whom he has transferred it, though coconut trees growing on that land belong to the lineage as a whole. Thus, the term ownership in this context refers to very limited rights of use and disposal. The lack of precision in the nature and duration of either leaves some room for maneuver and dispute.

Some land where arrowroot was planted has been left for many years unplanted and the planters have gone away. There is some difference of opinion about whether such land belongs to the lineage or to the absentee. Lineage heads maintain that anyone else could plant arrowroot on this land provided he first obtained the permission of the head. Continued ownership depends to some extent on use and can be inherited. Others maintain that it is only if the owner dies or goes away for a very long time without replanting and without reallocating it that it reverts to the lineage or to the lineage head for reallocation.

Here again, right is gained by effort expended and crops planted. I asked several people whether a person could plant sweet potato or some new crop on arrowroot land. All stated that the land belonged to that owner and he could plant any vegetable crops or food trees, excluding coconuts for copra which would belong to the whole lineage. I did not determine how far this assertion has been tested in practice.

There are several exceptions to the rule that coconut palms are owned in common by the lineage on whose land they grow:

Birth trees. When a child is born the placenta is buried, and a palm or tree, usually a sweet coconut, is planted over it. Sometimes a second palm is planted later with the withered umbilical cord. These trees become the sole property of the child for whom they were planted. Only he can climb them, give others permission to do so, and transfer them like other property. This custom probably originated with the Penrhyn wives, as birth trees are common in the Cook atolls. There is some confusion and dispute about ownership of many of the older birth palms—markings are irregular and memories uncertain.

Feeding palms. Earlier this century it was found that too many nuts were being used for food and drink, thus leaving an insufficiency for the making of copra, so it was arranged that two coconut palms would be set aside for each man, woman, and child on each of the main islets as feeding palms, which can be used at any time. Each person has an individual mark, an initial or initials, cut into such palms. Some people have extra feeding palms due to inheritance; some children have none allotted as yet. In the third lineage the share is ten palms per man and the headman uses the share of his brother in New Zealand also. The third lineage allows members to climb palms in its section more freely, probably owing to its small numbers and the relative abundance of palms.

Sweet coconuts. One variety of coconut has an edible husk and is called the sweet nut. A sweet nut palm is the private property of the person who plants it. I am not aware of any limitation on planting them.

In all the above cases, at copra-making time, any unused nuts are available for making copra. That is, for home consumption they belong to the individual, but for copra making the product is the property of the lineage as a whole. The stated rule is that any member of the lineage can use those palms for copra making, but in some cases only the owner of the palm concerned makes copra from it. In fact several young people maintained that such palms could only be used for copra making by the individual owner.

Other coconut palms, generally called sour nuts, are the property of the lineage irrespective of who plants them or where they are planted. If a person plants on the land of another lineage, the palms and their product belong to the lineage on whose land they are planted. This happened frequently when the first lineage planted much of the land of the third lineage at a time when most of the latter were away. The lineage which did the planting did not claim the palms or nuts, though it was alleged that they hoped that none of the third lineage would return and that they would get their lands.

Other trees include breadfruit, mangoes, limes, pawpaws, and custard apples.[30] Bananas, sugar cane, and such pandanus as is planted, can also be considered under this heading as the same rules apply to them. All belong to the person who plants them or inherits them. In the case of breadfruit several heirs may exercise joint rights.[31] They must be planted in the *Cyrtosperma* patch or other land of the person who plants them, or on other lineage land with the permission of the lineage head.[32] In the latter case the planter usually fences off a piece of land for his garden and either plants a hedge of hibiscus, coffee plant, or lilies, or he builds a wire fence around it.

Bamboo is planted in the *Cyrtosperma* patch or in the garden and belongs to the planter. It is used for fishing rods and the booms of sailing boats. It does not grow wild.

Trees and plants which grow wild on the land of the lineage belong to the members of that lineage in common. This includes the shrub *nono,* the fruit of which is eaten when other foods are scarce, and two types of scrub—*ngashu,* which is used at times for medicine, and *ngangie,* which is used for firewood and in some construction. The fruit of the pandanus is used for food, its wood for construction, and its leaves for making mats. Unlike the custom on some atolls, the leaves are not used for thatching. Most pandanus is self-propagated and belongs to the whole lineage.

Tamanu (*Callophylum*), 'native mahogany,' and other trees are used in the construction of houses, canoes, and furniture. Unless a tree is growing on someone's house site or garden, it can be used by anyone within the lineage. The fact that it is on someone's arrowroot land does not give that person the exclusive right to it. Some people, however, think that it does and that the owner of the land, if it is arrowroot land, should be asked for permission to use the tree. An individual can mark a tree for his exclusive use with the permission of the lineage if he wants to use it for making a canoe or building a house. It is not usual to go to another lineage for trees, though sometimes a particular tree is not available in one's own lineage land, in which case one must ask the head of the lineage on whose land it is growing. If he approves, then the tree is taken without payment. It is understood that no charge in cash or kind is made for any primary produce among Palmerston people.

Elders say that rights to fresh produce for on-the-spot consumption on islets other than Home Islet, particularly coconuts for drinking, can be obtained only from the land of one's lineage. Many young people, on the other hand, say that they can and do take them when and where they want for immediate consumption. In practice there is little the elders can do about it.

When a person wishes to erect a house, he selects a section of unused lineage land and obtains the approval of the lineage head to use it for his house site. He generally plants a hedge round it or trees at the corners. It is for him to determine its size and shape. The house site belongs to the person who cuts it out, and he can dispose of it within his lineage as with other property.

Within the limits imposed, garden pits, house sites, and arrowroot land may be considered private property in that the principal right holder may use them as he wishes and may transfer his rights in them to certain other people. Individual rights seem strongest in house sites, not quite so strong in gardens, and less strong in arrowroot lands.

RIGHTS IN FAUNA

Every household on the atoll has pigs and hens. Some geese and ducks are also kept. The pigs must be kept in pens on the land of their owners. Alternatively a piece of land may be cut out from unallotted lineage lands, and this becomes known as the land of that person for such time as he uses it for his pigpen. There are three levels of right here: those to the land penned, those to the pen structure, and those to the pigs. They are in some instances held by different parties.

Poultry are not penned, but are fed daily, and each person has a particular place where he feeds his poultry. It is said to be against the law to feed the poultry of another person, though there is no written law to this effect.

Bosun birds migrate to the atoll about June or July and leave between October and January. It is not permissible to take their eggs, and the birds themselves can be taken only at particular times decided on by the three lineage heads acting together. In recent years only one picking a month has been allowed. At one time each lineage picked on its own land and kept the birds it picked. In recent years, however, all lineages pick on their own lands but then pool the birds and divide them among the whole population. The usual quota is one or two birds per person, irrespective of age or sex. William Marsters's law that bosun birds should not be picked after Christmas Day is still adhered to.

Mr. Ned Marsters mentioned to the minister of island territories in New Zealand that the birds belonged to the lineage on whose land they were nesting. The minister replied that the birds belonged to the government, as with game in New Zealand, but that the people were entitled to control the catch and to divide it equally.

Frigate birds are often shot on the wing. Other birds are also shot occasionally. A bird shot on the wing belongs to the person who shoots it, and he is permitted to go onto any land to do so.

All birds other than bosun birds belong to the lineage on whose land they are sitting and can be taken by any members of that lineage at any time. *Ngoio* are commonly taken when nesting—there is no control on time or numbers—but it is against the law to take eggs. People used to take limited numbers of seagulls' eggs, but after the 1926 hurricane seagulls did not return.

Swimming turtles may be taken by any person at any time, but turtle meat is considered to belong to everyone, and representatives of all lineages help to cut the meat and share it equally among all people. The catcher owns the shell and usually sells it, for ten to twenty shillings in 1959, to someone on the trading schooner or by taking it to Rarotonga. If a live turtle were sold to a passing ship, the catcher could keep all the proceeds for himself.

Turtles on the beach, or laying eggs, may be taken by any person irrespective of whose land they are on.

Until about 1959 it was against the law to take turtle eggs. There were so many breaches of this law, however, that it was decided that the matter was one for the head of the lineage on whose lands the eggs were found. If there are sufficient eggs taken, they are shared by all people on the atoll.

If a young turtle is caught, it belongs to the finder. He feeds it for a few months, and it is then consumed by his household and some close relatives. It is not shared more widely because of the labor invested in feeding it and because it is not big enough for atoll-wide distribution.

Fish may be taken at any time and belong to the person who catches them.

Land crabs belong to the lineage on whose land they are found. However, it is usual for a special party to be made up and, with the permission of all three lineage heads, crabs are taken anywhere on a particular islet on a certain night. The catch is divided into household lots, with an equal share for each individual on the atoll.

COMMON LANDS AND WATERS

Legally, all land below high-water mark in the Cook Islands belongs to the crown.[33] The residents stress, however, that they have unrestricted rights to the reef and lagoon. These are like the economists' "free good" in that none of their resources is in short supply, the supply cannot be changed by the people, and the main requirement for exploitation is labor. An interesting change occurred about 1955, when a limited market appeared. The schooner *Tiare Maori* began to visit the atoll every three months to buy fish for sale in Rarotonga. The supply was relatively inexhaustible, but the market was scarce, as the ship's freezer could accommodate only half a ton. Accordingly, it was decided that fishing for this purpose would be done jointly by all residents and the payment divided equally.[34]

In another instance, scarcity of a resource for which there was an unlimited market was leading to a rationing of access to the resource. Pearl shell had been planted in the lagoon in the late 1950s, with the hope that harvesting would begin within a few years. It was not feasible to divide the lagoon so it was intended to allow each man to dive for a quota of shell.

It is difficult to define a precise legal high-water mark on beaches. The people regard bare sand as a beach and sand with vegetation as land. All beaches are regarded as common to all, but access to them is restricted by customary prohibitions. Such restrictions are never imposed on Home Islet though coconuts other than feeding nuts are placed under customary prohibition most of the time to protect the coconuts. In all other cases the whole islet, including the beach, is prohibited.

The three fish weirs in the lagoon are regarded as the common property of resident descendants. No new weirs have been built for decades. The weirs are little used and then only for fish drives involving the whole atoll. Fish are so easily obtained by other means that there is no incentive to build new weirs, and their effective use necessitates organizing a large team of people.

The distinction the Palmerston people make between a bank and an islet seems to be based both on size and on the extent of soil and flora. The main distinction between the laws relating to the two categories seems to result from the fact that banks have minimal resources. Islets are spoken of as being owned by the three lineages severally, but most sand banks are not spoken of as being owned jointly; they are there for everyone to use. The two largest banks, rather significantly, are owned by particular lineages.

It was originally thought that it was not worth planting banks with coconuts, but some years ago one lineage planted one of the unowned banks. When it was clear that they were growing well, another lineage went to plant other parts of the same bank, but the former lineage objected and pointed out that there were plenty of other unplanted banks and that they should use them. Several banks were subsequently planted but had not come into bearing at the time of my visit. Opinions varied on rights to such banks. This constitutes a possible source of future conflict. The recognition that the potential value of the banks could only be realized by investing labor in tree culture seemed to be leading to the emergence of a notion of rights, or at least priorities, in banks which could support useful stands of coconuts.

Apart from the beaches and sand banks, the only common land on the atoll is the main road, a vaguely defined strip less than one quarter of a mile long through the settlement. The road was built after the

1926 hurricane at which time it was agreed that it should be common land. Several young people, however, maintained that the section of road that ran through the land of the three lineages belonged to them severally. The matter is not of any consequence at this time.

All Home Islet, except those areas in use for graves, gardens, or buildings, is available for access to all persons at all times.

The people prefer that the government does not define the undemarcated ten acres which it reserved for public purposes but that the Palmerston people decide where public utilities will go on lineage land. They regard the school, church, radio station, and water catchment as being for public use, but with the landowning lineage holding a reversionary right. In the case of the new school erected in 1959, the government of the Cook Islands sent the materials and a foreman on condition that Mr. Ned Marsters, the resident agent and head of the first lineage, arrange land and labor.

It is agreed that public utilities should go on the land of each lineage in turn, but there was some disagreement about the placement of the school—some persons wanted the government to pay for the land as it did on other islands. Most, however, prefer the existing arrangement because the government could retaliate by defining its ten-acre entitlement, whereas at present it uses only about one acre in all.

The status of the land on which the church stands is special in some respects. Oral tradition on the atoll in 1959 had it that the land was given to the church by William Marsters and that it remains church property. When asked who owned that land, people replied that it was the church. But it is located within the land of the first lineage, and if the church were removed, that lineage would almost certainly be accorded reversionary rights both by the residents and the Cook Islands Land Court. This consideration is irrelevant at present, for the people do not conceive of a community without a church.

Until 1905 the dead were all buried in the center of the main islet. This area is still regarded as belonging to "all Palmerston people." After 1905 each lineage set aside its own burial place near the village. By 1959 it was felt that this was taking up too much land near the village so that people were considering burying inland again, with each lineage having its own cemetery on its own land.

Although land accretions normally belong to the lineage to whose land the accretion is attached, rights to flotsam vary with the size of the group which can benefit from it. Driftwood belongs to the finder, irrespective of the land it is washed up on. Stranded porpoises and blackfish likewise belong to the finder, but, though small fish may be consumed by his family or lineage, large ones are shared throughout the atoll. The oil, however, may be kept by the finder alone.

For wrecked ships, all able-bodied men on the atoll form a company to strip the wreck and share the materials gathered.

For those occasions that occur only once every few years, such as the visits of warships, the mission ship, or the resident commissioner, the heads of the three lineages agree on the contributions of coconuts, taro, and so forth, per head of population that will be needed to feast the visitors. Refusal to meet one's contribution is punishable by fine. I have no evidence on the actual implementation of this sanction.

DISTRIBUTION OF RIGHTS

From an original single form, or level, of right holding by a single party, the increasing involvement of other groups and individuals has led, even on this remote and minute area of infertile land, to no less than ten major kinds of rights, each held by different categories of institutions or persons. Although each kind of right is analytically distinct, they are probably not perceived in this way by the Palmerston people.

The rights of the United Kingdom under the protectorate passed to New Zealand in 1901 with its annexation of the Cook Islands. Palmerston became a part of New Zealand, which controlled and made laws for the atoll and which reserved to itself, in the act of 1954, the unspecified ten acres of land.

In August 1965, the Cook Islands became an internally self-governing territory within the boundaries of New Zealand. It is a moot point whether the reserved ten acres now belongs to the government of the Cook Islands or to that of New Zealand, but it is unlikely to become a matter of contention. The government of New Zealand retains control of external affairs and defense and could thus probably acquire land on the atoll as a military camp, tracking station, or observatory.

The Cook Islands Amendment Act, 1954, vested title to the atoll in those descendants of William Marsters who were then resident on it. That was only about 12 percent of his descendants, most having gone, decades before in many cases, to reside permanently elsewhere.[35] According to the act, persons who were resident in 1954, but left afterwards, retain their rights, as do their descendants. But the act could also be interpreted to accord rights to others as well for it stated that the land would be held under "native customary tenure," which has never been defined. On this ground, persons normally resident on the atoll, but absent in 1954, could claim reentry and resumption of rights. At least some returned after 1954 and resumed their former rights without question.

The Palmerston community on Rarotonga was mainly responsible for getting the atoll vested in the Marsters people.[36] They still act as informal agents for those on the atoll as well as accommodating visitors from Palmerston and sending gifts to the atoll. The leaders of this community assert unquestioned rights to return to Palmerston whenever they wish but base their claim more on the above criteria than on law. In practice both sets of criteria seem to be important. The legal limitation to residents, as of 1954, supports present residents in opposing others whom they do not want, but the moral obligations to certain nonresident clan members are such that they do not deny entry to those who have been helpful. Some of these visit Palmerston every few years, and one of them has lent his house site, garden plots, and personal trees to a non-Marsters government employee on the atoll.

By administrative arrangement with the Cook Islands administration, nonlandowners disembarking at Palmerston first required the permission of the resident agent, who was appointed by the Cook Islands administration but was in practice usually the head of the first lineage. This permission is usually sought by others, but few Marsters descendants bother to seek it. Heads of the other two lineages denied that the resident agent held or exercised any such power. In practice, however, the resident agent does seem to have at least some influence in such decisions. When members of the Marsters family go to Palmerston, it is not their membership in the clan that determines their rights, it is their membership in one of the three lineages.

Most advantages from the possession of land rights on Palmerston can only be enjoyed by those residing there. As described above, much is regarded as common property.

Residents who are not descendants of William Marsters include some wives of descendants; a few government staff members; occasional visitors like Commander Clark, who was shipwrecked there for nearly a year, or Captain Cambridge, who lived there irregularly in the 1940s; and the more numerous short-term friends or official visitors. Most long-term strangers are accorded benefits similar to those of the resident descendants, with the major psychological difference that they are there on sufferance, rather than by right.[37] This is so even for officials who have every right to be there, for their legal rights would entitle them only to access to the lagoon, the beaches and the settlement, and this would be unbearable in such isolation. In practice each is adopted into, or associated with, one of the three lineages, but their status is significantly different from that of true lineage members. Employed outsiders have relatively high cash incomes, some prestige, and some spare time. Properly handled, the relationships can be advantageous for all parties, but they are based on different criteria from family relationships. Any rights acquired by persons with no Marsters blood cease on their departure or death. To my knowledge, none has invested money or labor in building a house or making a garden pit.

One government official was given the use of food trees and garden pits by a clan member who was leaving by the ship on which the official arrived. About a year later, the head of that lineage forbade him to use the land any longer, allegedly for not cooperating adequately, and he abandoned it. For ten months he and his family had neither vegetables nor coconuts except for odd occasions when members of other lineages donated some. This is a powerful sanction indeed.

Shares in copra are likewise conditional. Some who have no blood ties receive full shares, some partial shares, and some no shares. One official, who was resident during my visit, had been told that he would do a full share of copra work but receive only a half share of the cash because he had not planted the trees. He claimed he had done his share of replanting, and the matter remained in dispute.

Through passengers on the schooner are usually accorded hospitality, mainly in the form of fresh coconuts, both to eat during the day or two of the ship's stopover, and to take with them on the onward voyage. This is done by heads of lineages acting individually. During my stay, any visitor who was given permission to collect nuts was told to stay within the boundaries of the donor lineage. Two young boys of the lineage were sent with the visitors to ensure that they did not take nuts from the land of others. Cook Islanders who have visited during the bird season have spoken of being given approval to catch a bird or two but only from the land of the lineage making the offer.

The rights of the lineages are perhaps the most important. With the exception of lands used only for copra production, however, it is all subdivided further. Even copra land is subdivided by the second lineage and has in the past also been subdivided by the other lineages.

Within a decade or two after William Marsters divided the atoll between the three lineages, it was subdivided into equal shares within each lineage for each of William Marsters's sons and daughters, irrespective of the number of children each of them had. This caused a lot of problems, as some lineage heads took control of shares derived from nonresident siblings or from resident women.[38] In 1959, the first and third lineages each worked as a unit in accordance with instructions of various visiting officials. These instructions have no legal validity, though residents assume they have. The second lineage continued to divide its copra land according to the shares of the six original children.

Most garden pits are dug by households but are usually spoken of in the name of the household head. Sometimes people refer to arrowroot lands belonging to households and sometimes to individuals. Cultivation and use is largely a household matter, and the question of proprietary rights seems to have little relevance or meaning apart from that of the household, except where divorce or separation occurs.

The same appears to be true for houses and house sites. A man wishing to build a new house consults the head of his lineage. All men of that family help to select and demarcate a plot for him and usually to build the house. The land so allocated is said to belong to the individual. If he goes away, he can transfer it to another member of his lineage. If he abandons it or dies without issue, it is said to revert to the lineage, but I did not record any such instance. Informants claimed that a house cannot be taken from a man while he is on the atoll. Nevertheless, this did happen in one case years ago. In several cases the same effect has been achieved by banishing people from the atoll or by making them so uncomfortable that they leave. In practice, though nobody states the situation in these terms, confiscation follows banishment and not vice versa.

Of the sixteen households on the atoll, only seven comprised a man with his wife and natural or adopted children. In each of two households there were two married couples, the second being a married son in both cases, plus other relatives. There were four extended families, that is, a married couple plus a variety of other relatives. There were two incomplete families, both unmarried women; one had several children plus other relatives while the other had a grandchild only. There was one solitary bachelor. Where the household comprised more than a nuclear family, the rights of the nuclear families were minor. They were clearly distinguishable in instances where component nuclear families constituted separate copra-making units or maintained distinct parts of household gardens.

Birth trees and feeding trees are the property of individuals, as are the few garden crops, but the distinction between individual, nuclear family, and household is blurred. Lands inherited by individuals will also remain identified for certain purposes with, and are spoken of as, the land of the individual heir.

Rights of individuals may be distinguished by seniority, sex, and descent. Heads of the three lineages are accorded a special status and are responsible for the allocation of land and for organizing its exploitation for copra making particularly. The rights of household heads, as such, are relatively insignificant, being restricted to the use of crops belonging to household members.

Women have a separate status from men with respect to land. They can inherit but, ideally at least, only while resident in the lineage concerned. As most marriages are exogamous, this greatly limits female inheritance. Also women living in lineages other than their born lineage, and viripatrilocal marriage makes this usual, should not use lands to which they do have nominal rights.

Descent is important both for inheritance of individual rights and for distinguishing Marsters's descendants from foreigners.

All the patrilineal descendants of William Marsters (i.e., those who carry the Marsters surname) whom I have met in Rarotonga, Aitutaki, New Zealand, and elsewhere claim that Palmerston is "their atoll" and that they have the right to live there if they wish. Some who are descended through women make no such claim or do not know. It is clear that most are only claiming a symbolic right, for the great majority have no wish for themselves or their descendants ever to live, benefit economically from, or even visit the atoll. They do benefit psychologically from the attachment—they are proud to be Palmerston people. This is not simply pride in having come from Palmerston or having Palmerston parents; it is pride in a sense of still belonging—more a feeling that "Palmerston belongs to me" than that "I belong to Palmerston."

The lease of 31 December 1941 said the lessees were to hold the atoll in trust for the issue of William Marsters who lived on or came to the atoll, but that persons coming in needed the approval of the residents, who could not refuse without "good reason." In a dispute, the resident commissioner in Rarotonga was to decide, but I am aware of only a few cases' having been referred to him.[39] The 1954 legislation, on the other hand, states that only persons resident on the atoll in 1954, and their descendants, have any rights.[40] Anyone who studies the law can see the situation clearly, but few if any have done so. The law is only one determinant of behavior even though some proponents of diverse interpretations say that the law supports their view.

Some members of the clan are effectively denied access to the atoll. William Marsters introduced the London Missionary Society, which was the only church until about 1930.[41] How the second church came in is uncertain. Some claim that a London Missionary Society pastor who was evicted from the island for alleged adultery became converted to Seventh Day Adventism and returned to Palmerston as an S.D.A. representative. Others claim that the first Adventist was a Manihiki man married to a woman of the second lineage. It is nevertheless significant, in view of the prominence of the first lineage in atoll affairs, that the splinter denomination should find its main support in the third and, to a lesser extent, in the second lineages. Great dissension developed, and all S.D.A. adherents resettled on Rarotonga and Aitutaki by order of the resident commissioner in answer to a request from the head of the first lineage. Many wished to return to the atoll, but this had been refused, at least until the time of my visit.[42] The one exception is an aged man who was allowed to return on the informal understanding that he not practice his religion.

A number of other individuals have been kept off the atoll, but usually by clear opposition from those in power on it, rather than by action of the resident commissioner.

The head of the first lineage maintained that land rights had always been subject to residence.[43] The rights of anyone who went away, apart from a short visit, the length of which he avoided specifying, were assumed by the head of that lineage and could be allocated by him as he thought fit. An absentee returning, he said, was entitled to have full land rights reinstated, though not necessarily to the same plots. Some others maintained that a departing person could allocate his rights to whomsoever he or she wished. This seems to be the usual practice, the head of the lineage being informed of the arrangement with which he normally concurs. Many who leave with the intention of a short absence never return. They may write to say who should use their land, or the head of the lineage or lineage section may allocate it. Usually, however, usage follows kin ties or other prior arrangements.

The rights of absentees are a matter of conflicting interests for which no rules have yet been made, but the conflict is modified by distance, difficulty of access, and the fact that the rights have no cash value and little noncash value. For instance, the head of one lineage maintained that the arrowroot lands of absent men of his lineage reverted to him, and he accordingly objected to my measuring them separately. Other members of the lineage were unsure, and some of the long-absent members interviewed on Rarotonga asserted that their individual rights to the arrowroot lands remained. But they were too far away to do anything about it. Since these lands were usually replanted at the time of harvesting, use by others constituted no great material problem, though at times it seems to have caused considerable psychological stress.

The intensity of attempts by absentees to maintain their rights, as well as the tacit acknowledgement of the continuation of such rights, is greatest with the land into which most labor has been invested: house sites, garden pits, and tree crops.

Those who were not born on the atoll must have a very strong case indeed to enable them to exercise any rights there. In 1930 Joel Marsters, Jr., son of the former headman, was refused permission to go to Palmerston on the ground that because his parents had left the atoll, they had lost all rights in it. Joel lived in Aitutaki. He claimed to be the rightful headman of Palmerston but not to have exercised the right or lived on the atoll as a matter of personal preference. The significant point is that few who were not born on the atoll have ever returned there for any length of time except as wives of residents.

There is a clear preference on the atoll for marriage within the Marsters clan. Marriage of Marsters men to non-Marsters women is simply considered less than ideal; marriage of Marsters women to non-Marsters men is considered very undesirable if they plan to live on the atoll. There were no instances of the latter at the time of my visit, and I am aware of only one earlier instance. This point, and the nature of the rights thus acquired, were not specifically explored beyond the fact that the land allotted to a foreign man who married a Marsters woman and lived on the atoll was his land, according to the head of the first lineage. He could not be deprived of it while the marriage lasted. If he were to become unwelcome, however, he would probably leave.

When a woman marries, she goes to live on her husband's land. The only exception in 1959 was that of the eldest daughter of the head of the first lineage. Her husband was the youngest son of a junior member of a junior line tracing from a daughter in the third lineage.

On marriage, a woman is supposed to relinquish all rights in her own lineage land. For most purposes this is followed in practice, but she sometimes continues to obtain fruit from personal trees, and she usually returns to her own lineage in the event of divorce or separation. This may not be a right so much as it is an expectation which public opinion would normally ensure was carried out.

In the event of remarriage, a divorcée will join her new husband's group, but cases noted show a wide variation in affiliation and inheritance by her previous children despite the law that they should inherit from their father unless adopted. An unmarried mother remains in her own lineage, and her children inherit land rights there unless paternity is acknowledged or the child is adopted.

Each lineage is supposed to be exogamous, but in 1959 two of the thirteen married couples were endogamous.[44] All thirteen current marriages were between descendants of the original William Marsters with the exception of two whose wives came from other islands in the Cook group.

Adoption is frequent but was not studied in detail. Adoption is said to occur most frequently within the lineage of the child and secondly within the child's mother's lineage. In the latter case the adoptee loses all rights in the father's property and acquires the same rights in the adoptive family and lineage as if he had been born there. In practice neither the separation nor the incorporation seems to be absolute. More frequently the adoptee makes primary connections and exercises his primary rights with his family of adoption but also often exercises some rights in the family of birth, which becomes a haven of refuge in times of trouble. Adoption is not registered. It varies from just 'feeding,' as all the children of the patriarch's third wife were fed by the first and second wives after the third died and as all Tahenga's children were fed when his wife died young, to full adoption. A child who was just 'fed' in another family may later return to his family of birth and exercise all his rights there. As clear-cut arrangements are not always made when a child changes residence, the decision about whether the 'feeding' is 'adoption' or not is often a post hoc one depending on length of residence and relative feeling of attachment to one or the other family and lineage. Several cases were recorded where people have changed their lineage affiliation along adoption lines during adulthood.

Scarcity of resources is sometimes a factor in adoption. For example, Tuatai James Marsters was born in the second lineage. His mother was a sister of the present head of the first lineage. He was adopted by the latter lineage and has lived sometimes with them and sometimes in the second lineage. Now that the second lineage has the largest population, Tuatai lives just inside its boundary but adjacent to the first lineage. He gets most of his food needs from land of the second lineage, but cuts copra as a member of the first—copra is the scarce and valued resource. One of his sons is fed by his maternal grandfather in the third lineage, but this son is very mobile and may settle in any of the three lineages. Apparently, adoption is an important mechanism of adjustment to material as well as social needs.[45]

Girls were said to be more in demand in adoption than boys,[46] who were considered to be the cause of trouble, including land trouble.

STRUCTURE OF PROPERTY RELATIONS

The laws which William Marsters wrote before his death laid a foundation for property relations thereafter. Some laws were modified and others added by the head of the first lineage after varying degrees of consultation with the heads of the other lineages or with the resident commissioner of the Cook Islands. All written laws were destroyed in the 1926 hurricane, and it is no longer possible to determine the precedents from which they were developed. Some minor features, such as birth trees and the use of customary prohibitions, probably originated from the Penrhyn wives. Although the Bible may have contributed important emphases, particularly in relation to the dominant rights of fathers and the marginal rights of women, the most important determinant of the laws was probably the physical structure of the atoll and the social and demographic structure of its people.

On 8 September 1946 the leading men of the first lineage made a written statement (see appendix 1) on the occasion of the departure of the headman. It implied that all shares were to be equal and that the rights of absentees were to be in abeyance during their absence.

The atoll had no written laws from 1926 until 28 October 1949 when the resident commissioner came to settle some disputes arising from uncertainty as to the law. He accordingly assembled the elders and asked them to record the laws for the future internal government of the atoll. They were recorded by the commissioner's interpreter (see appendix 2) but are incomplete as the elders could not remember them all. Laws about wills, adoption, succession, and other matters were not recorded at the time, though they are believed to have been included in Marsters's original code and are spoken of as laws. The primary emphases in all the laws seem to be the control of aggression and the distribution of property.

The laws recorded in 1949 were given additional legal significance by the 1954 legislation which vested the atoll in perpetuity in the resident descendants of William Marsters as "native customary land" to be dealt with in accordance with "native custom and usage." The 1949 recording would no doubt be a major criterion in any dispute over Palmerston land before the Cook Islands Land Court, which has exclusive jurisdiction over land ownership and inheritance. The court has not yet deliberated problems relating to Palmerston and has accordingly not defined what shall constitute "native custom and usage" for the atoll.[47] The written laws of the atoll would provide good prima facie evidence of "custom" in the sense of traditionally accepted principle. But they are incomplete, and at least some of them are not in accordance with "usage" in the sense of actual behavior. What would be upheld by the court in the event of conflict can only be a matter of conjecture.

Though not specifically mentioned in the written laws, *rahui* 'customary prohibitions on resource use' are a vital control mechanism. All islets except Home Islet are under 'prohibition' most of the time in order to protect the main resource, copra. Sand banks with few resources are not so controlled. When under 'prohibition,' which is placed by agreement among the three lineage heads, no person may land on an islet without prior arrangement. This would ideally be in the form of a ticket, note, or letter but in practice is sometimes only a verbal message. The purpose is to inform the other lineages at least one day in advance of where one intends to go and why. The other lineages cannot then stop the initiator from going, but they can send a representative at the same time to ensure that the land of each is respected. If one wishes to enter the land of other lineages while on the islet (e.g., to catch land crabs), one must obtain permission from the owning lineage. (The crabs are shared among all people of the atoll if enough are caught.)

Home Islet as a whole is never placed under prohibition, but the coconut trees are. That is, although one may walk among the trees and take other crops in the area, one cannot take coconuts for making copra or for food except by arrangement.

Customary prohibitions are also used to control access to such resources as birds, eggs, and emergency foods in short supply.

There are two separate concepts involved: that of 'prohibition,' which applies to owners as well as nonowners, and 'trespass,' which applies to nonowners only. The concept of trespass on Palmerston has two aspects: place and purpose. On Home Islet, for example, the land itself is never under prohibition, and one is said to be free to walk anywhere, on the land of any family. One is not free, however, to go on the land of others with intent to disturb their gardens or to take their produce. For this reason people keep clear of the garden pits of others for if one is in the vicinity, one is suspect. A person found in the garden pit of another without good reason would probably be accused of the crime most frequently spoken of on the atoll, "mischiefing," that is, the suspected causing of trouble, or committing (or intention to commit) an unidentified crime.

Despite the clear rule on customary prohibitions, several young men said that when they are out fishing, they do visit islets which are under prohibition and do walk through any lands. They say that so long as they only take an occasional nut for drinking, nobody minds. Some elders do mind, but there is not much they can do about it.

Another vital principle alluded to in the laws of Palmerston is that of shares. Commodities which are in limited supply but not fixed in space are allocated by means of shares whereby each person, usually irrespective of age or sex, is entitled to an equal quantity. This applies to birds, eggs, and fish caught in atoll-wide drives. It also applies where the scarce resource is fixed but where it is difficult to prove its place of origin such as breadfruit and coconuts for drinking. Theft is minimized by restricting people's access to their own resources to certain times, and even then allowing each to take only a specific share.

Copra is usually made by families and the income shared equally to all family members including those unable to help make it, especially the very young, the very ill, and the very old.

In addition to the laws, a number of underlying structural principles, never specifically spelled out but nevertheless fairly clear in every mind, pattern the distribution of land rights. The first question is whether one is or is not a descendant of William Marsters. If not, only marriage to a Marsters, government service, or such rare exceptional circumstances as shipwreck allow a person to even be on the atoll. But most of those descended from Marsters live elsewhere. To remain on Palmerston, in practice a descendant must have been born there, or be adopted by or be married to someone who was.

Status in relation to land on the atoll depends on whether a person is male or female. For men, it depends on whether he is resident agent, lineage head, household head, nuclear family head, or single. Age is important, but it may be more appropriately included in a compound factor which may be called experience, which is an amalgam of age, energy, skills, travel, and achievements. Age of itself means little for the several old men in poor health whose lives were not notable. Particularly in inheritance, where multiple choices are open, an almost entrepreneurial skill seems to lead some to acquire considerably larger shares than others.

The quality of leadership has been an important determinant of social organization in relation to land. William Marsters had autocratic control, but no subsequent individual has had his unique status as common progenitor, longest settler, lessee, and possessor of unique skills. Leadership had to be shared. The lineage functioned for a time as the unit organization, but once the third generation children were adult it was too often challenged so that all lineages at various times made the household or other subdivision the unit of landworking and landholding. The sheer number of persons who find it possible to agree may be a factor in this subdivision. The second lineage, for example, which is by far the largest, is today divided into three functional divisions for what the other lineages do as one.

It seems likely that fragmentation would have gone much further if the resident commissioner had not kept reinforcing the powers of the three lineage heads. Alternatively, if the atoll had been completely isolated from external sanctions, some of the crises would probably have been resolved by force, which might have led to much more centralized and unified control. Group action and equal sharing of effort and income is only feasible if leadership is strong and sanctions quickly enforceable.

The people of Palmerston seem always to have been burdened with anxiety and uncertainty. The disputes recorded in government files confirm the impressions of visitors of constant friction both within and between lineages and families.[48] I suspect that the problem is related to uncertainties, which were constant until 1953, about whether their occupancy of the atoll would be continued; about the validity of their laws and the difficulty of enforcing them; the recency of their traditions, none having become hallowed with time and usage; and the unpredictable and impermanent rulings of external officials, even though they visited the atoll only once in years.

Two of many examples of this concern may be noted. In 1901 the resident commissioner reported that the first lineage was quarrelling with the other two over the possession of the atoll. The parties had tried to get guns to effect their purposes. One man en route to Tahiti to buy guns was stopped by the commissioner.[49]

In 1942, Ronald Powell, a keen observer who lived on the atoll for nearly two years, reported that lineages were not prepared to thin out overcrowded coconut palms, because they believed that the government would give the whole atoll to that lineage which owned the most palms. There is some evidence that the first lineage had hoped to take over the lands of the third when its membership was low. They were especially hopeful because one head of the third lineage was adopted from the first, and a later head was the son of an Aitutaki father and a Palmerston mother.

Rights of all kinds are diminished by absence from the atoll, but the precise nature of the diminution is a matter of uncertainty and sometimes dispute. Acts of ownership are necessary for the perpetuation of rights to house sites and pigpen sites, but these are not lost automatically when structures are no longer standing on the site. Rather, if a site has not been used for a time and the former holder shows no likelihood of returning, the area may be allocated to, or taken over by, a relative, usually by arrangement.

Owing to the absence of written records and my very short stay, it was not possible to obtain any measurable indication of the nature and extent of disputes involving property. Rules are only one factor in this. Influence in the form of social, official, or economic status; numbers; location; and kinship links is also important. The headman of the lineage mediates in disputes, usually by discussion with the heads of component nuclear families. The head of the first lineage has usually also been the government-appointed resident agent and is accorded leadership of the atoll on both counts.[50] In the latter capacity he can help settle land disputes, though he cannot legally rule on boundaries or ownership. This can only be done by the land court, but it has never dealt with Palmerston lands.

If a person breaks a law relating to land, he is likely to be publicly criticized by the headman of his lineage or of the atoll.[51] If the offense is serious or warnings go unheeded, he may be brought to court. The most common punishment is a few days' hard labor clearing paths or tidying the settlement area. Ideally, this work is under the supervision of the constable. In the 1920s and 1930s some offenders dug garden pits as punishment. Although the pits became the property of the person who dug them, they provided the whole island with more emergency reserves in the event of hurricanes, and they reduced the temptation of offenders to steal food from the gardens of others.

Though the application of sanctions was not studied, it appears that the legal court machinery is not the main deterrent.

During the two years preceding my arrival, at least one person had been denied shares and another given a reduced share in the copra money as punishment for not cooperating. This was directly related to disobedience of the edicts of the lineage head concerning copra cutting, but both cases involved other interpersonal tensions. The threat to deny one's copra money is a very effective sanction.

Eviction from the atoll is another powerful sanction for some, though not for the many young people who would enjoy the trip and who know that their labor is needed on the atoll. If a solution is not readily found, the offender may be fined or pressured into leaving by the next ship. This is usually negotiated within the lineage, but in extreme cases the resident agent requests administrative action by the resident commissioner at Rarotonga. Judicial action through the high court or land court is never sought. Several years ago, a particularly able member of the clan was a government official on the atoll. His salary nearly equalled the total income of all other resident clan members put together. Problems arose as a result of his ability to modify the ideal leadership system under the lineage heads, and he was given a more senior post elsewhere by the resident commissioner at the request of the resident agent.

The more important day-to-day sanctions seem to lie in the desire to be accepted and to avoid criticism. These are far from fully effective, however, as interpersonal relations are in some instances such that individuals prefer to create tension rather than avoid it.

Work patterns have had a considerable influence on the developing tenure system. Gardening, pig and poultry keeping, and most fishing are done by households. Women collect reef foods, cook, make hats for sale, and make plaited ware for domestic use. Men fish, climb coconut trees, and build. Both sexes plant, cut copra, and cooperate in some kinds of fishing.

Copra cutting is usually done by households. At the time of my visit, a limit was set in the first lineage on the weight to be cut by each household each round, though one household was divided into two copra-making units. The limit was one hundred pounds per person in the household for the first round of any period of cutting, fifty pounds for the second round, and twenty-five pounds for the third. The other two lineages set quotas of one hundred nuts per person until the supply was low and then fifty nuts.

The nuts (only fallen nuts are used) are collected, husked, and then brought back to the settlement for opening and drying. Each household has its own drying racks. Once dry the copra is weighed and then pooled for storage in the copra shed of that lineage.

The three lineage heads must agree when to lift the 'prohibition' on entry to the coconut islets. Only one islet is worked in any one day to avoid the possibility of theft. Ideally, all lineages go together, but each works its own lands. As the area of planted land on each islet varies much more than the total area of land, and as the numbers in the lineages vary, the time taken by each lineage to cut the copra on any one islet varies considerably. When a lineage has collected all its nuts, it may change to another islet the next day. Then all lineages must work on that islet. A lineage cannot change islets unless it has either used all its nuts on that islet or worked there for three consecutive days (see appendix 2, law no. 13). There is a lot of friendly rivalry about who will be first to begin work on an islet and who will be first to complete work on it. Once a lineage has completed the round of all islets or has got the quota that it set, it must wait for the other two lineages to finish. Once all are finished, the second round starts. Again they stay only until the first of them has completed. Finally, the last lineage goes and finishes up. But one member of each of the other lineages will accompany the last lineage to obviate theft.

Although this is the law, it is not always carried out, even within lineages—households which are behind are sometimes left behind to catch up later, especially in the case of temporary sickness. Aged and chronically ill persons are not required to make copra if they do not wish to, but they receive an equal share of the proceeds.

Sorting and bagging copra and loading the schooner is done by the three lineages separately.

Two features were quite striking during my stay: the leisurely pace of work, for subsistence can be gained in a very short time and copra is limited in supply, and the high proportion of the work undertaken by children.

The above rules and behavior patterns are not absolute, though each determines behavior in varying degrees. Age, sex, and skills in personal negotiation modify their operation in practice. Nevertheless, formal rules may be more important than on other atolls in Polynesia, partly because Palmerston has a much smaller body of tradition to draw on. On Palmerston the law seemed to be on everybody's lips, though few had read it.

Behavior relating to the rights of government and the three lineages always seemed to take cognizance of the local law and of local understandings about the government's law, but behavior relating to the rights of individuals seemed to be conditioned much more by personal circumstances. Nevertheless, many personal circumstances were closely related to local laws about marriage, adoption, inheritance, and so on.

TRANSFER OF RIGHTS

The laws of the Cook Islands forbid the sale of land except to the government for public purposes. Leases are permitted, but no land on Palmerston has been leased. Permissive use of land has been granted by the separate lineages and by the Marsters's clan as a whole to residents who are not members of the clan, but the numbers are few and the rights accorded minimal. For practical purposes then, inheritance is the only means of transfer of land rights.

When asked who could inherit land rights on Palmerston, a group of the atoll dwellers said that anyone descended from William Marsters was entitled to do so. But when asked whether descendants not born on the atoll could inherit rights, they said that they could not unless they were adopted by or married to a resident or were given permission by the head of the lineage to which they belonged.[52] The claims of every man now resident on the atoll come from a parent who is or was also a resident. Questions about whether persons born on Palmerston but long absent from it could return and resume their rights were met with a diversity of answers. There is no ruling on the point, though some felt strongly that those who had been away too long should not be allowed back. There was lack of agreement as to whether this matter was determined by the head of the atoll, the head of the lineage, or the head of the family. In the actual cases noted, it had been negotiated individually with the lineage head. Several residents had earlier been absent from the atoll for as long as ten years, but in at least one case some persons considered that the former absentee should not have returned because he had been away so long.

Absence obviously diminishes one's rights. Those not born on the atoll almost never acquire rights there. This could be because of the difficulty of getting to Palmerston, the lack of desire to go there, or to resistance from those on the atoll. In this regard, it should be noted that the annual schooner calls at many islands and seldom has room for all who wish to travel.

Mr. Ned Marsters explained the present unwritten law about wills. This was confirmed by several other elders, except where noted. When a man thinks he is going to die, he should at least call together all his nuclear family plus the head of his lineage. Any of his issue or siblings who have married into other lineages should also attend. The dying person says what is to be done with his lands, house, trees, and other property, though most of these things are already known and have been taking shape for some time. The house will remain with other members of the household, and the children or others supporting him from the land will usually get the land. Trees can be allocated to various individuals. But if the important members of the lineage disagree with anything the dying person says, then it may be changed to accord with their view. Minority views not supported by the head of the lineage are usually disregarded.

The will should be written and three witnesses should sign it, but this is seldom done in practice, oral wills being more usual. Approximately equal provision should be made for resident children who have not married out or been adopted out. Special provision is commonly made for individual close relatives who have been particularly friendly or helpful. Thus, if a particular person has cared for a dying man during old age or a long final illness, it is proper to remember him with a larger share of land and trees. Provided he bequeaths within his lineage, the dying person seems to have considerable choice. One case was cited several times as an example of a bad will in which a man gave most of his lands and all his trees to his favorite grandchild. Though several members of the lineage, including his successor, thought him wrong in this, nobody objected and the grandson has the land and trees now. It may have been significant that the deceased was a lineage head and a strong personality.

Food trees can be, and often are, willed separately from land. Likewise an arrowroot crop can be willed separately from the land on which it is growing, but no replanting is permitted without the approval of the landowner.

Women have little to transmit. They are not regarded as landowners, and few have more than some food trees to will. A man's will is not supposed to take effect during his wife's lifetime, for William Marsters is said to have ruled that a wife inherits the *use* of everything from her husband for her lifetime. In practice, the effect of this ruling varies depending on the age of the wife and children. Many older women allow the will to take full effect and are thereafter supported by the beneficiaries.

Although the oral law says that one cannot will property outside one's lineage, it does occur in some cases where a beneficiary has marginal status in more than one family either by uxorilocal residence, of which there was one case in 1959, or by adoption, which is common.[53] It is also considered proper for land to be given to facilitate the return to the lineage of a former adoptee or a woman who wants to divorce or separate. The beneficiary is not supposed to exercise such rights until he or she shifts residence to the lineage in which the rights are held.

When land rights are willed, the lineage head is supposed to ensure that adequate provision has been made for all resident children of the testator and that the distribution is equitable. Nevertheless, it seems that decisions on transfer are not only a matter of rights, but also of relative influence. Examples of persons who died or left the atoll without resident issue show that lineage heads and forceful individuals often inherited at the expense of closer kin.

Even though the three lineages are based on descent from one or another of the three original mothers, descent and inheritance thereafter are universally stated to be patrilineal. However there are many exceptions. Though most adoption is within the lineage, many children have been adopted into other lineages, in which case they inherit through that lineage rather than in their families of birth. Children of divorced, separated, or unmarried mothers sometimes inherit from them as do resident children whose fathers are not of the Marsters clan. But these cases are rare.

Land is sometimes lent. William Marsters laid down that no money shall pass between clan members for land or produce. For loans of garden plots, however, it is now considered appropriate that the donee make a small gift of produce to the donor. Most garden land is in constant use due to the steady increase in population, and more pits are dug from time to time. If land pressure increases, the size and obligatory nature of the gift seem likely to increase.

All resident descendants are considered to have the right to remain and to transmit their rights to their progeny. All persons I asked denied any preferences or selective processes to force or encourage any category of persons to leave the atoll or to remain. The data suggests, however, that selective processes have been at work, whether consciously or not. William Marsters had seventeen children from his three wives, but all persons resident on the atoll in 1959 trace descent from only eight of them. Though many of the progeny of these eight live elsewhere, none of the progeny of the other nine live on Palmerston. Of the eight from whom descent is traced, four were men and four were women, but of the eighty-four resident descendants plus their wives, seventy-one trace their line to the four men and only thirteen to the four women. Of the thirteen who trace from women, a considerable, but undeterminable, proportion trace from women who were divorced, separated, or unmarried. This is not unexpected in that the original children, all being half-siblings, had to seek spouses off the atoll. A number of men brought their wives back to the atoll, but, as far as I know, all the women who married out remained on the islands of their husbands.

A similar trend showed up in those persons claiming rights, either by descent or by marriage to a descendant, from persons of the second generation from William Marsters. The eighty-one persons concerned claimed these rights from nine men and two women,[54] but seventy-nine of the eighty-one claimed from the men and only two from the women.

The rigid division of land on Palmerston into three portions has remained constant. The lineages began at approximately the same size with the three wives having six, six, and five children, respectively.

However, the idiosyncracies of human fertility have led to considerable flux in the size of lineages and, in the case of the second lineage, among lineage sections.

A fixed resource base combined with a fluctuating population of component groups requires flexibility if opportunities are to be made more equal and production maximized. The mechanisms of flexibility on Palmerston are migration, adoption, wills, uxorilocal marriage, and ad hoc arrangements, usually rationalized in terms of matrilateral or quasi-adoptive links.

CONCLUSIONS

Rights to use have become subdivided by both area and number of right holders more quickly than rights of a proprietary kind. Rights in consumer produce, especially foods, were shared equally on a communal basis until the death of William Marsters, then on a lineage basis. At present they are generally on a household basis though there are some individual rights such as in food trees. Rights in export produce were first autocratically controlled by William Marsters, who also determined the expenditure of income. In the latter part of his life, export produce was put on a share basis whereby the producer received a part of the income from his products. It will be noted that rights in consumer produce fragmented much later than those in relation to export incomes. The fragmentation of land use rights led, after a period of close identification and labor investment, to the recognition of rights of a proprietary kind.

Each problem which has arisen has been resolved, usually after considerable trouble and experimentation, by the acceptance of a law or principle which defines rights with greater specificity and restriction. This is illustrated in table 20.

The various levels at which different categories of rights on Palmerston are held are the product of a balance of forces. The processes tending toward the holding of rights by smaller units and by individuals include the following:

(1) Demands for differential rights in accordance with differential effort, particularly where the results of differential effort were demonstrably different.

(2) Disputes over rewards for land-based resources, whether the dispute was based on effort, inheritance, or affiliation.

(3) Wish to work in smaller rather than larger groups, the smaller ones being more closely tailored to individual needs and idiosyncracies.

(4) Defects in personal leadership.

TABLE 20 Increasing Diversification and Precision of Rights on Palmerston Atoll

Period	Use Rights to Consumer Produce	Exploitation Rights to Export Produce	Proprietary Rights to Capital Assets
Pre-1870s	Communal	Communal	Autocratic
1870s–1899*	Communal	Partly communal, partly individual	Autocratic
Early 1900s	Communal below high water. Lineage on land. Individual for tree crops.	Partly lineage, partly individual	Communal below high water, road, and church. Lineages for land. Individual for trees.
Present	Communal below high water. Lineage for foraging and hunting. Household for garden crops. Individual for tree crops.	Partly lineage, partly individual	Communal below high water, road, and church. Lineage for lands. Household for gardens. Individual for trees.

*William Marsters died in 1899.

The processes tending toward the holding of rights by larger units include the following:

(1) The ethic of sharing and the feeling of common identity. William Marsters laid down, and the Bible is frequently quoted to reinforce the view, that Palmerston people are all one family and should work and share together.

(2) The formal structure of leadership. The government has always

supported the resident agent, a post usually held by the head of the first lineage, as paramount. The existence of an atoll head, a head of each of the three lineages, and of each household is accepted by all, though the extent of authority ideally held at each level is not always agreed on.

(3) The tendency to suspect the motives of others when alone or in small groups leads to larger groupings than necessary to undertake almost any activity on islets other than Home Islet, and is conducive to larger landholding units. If everyone were confident that people would not steal nuts or other supplies, it is likely that the islets would have been divided into individual or nuclear family units.

(4) The fear of hurricanes, tsunami, and erosion. These do not do equal damage to all land areas; they increase the lands of some, decrease others, and damage crops in some areas more than others. The allocation of a single area of land to each individual or nuclear family would leave them vulnerable to carrying all the losses. It would also deny people access to all islets but the one on which their land was located. On an atoll which already provides few places to go, this would further restrict a degree of movement which people obviously enjoy.

Several factors lead to preferences for intermediate groupings. The vulnerability of the individual leads to the strengthening of units larger than the individual, but smaller than the atoll or even the lineage. One may get sick, old, or leave the island temporarily. Most do not trust those far above them in the hierarchy as much as they trust those whose identity and interests are more closely bound with their own. This lends cohesiveness to the sibling group, the nuclear family, and the sections of the lineage. Because there are many islets, boats are essential. They can best be made and handled by more than one person, but the population of the whole atoll or even of the whole lineage would be far too large a unit for this purpose.

Copra is worked by intermediate groups, but it is difficult to determine whether it would be more or less efficiently worked by individuals or by the population as a whole. The present processes of gathering, husking, splitting, and sun-drying can be done as efficiently by nuclear families as by work groups. In fact, households are the most usual copra-making units as distinct from the unit holding the copra lands—the lineage (except in the case of the second lineage).

Appendix 1

Agreement dated 8 September 1946

Agreement made by William Marsters [whether the original William Marsters or his son is referred to is not clear] not to be change:—

(1) In our share every body will be the same.

If any one gets a coconut every one will have the same.

Earning on the Island belong to every body. If anybody wants to depart on the Island his share will be put together to the one who stops on the Island till he arrives back.

(2) Everything I been controlling on Palmerston is handle over to Ned, till to the season Carl wants to return back, Ned will handed over to him (Carl). If any of these two boys wants to go out the one stops on the Island will take the place.

If all these two boys passes away the ruling of the Island will be handed over to Carl Junior (Jnr.)

No Resident Agent is allowed to come on the Island and rule, picked by the Commissioner. Palmerston will pick its own Resident Agent to rule the Island not by the Government.

```
              Signed by  =  WILLIAM MARSTERS
                            [the second]
                         =  NED MARSTERS
                         =  CARL MARSTERS (JNR.)
                       ⎧ =  TUTAI MARSTERS
              Witness  ⎨
                       ⎩ =  JOHN TARIAU
                            [Radio Operator]
```

The Secretary,
Department of Island Territories,
WELLINGTON.

Copy for your file.

    (sgd.)   A. McCARTHY,
               Dep. Res. Commr.,
               4.10.1946.

Appendix 2

Laws dated 28 October 1949

These are written in the Rarotongan language in a book held by Mr. Ned Marsters, resident agent and head of the first lineage. They were copied with his permission on 20 November 1959. The portions relevant to land tenure are presented below translated into English:

1. *The law relating to the three lineages:* It shall not be lawful for any person to separate himself (or herself) from his or her lineage. When manufacturing copra, or picking green or dry coconuts or anything else whatsoever, he must inform all of his intention.

2. *The law on visits to islets:* It shall not be lawful for any lineage to visit any islets without prior notification to the other lineages. A penalty of ten days shall be imposed (i.e., ten days hard labor).

3. *The law about bosun birds:* It shall not be lawful to catch bosun birds except with the consent of all three lineages during the period it is lawful to catch them for distribution among all the people. Any person seen catching bosun birds when it is not lawful shall be liable to a penalty of ten days together with one bird.

4. *The law about coconut leaflets used in hat-making:* Any person seen cutting leaflets belonging to another lineage shall be liable to a penalty of ten days, as will any person tampering with leaflets belonging to his own lineage. It is lawful for a person to cut one leaflet, but thereafter that palm is not to be touched until there are at least four leaves on it before cutting another leaflet therefrom.

5. *The law about palms overhanging the property of another lineage:* Any coconut falling from a palm which overhangs the property of another lineage shall be returned to owners of the property upon which such palm is growing. The penalty for taking such a coconut is ten days. [Mr. Ned Marsters stated that the minister of territories had told him in New Zealand in 1958 that this law should be changed to the New Zealand law whereby the produce would belong to the person whose property it overhung. Mr. Marsters informed me that the New Zealand law would be the law but noted

that the Palmerston custom, which follows the Penrhyn Island precedent, would probably be followed by the people in practice.]

The laws of Palmerston were first written out by William Marsters II though many date from the time of William Marsters I. Those laws were destroyed in the 1926 hurricane. In 1949 the resident commissioner came and asked about the laws. He had the above (plus some others) written for the Palmerston people according to what they said were the old laws.

Additional laws on loose paper in the book (paraphrased)

13. *The law about going to the islets to make copra:* Any lineage going to an islet is to notify other lineages and all are to go to that one. It is not permitted to work more than one islet any one day. After three days on one islet they can change to another, but any lineage which has *completed* its copra on one islet can go to another after one day. Any lineage finished should still send some representative to an islet if any other lineage is working there. Only after all lineages complete all islets can they start ticketing again for the next round.

14. *The law about shooting birds:* Nobody is allowed to go to the islets to shoot birds.

15. *The law about the life of the people:* If one person gets a coconut, every person must get one.

NOTES

1. I collected most of the data during a thirty-day visit to Palmerston in November and December 1959. Unless otherwise stated, this chapter describes the situation at that time. The visit was possible because the schooner which serviced the atoll, usually once a year, on this occasion unloaded at Palmerston en route to the northern atolls and called back to load on its return to Rarotonga a month later. Supplementary data was obtained from government files and from John Burland, who has studied the history of the atoll and spent several months there during 1960. The help and kindness of Ned Marsters and all members of the Marsters clan both on Palmerston and Rarotonga is acknowledged with sincere thanks. Other persons who have kindly assisted with information, advice, or editorial comment, include John Harre, Robin Hide, Amirah Inglis, Michael Lieber, Henry Lundsgaarde, Louis Marsters, Gerard

Nash, M. Paget, Ron Powell, and Susan Tarua. The maps were kindly provided by courtesy of the New Zealand surveyor-general, R. Gough.
2. The word *family* is used on Palmerston for what I here call lineages. As Palmerston people use the word *family* to refer either to all of Marsters's descendants or to the descendants of any wife or subgroups of such descendants or for nuclear families, I will refer to the descendants of any one of the three original wives, the most important divisions, as a lineage.
3. It lies at 18°04' south latitude and 163°10' west longitude. Its nearest neighbors are Aitutaki, 195 miles southeast; Suwarrow, 280 miles north; Pukapuka, 480 miles northwest; and Niue 400 miles west.
4. In 1964 the atoll had about 173 persons per square mile compared with an average of about 313 per square mile for other inhabited atolls of the northern Cooks, and 457 persons per square mile in the neighboring Tokelau atolls.
5. Waves generated by submarine earthquakes.
6. Large numbers of Marsters's descendants live on Rarotonga, Aitutaki, Penrhyn, Manihiki, and Rakahanga. There are probably a few on every other island in the Cook group. There are many in New Zealand, some in Australia and Tahiti, and probably others elsewhere. The total number of descendants from Marsters and his three wives was estimated from Mrs. M. Paget's comprehensive genealogy to be about 800 in 1959, of whom only 95 lived on the atoll. The total today must be close to 1,200.
7. For fear that it will be used to demarcate the government's ten acres (see page 235).
8. The main crop grown is *Cyrtosperma chamisonnis*, a large cultivated tuber grown in brackish swamp in man-made garden pits.
9. For the seven years, 1953–1959 inclusive, copra exports averaged 19.7 tons per year. Assuming that the islanders were paid an average of $NZ60 per ton, this would yield a per capita income from copra of only $NZ12 per year.
10. I would guess that these seven officials were paid an average of about $NZ300 per year each.
11. This control seems to have been accepted in the earlier years, but it became increasingly necessary to reinforce it as he grew older and his sons reached manhood. The fact that this lonely man with several wives had to guard himself with dogs and a rifle (Gill 1885:39) may have Freudian significance. The fact that he sought the introduction of Christianity to restore peace to a community formerly without religion may support Durkheim's view of the function of religion as a means of social control.
12. The two teachers, who were brothers, were Aitutakians. They were cousins of a member of the third lineage who had been resident on the atoll at the time of their arrival and were regarded for certain purposes as members of this lineage. Likewise, the medical assistant, from Rakahanga, was a nephew of the deceased wife of the head of the first lineage.
13. These rights and titles had little legal basis as Palmerston was not within the domains of any sovereign power.

14. Oral tradition on the atoll today simplifies this very complex period and states that Marsters joined Strickland on the atoll but that Strickland left and handed over his rights to Marsters to annul Strickland's debts.
15. Under the Western Pacific Order in Council of August 1877.
16. Marsters's acceptance of a lease was technically inconsistent with his claim of ownership, but in the circumstances there was no way in which he could legally assert ownership. A crown lease was the only legal way he could exclude his competitors.
17. Morrell 1960:287. Palmerston had been leased in 1867 to a Mr. Lavington Evans of Australia by the British government, but the lease was never taken up (Burland, personal communication).
18. On 31 December 1941 the crown leased the atoll to the then heads of the three lineages by personal name "and their survivors." This could be read as implying that nonmembers of the lessees' lineages, particularly nonresidents, had no legal rights, but a later section of the lease stated that the lease granted exclusive rights of occupation to the lessees "and others the issue of William Marsters deceased." The lease was for twenty-one years, at a rental of £50 per year, renewable for a further twenty-one years on the same terms. The New Zealand government reserved the power to cancel it and take over the atoll, without compensation, provided it gave one year's notice. The lessees were not to let or mortgage the lease, or any right under it, without the approval of the minister of island territories. The backlog of unpaid rent was wiped out.
19. Cook Islands Amendment Act 1954, section 2.
20. Present population is given in the socio-cultural context above.
21. A number of descendants have been given the same name, but when used here, the name William Marsters refers to this original patriarch.
22. Home Islet is legally named Palmerston Islet, but as the latter name is also used for the atoll as a whole the colloquial name of Home Islet is used.
23. The village site on Home Islet was divided separately, the first lineage being given the central portion and the other two lineages placed on the east and west sides, respectively. One or two houses had to be shifted to the land now allocated to their owners.
24. Persons resident on Palmerston whose mothers came from outside the atoll retain links with their mothers' kin, but the extent to which these links include land rights is seldom defined. In practice, the nature and extent of rights are likely to depend on supplementary ties, such as reciprocal gift giving, visiting, or adoption of children, and, particularly, on need.
25. The governor-general had no legal authority to make such rules, but because of his towering prestige and the islanders' assumption that he had almost infinite power, this was not questioned.
26. As an administrative officer, the resident commissioner had no authority to tell people how to allocate their business profits, but again the people assumed he had the authority. Had he been challenged by somebody off the island, which is most unlikely, the commissioner would no doubt have said that his was only a suggestion, though he must have known that the people would regard it as an instruction.
27. For the making of copra see p. 250.

28. Thus one person may be spoken of as the owner of a pit or a plot within it but may allow another to plant a garden in some or all of it. Ideally, both parties should be of the same lineage, but there are some exceptions.
29. It existed only in small quantities until the death of William Marsters, for the pigs were not penned until then.
30. Breadfruit is a very important source of food, and the people use it extensively to save coconuts for copra making.
31. In such cases, equal quantities are picked by each owner at prearranged times.
32. See p. 231.
33. Though the lease of 31 December 1941 specifically included the reef.
34. The schooner left the Cook Islands shortly afterwards, and the scheme was discontinued.
35. See page 217 and footnote 6.
36. The act resulted from continued pressure by Mr. W. H. Watson, a member of the Cook Islands legislative council, which was formed in 1946. Mr. Watson's electorate, mainly on Rarotonga, also included Palmerston Atoll, but most of the pressure for the new legislation came from Palmerston people who lived permanently on Rarotonga.
37. Those benefits include shares of the product of communal drives for fish or crabs, a share of turtles' eggs, and in some cases a share of income from copra.
38. A letter of 16 December 1934 in the secretariat, Rarotonga, contains a complaint by a Palmerston woman that her father's share had been usurped by the head of the lineage.
39. I did not find any written cases of this kind, but one which indicated the acceptance of the resident commissioner's control over movement occurred in 1908 when Joel Marsters, then headman on the atoll, wrote asking the resident commissioner's permission to go to Aitutaki and plant his wife's land. The permission was granted and he went.
40. Cook Islands Amendment Act, 1954.
41. A Congregational church now known as the Cook Islands Christian Church.
42. The legality of the resident commissioner's action and his refusal to permit S.D.A. adherents to return was doubtful indeed. However, as they were not on the atoll when the 1954 legislation vested it only in those who did reside there, the exclusion of those banished is now legalized. People on the atoll with whom this was discussed, however, did not see it in these terms at all, but in terms of a law which forbids S.D.A. adherents. No such law exists except in the colloquial sense that Palmerston people tend to refer to accepted understandings of this kind as laws. Those with whom I spoke, however, considered its power derived from the fact that it was a ruling of the resident commissioner of Rarotonga. This was to a considerable extent true formerly, but with self-government of the Cooks in 1965 this post was abolished. Many of those who were resettled, and their descendants, claim that it was a voluntary resettlement at a time of food shortage. There is probably some truth in both views, but the Adventists have stayed away in any case.
43. This is supported by the law recorded on 8 September 1946 that "if

anybody wants to depart on the Island his share will be put together to the one who stops on the island till he arrives back." Records in Rarotonga, however, show that this has been a matter of contention for decades. Joel Marsters, who had been absent from the atoll for five years, wrote to the resident commissioner describing himself as the "Resident Agent and lessee of Palmerston" and claiming two pounds sterling per ton on all copra exported from Palmerston. He offered to accept responsibility for continued planting and production on Palmerston despite the fact that he lived on Aitutaki. The records do not show whether his requests were granted, though probably they were not.

44. In one case they were cross-cousins by adoption, the husband having been born in another lineage. In the other case the blood relationship was also relatively distant, the wife being the husband's mother's father's brother's son's daughter. Both these marriages were within the largest lineage.
45. John Fernandez, William Marsters's lifelong friend and helper, brought two wives to the atoll at different times and had children there. Within a short time after his death in 1898, however, Fernandez's issue had either been absorbed by adoption into one or another of the three Marsters families or left the atoll. His eldest son was adopted by Marsters himself and became head of the third lineage.
46. By contrast, boys are more commonly preferred elsewhere in the Cook Islands.
47. There have been a few applications for land court sittings on Palmerston, but, owing to a heavy backlog of work on larger islands, they have not been heard.
48. The fear of hurricanes and droughts may be a factor, though it does not seem to have this effect on the people of Pukapuka which is the nearest inhabited atoll. For a description of Pukapuka, see Beaglehole (1938). Ronald Powell observes that very few who have lived for many years outside Palmerston wish to return there to live, because of the "continuous tension and strain of living in this small isolated community."
49. *New Zealand Parliamentary Papers*, A.3, 1902.
50. As resident agent, he has jurisdiction as a commissioner of the high court, which enables him to try minor offences.
51. The most common offences relate to visiting or taking produce from areas under prohibition.
52. As noted on page 242 the legislation restricts the rights to persons resident in 1954 and their descendants, but nobody quoted the legislation on the point, and, apart from the head of the first lineage, nobody may have been aware of it.
53. See pages 243–244.
54. Though in one marriage of adopted cross-cousins, the inheritance is claimed as being from both the mother, who was the eldest child of the eldest son of the second lineage, and the father, who was adopted by a woman of that lineage.

PACIFIC LAND TENURE IN A NUTSHELL

Henry P. Lundsgaarde

As empirical data on systems of land tenure in Oceania accumulate, it becomes both necessary and possible to sharpen the conceptual tools that will clear the way toward general theory. Although much work still lies ahead before such a theory can be constructed, we have reached a significant threshold. It is the purpose of this concluding chapter to discuss some of the land tenure principles that have emerged in the previous chapters.

Comparative analysis of different land tenure systems is rewarding, as one does not encounter as many obstacles to comparison as with many other aspects of culture. This does not mean that the structure of any given tenure system reveals itself without much effort. On the contrary, each contributor to this volume has demonstrated how knowledge of land tenure is acquired by detailed empirical analysis of both social organization and total cultural context. Clarity and explanation, therefore, are not derived from simplicity of data but from the discovery of general principles in otherwise diverse settings and circumstances.

Although the description, classification, and analysis of land tenure variables can begin from any base, it would be appropriate to sequence the study in order of relative difficulty. One might start with a description of terrestrial physiography and general ecology, continue with a description of land use and resource allocation, and conclude by an analysis of the ideological rules which define the different obligations that attach to forms of individual or collective ownership. This sequence corresponds roughly to the three foci of all land tenure systems: the territorial resource base essential to survival, the socio-economic institutions necessary for efficient exploitation, and the ideological base imperative to cultural continuity. It will be assumed that these foci are both universal and elementary to cross-cultural generalization. The variety and diversity of land tenure systems found in Oceania represent a formidable challenge to the soundness of these assumptions, yet it should not be difficult to test their efficacy against land tenure data from other culture areas.

Serious objections against any general model or analytical perspective may easily arise, however. The numerical increase in anthropological and other researchers will challenge any generalist, because empirical analysis of individual systems provides the only input for a general theoretical system. Unless new data can be incorporated into the system, the theoretical system itself must be changed. At the same time, however, it is essential to begin with a general perspective. To put the matter simply, we have reached the point in studies of Pacific land tenure systems which separates a past phase dominated by particularistic studies of individual societies from an emerging phase which adds a generalizing dimension.

The most serious of the remaining problems is epistemological. For example, to what extent does a researcher's own conceptions of land tenure distort his observations of a foreign tenure practice or, conversely, to what extent may his emphasis on understanding native conceptions obscure the universal by focusing on the particular? Very few, if any, subscribe to the extreme theoretical absurdity that because analytical concepts are developed within one intellectual tradition they must be considered ethnocentric and inapplicable to other systems. The substantive chapters in this volume suggest how one may reach a balance between the folk and analytical concepts of tenure without, in my opinion, distorting the data too severely in either direction.

A related problem is the absence of clearly defined cultural and analytical boundaries between land tenure and other institutions. Also, there may be no exact native equivalents for traditional Anglo-Saxon land tenure categories or any separate cultural concepts which parallel ours. It is therefore only in the abstract that we can speak of land tenure in Oceania as something separate from kinship, social obligation, politics, or family law.

The concept *land tenure* refers to a multitude of reciprocal rights and duties that arise in relation to real property. To make it operational and apply this broad definition in different cultural contexts it is necessary to explore each of the following questions: What aspects of the natural environment are categorized as real property? What proprietary rights and duties are said to correspond with each such category? How are such rights and duties acquired, upheld, and alienated? If data from different tenure systems prove sufficiently uniform on these points, one can develop a generally valid conceptualization of land tenure for the culture area as a whole.

For Oceania in general it makes good sense to group various forms of real property into three categories: above surface, surface, and subsurface. Properties in the first category include those trees and plants which are economically important to arboriculture and technologically significant as raw material for artifacts and shelter. Surface properties include surface soil and in some settings the lagoon or reef areas contiguous in space with land. It should be noted that surface space should technically be defined as horizontal territory, enclosed within a culturally defined set of boundaries, rather than as real property. Subsurface properties include such man-made improvements as garden pits, wells, and fishponds. The food products derived from horticulture can also be categorized as subsurface property. Each category may in turn be divided further into improved and unimproved property.

It is important to emphasize that these categories of property correspond rather closely with three general kinds of proprietary rights. Trees, palms, and garden pits can be owned by someone who does not have surface rights to the space where these may be located, and conversely, a person can have surface rights only. In that case he would not possess any rights which would allow him to harvest the plant products grown within his territory. The confusion over use and territory rights that could result from a rigid system of tripartite categorization of tenure rights, if such rights were held by different persons, is avoided in part by such mechanisms as corporate ownership, concurrent possession, and subdivision of spatial land units into family estates.

It may be said that the different number and kinds of tenure rights applied to any category of real property multiply in direct relationship to the number of right holders. Yet when we look at the evidence it becomes necessary to discriminate between an infinitesimal variety of different rights that may apply to any given form of real property. This has proven one of the most difficult problems to be resolved for each society. Crocombe's description of tenure rights on Palmerston Island illustrates how one can address the problem. He provides an inventory of the rights that apply to various kinds of property together with a descriptive account of how these rights are distributed among individuals, social groups, and institutions. But this procedure proves cumbersome for comparative and general analysis.

The variety of tenure rights found within every society is multiplied and compounded by comparative analysis. The right of a Palmerston islander to harvest coconuts from one tree is different from the parallel right of a Lamotrek native. The right of each is subject to societal or contextual definitions of rights and duties. However, awareness of these subtle differences in contextual meaning need not take us back full circle to the epistemological contrast between native and analytical terms. There is to my knowledge no language in Oceania which contains a lexical term exactly parallel to the English term *right*. The English term itself is polysemous. Even in the field of jurisprudence, where one might expect to find a more precise definition of legal right, there is only superficial agreement to conceptualize right as a positive legal quality (Hohfeld 1919).

Terminological ambiguity or the absence of precise lexical definition can partly be resolved by the ethnographer. He simply operationalizes the English terms which he finds useful for the description of contextually or culturally bound usage. A more serious hurdle presents itself as soon as we seek to describe the similarities between different cultural systems. I proceed toward the goal of generalization with two assumptions. First, it is assumed that the application of time-tested ethnological and jurisprudential concepts to data on different tenure systems can expose the most significant similarities and differences in tenure principles. Neologisms, folk conceptions, or other similar ways to "objectify" particular data are by and large unnecessary when we talk about land tenure in general. Second, the application of basic Anglo-Saxon tenure and property conceptions to Pacific tenure systems can facilitate additional insight by way of contrast and analogy.

Everywhere in Oceania it is possible for men and women alike to acquire and exercise some kinds of proprietary rights. The distribution of such rights among the members of any given society generally correlates with well-defined social categories. These categories, which are surprisingly limited in number, can be arranged on a hierarchical scale.

PACIFIC LAND TENURE IN A NUTSHELL

The apex and base of this scale represent extremes on a continuum of generality and specificity. Proprietary rights in the most general category thus represent those kinds of rights that are shared by many different persons who in turn may not share other rights in common. This point can be illustrated by reference to the social rules which serve to differentiate the proprietary and other related rights and duties in every society. These rules, in brief, are founded on such universally recognized principles as: descent (patrilineal, matrilineal, or cognatic), social status differentiation by relative social rank (vertically stratified or broadly egalitarian), relative age (birth order and generational affiliation), or sexual identity. Within each of these categories there may be other attributes such as the degree and closeness of relationship, consanguineal or affinal status rank, or status connected with plural marriage, concepts of legitimacy, and various forms of friendship and adoptive relationships.

The empirical foundations for this scheme are well illustrated in the previous chapters. To simplify the discussion of how this analytical scheme applies to concrete social fact, I will rely on my own data from the southern Gilberts. The situation here is much less complex than in other regions, because these societies are unstratified, classless, and egalitarian. To categorize the proprietary rights and duties of a Gilbertese person, one would merely have to identify his kinship status. This status is well defined by his inclusion in a particular cognatic descent category; his rank within a kin group based on such factors as age seniority, individual leadership ability, and marital status; and his or her sex. The relative allocation or distribution of proprietary rights and duties associated with the individual's status are outlined in my previous chapter. Here it is sufficient to point to the important nexus between the distribution of proprietary rights and the societal rules which define social status.

It is now possible to show how two seemingly unrelated social patterns converge and thereby reveal the distribution of proprietary rights in a land tenure system. The categories of real property broadly define which aspects of the productive environment are important enough to be subjected to rules of ownership and tenure. On the other hand, the principles of social organization specify the criteria by which proprietorship for each category of real property can be established.

One can say that any system of land tenure arises from the categorization of differentially productive resources into classes of property. Each of these classes is subject to different forms of ownership and possession. Finally, the forms of ownership and possession are defined by the unequal distribution of proprietary rights among persons of unequal social status.

We can now ask if the distribution of proprietary rights for all Pacific tenure systems taken as a whole correspond to any parallel or analogous distribution of rights in Western tenure systems. If they do correspond in principle to such historically unrelated systems it clears the way for ready comparison. If they do not correspond to anything that we already know about, it will be necessary to invent a new vocabulary and conceptual framework to accommodate the description of novel tenure patterns. The latter alternative is unnecessary for comparative analysis at this level of abstraction.

Proprietary rights may be discussed as different forms of tenure. We have seen how different proprietary rights arise and it is now time to consider in more detail what these rights are. Similar kinds of rights can be collectively described as a particular form of tenure. Different tenure forms can be found, in greater or lesser number, in all Pacific island societies. We need to know what these forms are for each society as well as for all the societies viewed collectively. To accomplish what can only be regarded as a simplification and overview, I will attempt to characterize the various estate interests in land that characterize different tenures. These tenures will be discussed in order of their exclusiveness. It should also be noted that the analysis excludes any consideration of public or overall societal interests in land. Estate interests are said to reside exclusively with private persons or social groups that are contextually conceptualized as single entities.

There are no societies in Oceania that can be said to allow persons to hold a fee simple estate interest in land. A fee simple interest in land is potentially of infinite duration (for a detailed description of Anglo-Saxon estate principles see the legal treatises by Moynihan 1962, Casner and Leach 1969). The fee simple also implies a maximization of tenant ownership rights and a minimization of duties in relationship to the state or other centralized authority. All landowners in Oceania sustain their ownership rights, which in some societies amount to the exercise of political power, primarily because they manage to balance their rights with the performance of well-defined duties. The most compelling evidence against the recognition of the fee simple interest resides with the universally recognized limitation on alienation, that is, landowners cannot dispose of their lands as they may please. Although Murdock and Goodenough (1947:331–343) and Goodenough (1961) convincingly argue that the members of a Truk lineage hold what they call a "lineage fee simple" interest in all lands within its traditional territory, they also state that the paramount chief could confiscate lineage lands if the members of the lineage failed to fulfill their duties to the district chief. The presence of such reciprocal right and duty relationships are, as they put it, ". . . somewhat reminiscent of subinfeudation in European feudal land law" (Murdock and Goodenough 1947: 337). The estate interest thus described falls far short of meeting the criteria of the fee simple tenure form.

It is fruitless to search for Pacific parallelisms to the fee simple estate, but the analogy between fee tail and life estates, which represented less than fee simple interests in early English property law, may be considered advantageously. Both a fee tail and a life estate limit the ability of a landowner to alienate his estate as he may please. An entailed estate restricts conveyance to the owner's lineal descendants. Similarly, the life estate limits the rights of ownership and possession to the duration of a person's life. The tenure principles attributed to these two estate interests can be merged into what might be called an "ancestral estate."

An ancestral estate can be characterized as a cluster of proprietary rights that can be held by persons who acquire these rights by virtue of common descent, who exercise their rights during a lifetime, and who can reconvey such rights only through inheritance. The widespread use of land conveyancing as a form of gift in the Pacific does modify the analogy, but only partially. Such gift conveyances are usually contingent upon all or most of those who share common proprietary interest in an estate giving their consent to such a transfer. The rights held by a particular person during his own lifetime generally revert to the ancestral estate if he dies without issue. The recognition of complex descent rules does not significantly alter this definition of the ancestral estate. It remains to be shown how proprietary rights in an ancestral estate are distributed among those who claim such rights. Generational differences, relative age and sex attributes, or degrees of genealogical distance may be important variables, as are relative need and social or political pressure. If rights in ancestral estates are determined largely by rules of descent, we also need to know specifically how such rules discriminate among those descendants who are said to belong or not belong to the category of proprietor. The problem would be much simpler if all persons of common descent acquired rights in ancestral estates, which of course is not the case for any known society. We therefore need to know for each society exactly how a particular rule of descent circumscribes the category of proprietors who can exercise rights in a common ancestral estate. It is also necessary to establish what rules govern the unequal allocation of rights among the persons assigned to a common descent category. Since these rules vary in accordance with the prevailing mode of recognizing descent, it is desirable to treat the three most common descent types separately. Discussion of these types is facilitated by ready reference to the descent systems described in the previous chapters.

Patrilineal and matrilineal descent systems generally assign rights and privileges in accordance with the prevailing rule of unilineal descent. A person becomes a proprietor in one lineage only. The exclusive principle applies to proprietorship and does not necessarily preclude the assignment of lesser privileges to persons who are not lineage members. This practice allows a man in a matrilineal system, and by extension his spouse and children, to harvest from the estate of his father's matrilineage. But it precludes a son from succeeding to proprietary status within his father's matrilineage. The same principle, in mirror image, applies to a patrilineal system. Unilineal descent systems thus assign proprietary rights on the basis of lineage membership and lesser use privileges on the basis of formal affiliation with a lineage member. The use rights, by definition and in actual practice, reside in the person who is consanguineally related to a lineage member. The spouse(s) and children of such a person may be said to exercise use privileges that amount to a very restricted form of tenure.

The situation is much the same for persons in a cognatic system. Although a person can here succeed to the proprietary rights in two different ancestral estates, namely that of his mother and father, he cannot significantly change the use privileges generally accorded to a spouse in a lineal descent system. Unlike his patrilineal or matrilineal status equivalents, he can in some instances transfer a form of life estate interest to his spouse. In the Gilbertese case, for example, a person can under some circumstances create what amounts to an estate interest in his spouse. This occurs most frequently when a man makes a testamentary disposition of his holdings in the ancestral estate to his wife. If the couple has children, the rights thus transferred are exercised by the man's wife on behalf of their children, or if the couple is childless, a man may leave his share of the family estate to his wife for as long as she lives. In either case, the rights in the ancestral estate extended to a nonrelative in this way automatically revert to the estate when the person dies.

Exceptions to all of the above-mentioned rules may well be found. However, if tenure rights other than simple use privileges are conveyed to persons who are not directly categorized as descendants, the conveyance has established a new and separate ancestral estate in another person. Although the division and subsequent multiplication of ancestral estates by these means is found, it is not common.

Goodenough (1955:73-76) feels that nonunilineal descent groups combine flexibility in membership size with an equitable distribution of individual landholdings. Unilineal descent groups, on the other hand, may create intolerable inequities in landownership, because they permit a few persons to control the land resources needed by many. But it is not very difficult to see how ancestral estates can function effectively in both unilineal and cognatic societies. The economic advantages of one type of descent principle over another are not altogether clear. Since ownership rights in Pacific societies have never allowed all tenure rights to reside with one person or with specially favored kin groups, it is difficult to see exactly how unworkable inequities would arise in landholdings. Proprietary rights seem to have been distributed in such a way that few persons, if any, were ever deprived of all rights. The differential allocation of proprietary rights within, as well as between, kinship and social status categories leads to the recognition that tenure rights vary in both kind and degree. Some kinds of landownership are more readily distinguished from mere use and physical possession. Most proprietary rights are tempered by corresponding duties and are often enforced after other remedies to an inequitable situation have been explored.

In summary, the most apparent cluster of proprietary land rights in all Pacific societies has been characterized as an ancestral estate. Such an estate lacks the attribute of free alienation of proprietorship associated with the classic conception of a fee simple interest, but as already stated, it combines the major proprietary features associated with early English fee tail and life estates.

There are, of course, many other forms of proprietary interests to be found among the cultures of Oceania. Most of these, with the exception of such very recent changes in tenure practices as title registration, purchase, and introduction of foreign laws, can best be described as interests that are less than estates. Various easements permit persons to exercise above surface or subsurface rights in areas where they do not hold surface rights. Some societies permit arrangements by which a caretaker obtains the equivalent of possession while others recognize landlord-tenant agreements as contractual in nature.

The evolution of proprietary rights is likely to change its course from a concern with the cultural continuation of ancestral estate interests to new forms of landownership that involve less than estate interests in realty. The direction today in many Pacific tenure systems is toward the implementation of landlord-tenant leasing arrangements, in which the government is the most common landlord; the recognition of title by adverse possession of abandoned or unused land parcels; the legally enforced consolidation of noncontiguous landholdings; and the registration of titles in order to maximize the rights of primary descendants and minimize those of others. Before these innovations take root, it will be necessary to effect some major changes in the basic ideology and value structure that underlie present-day tenure practices. Enough is known about this ideology from anthropological sources to say that ownership of land is taken as a close correlate of social status and that the ability to exercise a variety of proprietary rights is an important basis for the achievement of identity, political power, and leadership.

There is a final and perhaps speculative point to be made regarding the possible consequences that might follow if Pacific land tenure problems in the future only become resolvable by strictly legal mechanisms such as court litigation and administrative enforcement of written statutes. Such a direction for change away from a willingness to cope with a complex of social customs will only permit an occasional and superficial reference to general cultural principles. This change and legal formalization of tenure principles may not be in the best interest of indigenous populations.

It is not because of some dislike for the systematization of tenure principles associated with courts and legislatures that leads to this conclusion. In fact, it is genuinely puzzling how some of the societies have managed for so long without this additional formalization of land tenure practices. The answer must be sought in the data presented in this book. These data, as noted, did not clearly separate and discriminate among such tandem categories as status and estate, proprietary right and kin group seniority, or ownership and social rank. The native peoples of Oceania seem to have evolved a form of social and legal organization which precludes understanding and study of land tenure as a separate element of culture.

REFERENCES

Alkire, William H.
    1965   *Lamotrek Atoll and Inter-Island Socioeconomic Ties.* Illinois Studies in Anthropology, no. 5. Urbana: University of Illinois Press.
    1970   "Systems of measurement on Woleai Atoll, Caroline Islands." *Anthropos* 65:1–73.

Ardrey, Robert
    1966   *The Territorial Imperative.* New York: Atheneum.

Barnes, J. A.
    1955   "Seven types of segmentation." *The Rhodes-Livingston Journal* 17:1–22.
    1962   "African models in the New Guinea Highlands." *Man* 62:5–9.

Bateson, Gregory
    1972   *Steps to an Ecology of Mind.* New York: Ballantine Books.

Beaglehole, Ernest, and Pearl Beaglehole
    1938   *Ethnology of Pukapuka.* Bernice P. Bishop Museum Bulletin 150. Honolulu: B. P. Bishop Museum.

Bedford, R. D.
    1967   "Resettlement: solutions to economic and social problems in the Gilbert and Ellice Islands Colony." Master's thesis, University of Auckland.

Brady, Ivan A.
    1970   "Land tenure, kinship and community structure: strategies for living in the Ellice Islands of Western Polynesia." Ph.D. dissertation, University of Oregon.

Brookfield, H. C.
    1968   "The money that grows on trees: the consequences of an inno-

vation within a man-environment system." *Australian Geographical Studies* 6:97–119.

Brookfield, H. C., and Paula Brown
    1963   *Struggle for Land: Agriculture and Group Territories among the Chimbu of the New Guinea Highlands.* London: Oxford University Press.

Bryan, Jr., E. H.
    1965   *Life in Micronesia: The Marshalls and the Pacific.* Kwajalein, Marshall Islands: Hourglass Newspaper Co.

Buck, Sir Peter H.
    1950   *The Material Culture of Kapingamarangi.* Bernice P. Bishop Museum Bulletin 200. Honolulu: B. P. Bishop Museum.

Burland, John
    1966   Untitled and unpublished manuscript pertaining to the history of Palmerston Atoll, located in the Alexander Turnbull Library, Wellington, New Zealand.

Carpenter, C. R.
    1958   "Territoriality: a review of concepts and problems." In *Behavior and Evolution,* edited by Anne Roe and George Gaylord Simpson. New Haven: Yale University Press.

Carroll, Vern
    1968   "Nukuoro kinship terms." Paper presented at the 67th annual meeting of the American Anthropological Association, Seattle, November 1968.

Cartland, B. C.
    1949   "Lands settlement: Ellice Islands." Unpublished memorandum, located in the files of the Lands Commission, at the Secretariat, Tarawa, Gilbert Islands.
    1952   "Memorandum on land hunger in the Gilbert and Ellice Islands." Unpublished report, located in the files of the Lands Commission, at the Secretariat, Tarawa.

Casner, A. James, and W. Barton Leach
    1947   *Cases and Text on Property.* 2nd edition, 1969. Boston: Little, Brown and Co.

Catala, Rene L. A.
    1957   *Report on the Gilbert Islands: Some Aspects of Human Ecology.* Pacific Science Board Atoll Research Bulletin 59. Washington, D.C.: National Research Council.

Cook Islands Government
    n.d.   Files relating to Palmerston Atoll, located at government headquarters, Rarotonga, Cook Islands.

Couper, A. D.
    1967   "The Gilbert and Ellice Islands Colony: implications of regional trading anomalies." *Pacific Viewpoint* 8:68–86.

Crocombe, Ron G.
 1968 "Observations on land tenure in Tarawa, Gilbert Islands." *Micronesia* 4:27–37.
Crocombe, Ron G., ed.
 1971 *Land Tenure in the Pacific*. Melbourne: Oxford University Press.
DeBrum, O., and Henry Rutz
 1968 "The mode of succession and political organization in Laura." In *The Laura Report*, edited by Leonard Mason. Honolulu: University of Hawaii.
Department of Maori and Island Affairs
 n.d. Files relating to Palmerston Atoll, located at the Department of Maori and Island Affairs, Wellington, New Zealand.
Dias, R. W. M.
 1957 *Jurisprudence*. 2nd ed. 1964. London: Butterworths.
Eilers, Anneliese
 1934 *Inseln um Ponape: Kapingamarangi, Nukuor Ngatik, Mokil, Pingelap*. Ergebnisse der Südsee-Expedition 1908–1910, series 2B, vol. 8. Hamburg: Friedrichsen, De Gruyter & Co.
Emory, Kenneth
 1965 *Kapingamarangi: Social and Religious Life of a Polynesian Atoll*. Bernice P. Bishop Museum Bulletin 228. Honolulu: B. P. Bishop Museum.
Epstein, A. L.
 1969 *Matupit: Land, Politics, and Change Among the Tolai of New Britain*. Berkeley and Los Angeles: University of California Press.
Firth, Raymond W.
 1957 "A note on descent groups in Polynesia." *Man* 57:4–8.
Gilbert and Ellice Islands Colony
 1963 "The native lands ordinance, 1956." *Western Pacific High Commission Gazette* 32:187–198.
Gill, William W.
 1885 *Jottings from the Pacific*. London: Religious Tract Society.
Goodenough, Ward H.
 1955 "A problem in Malayo-Polynesian social organization." *American Anthropologist* 57:71–83.
 1961 *Property, Kin and Community on Truk*. Yale University Publications in Anthropology, no. 46. New Haven: Department of Anthropology, Yale University.
 1963 Review of *Matrilineal Kinship*, edited by David M. Schneider and Kathleen Gough. *American Anthropologist* 65:923–928.
Goody, John R.
 1956 *The Social Organization of the Lo-Wiili*. Colonial Research Studies, no. 19. London: Her Majesty's Stationery Office.

Great Britain, Colonial Office
   1950–1968   *Annual and Biennial Reports for the Gilbert and Ellice Islands Colony.* London: Her Majesty's Stationery Office.
Grimble, A. F.
   1929   *Instructions and Hints to District Officers, Deputy Commissioners, and Sub-Accountants.* Suva, Fiji: Government Printer.
Hainline, Jane
   1965   "Cultural and biological adaptation." *American Anthropologist* 67:1174–1197.
Hanson, F. A.
   1971   "Nonexclusive cognatic descent systems: a Polynesian example." In *Polynesia: Readings on a Culture Area*, edited by Alan Howard. Scranton: Chandler Press.
Hart, C. F. D.
   1969   "Lands administration in the Gilbert and Ellice Islands Colony." Unpublished report, located in the files of the Lands Commission, at the Secretariat, Tarawa, Gilbert Islands.
Hohfeld, Wesley Newcomb
   1919   *Fundamental Legal Conceptions.* 3rd printing, 1964. New Haven: Yale University Press.
Keesing, Roger M.
   1968   "Nonunilineal descent and contextual definition of status: the Kwaio evidence." *American Anthropologist* 70:82–84.
Kelly, Raymond C.
   1968   "Demographic pressure and descent group structure in the New Guinea Highlands." *Oceania* 39:36–63.
Kennedy, Donald G.
   1931   *Field Notes on the Culture of Vaitupu, Ellice Islands.* Polynesian Society Memoir, no. 9. Wellington: The Polynesian Society.
   1953   "Land tenure in the Ellice Islands." *Journal of the Polynesian Society* 64:348–358.
Kiste, Robert C.
   1968   *Kili Island: A Study of the Relocation of the Ex-Bikini Marshallese.* Eugene, Oregon: Department of Anthropology, University of Oregon.
Knudson, Kenneth E.
   1964   *Titiana: A Gilbertese Community in the Solomon Islands.* Eugene, Oregon: Department of Anthropology, University of Oregon.
Lake, A. G.
   1948–1949   "Cartland Lands Commission minutes." Volumes I and II, unpublished. Located at the Central Archives of the Western Pacific, Suva, Fiji.
Lambert, Bernd
   1966   "Ambilineal descent groups in the Northern Gilbert Islands." *American Anthropologist* 68:641–664.

1970 "Adoption, guardianship, and social stratification in the Northern Gilbert Islands." In *Adoption in Eastern Oceania,* edited by Vern Carroll. A.S.A.O. Monograph Series, no. 1. Honolulu: University of Hawaii Press.

1971 "The Gilbert Islands: micro-individualism." In *Land Tenure in the Pacific,* edited by Ron G. Crocombe. Melbourne: Oxford University Press.

Langness, Lewis L.
1964 "Some problems in the conceptualization of Highlands social structure." *American Anthropologist* 66:162–188.

Lawrence, Peter
1967 "Garia land tenure." In *Studies in New Guinea Land Tenure,* edited by Ian Hogbin and Peter Lawrence. Sydney: Sydney University Press.

Leach, Edmund R.
1961 *Pul Eliya: A Village in Ceylon.* Cambridge: Cambridge University Press.

Leahy, M. J., and M. Crain
1937 *The Land That Time Forgot.* London: Hurst and Blackett.

Lieber, Michael D.
1968 "The nature of the relationship between land tenure and kinship on Kapingamarangi Atoll." Ph.D. dissertation, University of Pittsburgh.

1970 "Adoption on Kapingamarangi." In *Adoption in Eastern Oceania,* edited by Vern Carroll. A.S.A.O. Monograph Series, no. 1. Honolulu: University of Hawaii Press.

Lorenz, Konrad
1966 *On Aggression.* Translated by Marjorie Kerr Wilson. New York: Harcourt, Brace and World.

Lundsgaarde, H. P.
1966 *Cultural Adaptation in the Southern Gilbert Islands.* Eugene, Oregon: Department of Anthropology, University of Oregon.

1968a "Some transformations in Gilbertese law: 1892–1966." *Journal of Pacific History* 3:117–130.

1968b "The strategy and etiology of Gilbertese property disputes." *American Anthropologist* 70:86–93.

1970a "Some legal aspects of Gilbertese adoption." In *Adoption in Eastern Oceania,* edited by Vern Carroll. A.S.A.O. Monograph Series, no. 1. Honolulu: University of Hawaii Press.

1970b "Law and politics on Nonouti Island." In *Cultures of the Pacific: Selected Readings,* edited by T. G. Harding and B. J. Wallace. New York: The Free Press.

Lundsgaarde, H. P., and Martin G. Silverman
1972 "Category and group in Gilbertese kinship: an updating of Goodenough's analysis." *Ethnology* 11:95–110.

Mason, Leonard E.
   1947   *The Economic Organization of the Marshall Islanders.* U.S. Commercial Company Economic Survey of Micronesia, no. 9. Washington, D.C.
Mason, R. R.
   1960   *Some Aspects of Agriculture on Tarawa Atoll, Gilbert Islands.* Pacific Science Board Atoll Research Bulletin 73. Washington, D.C.: National Research Council.
Maude, Alaric
   1965   "Population, land and livelihood in Tonga." Ph.D. dissertation, Australian National University.
Maude, Harry E.
   1937   "Settlement of land disputes by administrative officers." Unpublished government document, located in the files of the Lands Commission, at the Secretariat, Tarawa, Gilbert Islands.
   1947   "Lands commission notes." Unpublished memorandum, located in the files of the Lands Commission, at the Secretariat, Tarawa, Gilbert Islands.
   1963   *The Evolution of the Gilbertese Boti. An Ethnohistorical Interpretation.* Polynesian Society Memoir, no. 35. Wellington: The Polynesian Society.
   1968   *Of Islands and Men: Studies in Pacific History.* Melbourne: Oxford University Press.
Maude, Harry E., and Marjorie Crocombe
   1962   "The Rarotonga sandalwood trade." *Journal of the Polynesian Society* 71:32–56.
McArthur, Norma, and J. B. McCaig
   1964   *A Report on the Results of the Census of the Population, 1963.* Suva, Fiji: Government Press.
McKee, Edwin D.
   1956   *Geology of Kapingamarangi Atoll, Eastern Caroline Islands.* Pacific Science Board Atoll Research Bulletin 50. Washington, D.C.: National Research Council.
Meggitt, M. J.
   1965   *The Lineage System of the Mae-Enga of New Guinea.* Edinburgh: Oliver and Boyd.
Montagu, M. F. Ashley, ed.
   1968   *Man and Aggression.* New York: Oxford University Press.
Morrell, William P.
   1960   *Britain in the Pacific Islands.* Oxford: Clarendon Press.
Morris, Desmond
   1967   *The Naked Ape.* London: Jonathan Cape.
Moynihan, Cornelius J.
   1962   *Introduction to the Law of Real Property.* St. Paul: West Publishing Co.

Murdock, George P., and Ward H. Goodenough
    1947   "Social organization of Truk." *Southwestern Journal of Anthropology* 3:331–343.
Murray, Archibald W.
    1876   *Forty Years' Mission Work in Polynesia and New Guinea, from 1835–1875.* London: Nisbet & Company.
Newton, W. F.
    1967   "The early population of the Ellice Islands." *Journal of the Polynesian Society* 76:197–204.
Niering, William
    1956   *Bioecology of Kapingamarangi Atoll, Eastern Caroline Islands.* Pacific Science Board Atoll Research Bulletin 49. Washington, D.C.: National Research Council.
Paget, Margaret
    1959   Unpublished genealogy and census of Palmerston, located in the Land Court, Rarotonga, Cook Islands.
Panoff, Michel
    1970   "Land tenure among the Mae-Enga of New Britain." *Oceania* 40:177–194.
Pollock, Nancy J.
    1970   "Breadfruit and breadwinning on Namu Atoll." Ph.D. dissertation, University of Hawaii.
Pollock, Nancy J., J. M. Laloulel, and N. E. Morton
    1972   "Kinship and inbreeding on Namu Atoll." *Human Biology* 44:459–474.
Pospisil, Leopold
    1965   "A formal analysis of substantive law: Kapauku Papuan laws of land tenure." *American Anthropologist* 67:186–214.
Pusinelli, F. N. M.
    1948   *A Report on the Results of the Census of the Population, Gilbert and Ellice Islands Colony, 1947.* Suva: Government Printer.
Rappaport, R. A.
    1968   *Pigs for the Ancestors: Ritual in the Ecology of a New Guinea People.* New Haven: Yale University Press.
Rhodes, Fredrick C.
    1937   *Pageant of the Pacific . . .* 2 vols. Sydney: F. J. Thwaites Ltd.
Roberts, R. G.
    1958   "Te atu tuvalu: a short history of the Ellice Islands." *Journal of the Polynesian Society* 67:394–423.
Sahlins, Marshall D.
    1958   *Social Stratification in Polynesia.* American Ethnological Society. Seattle: University of Washington Press.
    1965   "On the sociology of primitive exchange." In *The Relevance of Models for Social Anthropology,* edited by Michael Banton. A.S.A. Monographs, no. 1. New York: Praeger.

Salisbury, R. F.
  1962   *From Stone to Steel.* . . . Melbourne: Melbourne University Press.
Silverman, Martin G.
  1970   "Banaban adoption." In *Adoption in Eastern Oceania*, edited by Vern Carroll. A.S.A.O. Monograph Series, no. 1. Honolulu: University of Hawaii Press.
  1971   *Disconcerting Issue: Meaning and Struggle in a Resettled Pacific Community*. Chicago: University of Chicago Press.
Souter, Gavin
  1963   *New Guinea: The Last Unknown*. London: Angus and Robertson.
Spoehr, Alexander
  1949   *Majuro, a Village in the Marshall Islands*. Fieldiana, Anthropology, vol. 39. Chicago: Chicago Natural History Museum.
Steward, Julian
  1955   *The Theory of Culture Change*. Urbana: University of Illinois Press.
Strathern, A. J.
  1968   "Descent and alliance in the New Guinea Highlands." *Proceedings of the Royal Anthropological Institute* (1968):37–52.
  1971   *One Father, One Blood: Descent and Group-Structure Among the Melpa People*. Canberra: Australian National University Press.
Strauss, Hermann, and Herbert Tischner
  1962   *Die Mi-Kultur der Hagenbergstamme im ostlichen Zentral Neuguinea: Eine Religions-Soziol. Studie*. Hamburg: Cram, De Gruyter and Co.
Tobin, Jack A.
  1958   "Land tenure in the Marshall Islands." In *Trust Territory Land Tenure Handbook*, edited by John de Young. Agana, Guam: Office of the High Commissioner of the Trust Territory of the Pacific Islands.
Townsend, Michael M.
  n.d.   "Land customs, Beru Island." Unpublished memorandum, located in the Government Archives, Tarawa, Gilbert and Ellice Islands Colony.
Western Pacific High Commission
  1875–1891   Registers of correspondence, located in the Government Archives, Suva, Fiji.
White, G. M.
  1965   *Kioa: An Ellice Community in Fiji*. Eugene, Oregon: Department of Anthropology, University of Oregon.
Wiens, Harold
  1962   *Atoll Environment and Ecology*. New Haven: Yale University Press.

Wurm, S. A.
   1964   "Australian New Guinea Highlands languages and the distribution of their typological features." *American Anthropologist* 66: 77–97.

Wynne-Edwards, V. C.
   1962   *Animal Dispersion in Relation to Social Behaviour.* New York: Hafner Publishing Co.

Zwart, F. H. A. G., and K. Groenewegen
   1970   *A Report on the Results of the Census of the Population, Gilbert and Ellice Islands Colony, 1968.* Suva: Government Printer.

CONTRIBUTORS

WILLIAM H. ALKIRE has been an associate professor of anthropology at the University of Victoria, British Columbia, since 1970. He received his M.A. from the University of Hawaii in 1959 and his Ph.D. from the University of Illinois in 1965. His fieldwork in Micronesia includes trips to Lamotrek (1962–63), Woleai (1965), and four months on Saipan (1971).

IVAN BRADY is associate professor of anthropology at the State University of New York College, Oswego. He received his Ph.D. from the University of Oregon in 1970, and was assistant professor of anthropology at the University of Cincinnati from 1970–1973. He conducted field research in the Ellice Islands in 1968, 1969, and 1971 for a total of fifteen months.

RON CROCOMBE is professor of Pacific studies at the University of the South Pacific, which serves the ten Pacific island countries and territories from its main campus in Suva, Fiji. He has worked on various Pacific islands almost continuously since 1951, first as an administrator (1951–58) and then in academic research and teaching mainly for the Australian National University (where he completed his Ph.D. in 1961 and was for five years field director of the New Guinea Research Unit) and also at the University of the South Pacific and the University of Hawaii.

MICHAEL D. LIEBER is an associate professor at the University of Illinois at Chicago Circle. He was educated at Trinity College (A.B. 1960), Indiana University (1960–62), and the University of Pittsburgh (Ph.D. 1968). He conducted fourteen months of field research on Ponape and Kapingamarangi in the Trust Territory of the Pacific Islands, and he has since compiled a lexicon of the Kapinga language.

CONTRIBUTORS

HENRY P. LUNDSGAARDE is professor and chairman of anthropology at the University of Kansas, Lawrence. He attended the University of California at Santa Barbara (B.A. 1961) and the University of Wisconsin (M.S. 1963, Ph.D. 1966). His field research includes fifteen months in the Gilbert Islands.

NANCY POLLOCK is a senior lecturer in anthropology at Victoria University, Wellington, New Zealand. She received her B.A. degree from Colorado College, and her M.A. and Ph.D. (1970) degrees from the University of Hawaii. Her field research includes a brief visit to Jamaica (1964) and two visits to the Marshall Islands in 1967 and during the year 1968-69.

ANDREW STRATHERN is a professor of social anthropology at the University of Papua New Guinea. He studied anthropology at Cambridge University (B.A. 1962, Ph.D. 1966). His fieldwork, from 1964 through 1972, has taken him to the Mount Hagen and Pangia areas of the Western and Southern Highlands districts in Papua New Guinea.